THEN & NOW®

# COCOA BEACH

**OPPOSITE:** A girl relaxes on the beach in this *c.* 1950 photograph in Cocoa Beach. A long time ago, one could see planes landing on the beach, cars driving right down to the water, and people gathering to get a close-up view of sea turtle eggs as they hatched. The closest beach to Orlando's Walt Disney World today attracts millions of tourists. (Courtesy City of Cocoa Beach.)

THEN & NOW®

# COCOA BEACH

Wade Arnold

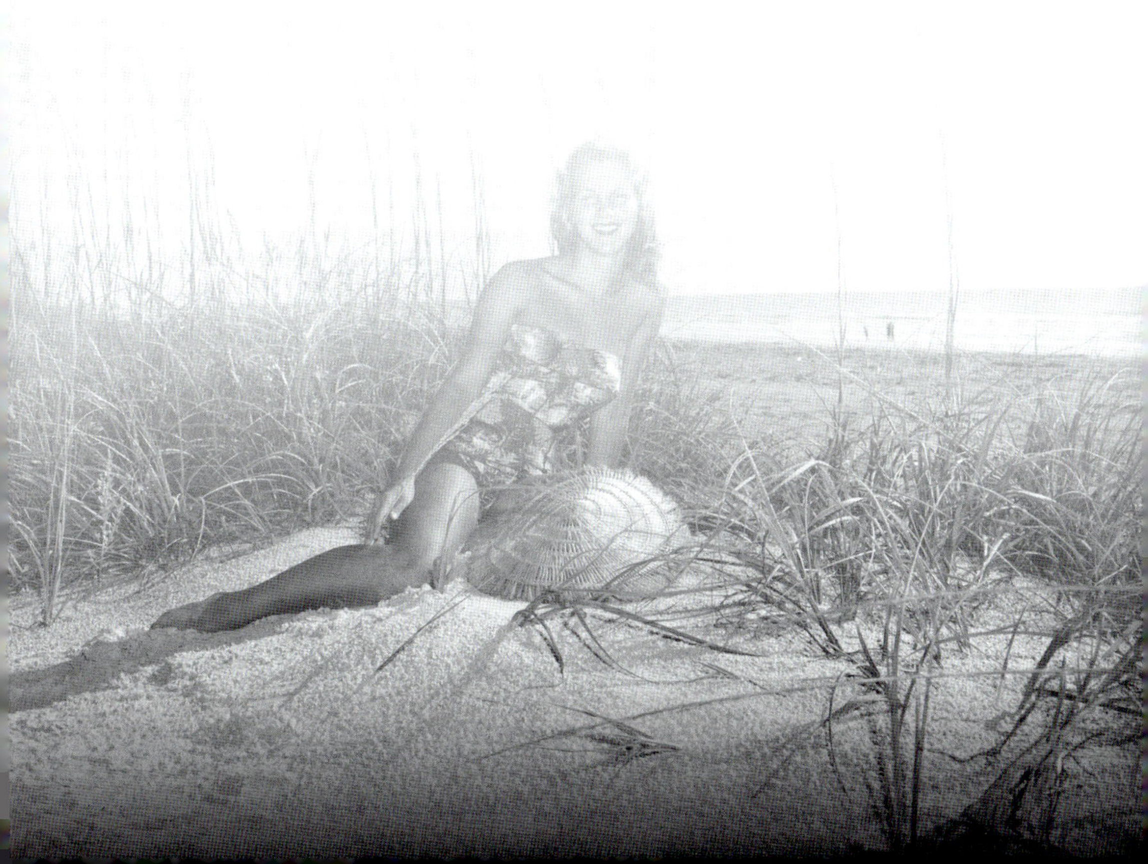

*For Lisa: Your support and encouragement made it all possible.*


ISBN 978-0-7385-6806-5

Library of Congress Control Number: 2008940168

Published by Arcadia Publishing
Charleston, South Carolina

Printed in the United States of America

Then and Now is a registered trademark and is used under license from Salamander Books Limited

For all general information contact Arcadia Publishing at:
Telephone 843-853-2070
Fax 843-853-0044
E-mail sales@arcadiapublishing.com
For customer service and orders:
Toll-Free 1-888-313-2665

Visit us on the Internet at www.arcadiapublishing.com

**On the Cover:** This photograph shows just how popular Canaveral Pier, now called Cocoa Beach Pier, was after its construction in 1962. Located at 401 Meade Avenue in Cocoa Beach, the 800-foot-long pier still attracts thousands of tourists and surfers today. Visitors enjoy restaurants like the Atlantic Ocean Grille, Oh Shucks Seafood Bar, and the Mai Tiki Bar, located on the far end of the pier. (Courtesy City of Cocoa Beach.)

**On the Back Cover:** Cocoa Beach has its first parade. Residents having a good time in this picture probably had no idea that things were about to change for the sleepy beach town. The space race was just around the corner, and Cocoa Beach would grow along with America's space program. Somehow, though, the city has always managed to keep that small-town atmosphere alive. (Courtesy Pete Godke.)

# Contents

# Acknowledgments

There are so many ways in which the writing of this book was made possible by people who had no incentive, other than their love of history, to help in its creation. But let me take a step back, just for a moment.

In the middle of winter, in a small-town Illinois classroom, a girl raised her hand to get the teacher's attention. "Can we close the windows? I'm fr-fr-freezing," she said. Several of her classmates nodded in agreement.

It was somewhere below 32 degrees outside, and the school's heater just could not compete with Mother Nature—especially when the windows really were open. Finishing what he was writing on the chalkboard, John Zerjal turned around to face the class.

"You can't fall asleep when your teeth are chattering," he laughed with a kind-hearted smile.

How do I know this story? Because I was there. Mr. Zerjal was my history teacher at Mascoutah High School, and his intention was simple. He was dedicated to teaching his students, even if it meant making sure an overactive heater did not help everyone to a cozy nap. I didn't know it then, but his class started my lifelong fascination with history. Sue Zerjal, his wife, another of my teachers, taught me a lot about expressing myself. This is really where this book started, and although it is about 20 years late, I want to thank them.

Back to the present, with the exception of Chapter Two, all of the "Now" images were photographed by me, and the "Then" images would not have been possible without the help of the Florida Historical Society, including Dr. Ben Brotemarkle, Debra Wynne, Barbara West, all the staff, and volunteers. They gave me so much of their time; my thanks are endless. I also want to thank Cocoa Beach city clerk Loredana Kalaghchy and her staff, Stuart Fergusen of the Historic Rossetter House Museum, retired teacher Mike Ferger, the staff of Cape View Elementary, the Holiday Inn Cocoa Beach Oceanfront Resort, and the staff of Our Saviour Catholic School. There are also a few local history experts that helped immensely, namely George "Speedy" Harrell, Pete Godke, Joe Morgan, and Al Trafford. Their knowledge and stories could captivate me for days. To everyone else I did not mention here, I thank you.

Finally, I am so grateful for the support of my family. Without them, I could not have done it.

# INTRODUCTION

Cocoa Beach has a lot of history, but unlike other cities and towns across the country, much of it has been compressed in decades instead of centuries. Its history is intertwined with its surrounding neighbors, like Merritt Island, Cocoa, Melbourne, and other communities. It also has a strong connection to America's space program. No one knows the true population before development in 1925, but reports indicate that, by 1940, it was just 49 people. Not long after, the space race would hit the area and with it a new popularity. Today 12,800 people call Cocoa Beach their home, but that does not tell the whole story. It is a sleepy beach community that during peak tourist season grows to a population of about 30,000. It also has become a popular destination for another 2.4-million visitors per year. The weather, beach, and the National Aeronautics and Space Administration (NASA) are all major attractions for tourists and residents alike, but being less than an hour from Walt Disney World in Orlando, Florida, does not hurt much either.

Cocoa Beach is part of Brevard County, which was once known as Mosquito County. You can guess why. At first, the county was much larger and included Lake Okeechobee to the south in addition to parts of other surrounding counties. The first settlers to the area were a family of freed slaves, but the arrival of a hurricane in 1885 proved too much for the settlement. Then in 1888, the entire tract of land encompassing Cocoa Beach was purchased by a group of men from neighboring Cocoa. It would be largely undeveloped until around 1925, when Cocoa attorney Gus Edwards bought and started to develop the area. Edwards would later become known as a real estate pioneer who foretold of a thriving Cocoa Beach. Within a short time, the secretary of state would sign the town charter, and eight ballots were cast for the first election. Wildlife, including rattlesnakes, panthers, and deer, was in greater number than the residents.

In the beginning, the only way to reach the town was by travelling on the Banana River. With the development of a community, a wooden bridge was built that linked nearby Merritt Island to Cocoa Beach. Unfortunately, it was prone to fire, especially because drivers would throw cigarettes out of car windows as they crossed. Water barrels and buckets were placed on the bridge, and they were put to good use.

One of the early residents of Cocoa Beach was Paul C. Godke. He reported that his family came to Cocoa Beach on a Sunday afternoon, only to drive endlessly without finding it. They even wondered if it existed. "We went over bad roads, dirt roads, narrow bridges, wooden bridges, and I don't know what all and finally decided that there must not be a Cocoa Beach. So we returned home and never saw it until some years later," he said in a published account.

In 1939, the Godke family would move to the area for good. Pete Godke brought his wife and two sons and got employment as a manager at a hotel called the Ocean Lodge. It had just 20 rooms. The only buildings existing at that time were the hotel, a gas station, and a post office. No school existed, no church existed, and it was only later that one policeman was added. "Not that it was needed especially, but it seemed to be a necessary step in the building of a city," Godke said. Their first major accomplishment, he said, was the founding of the nondenominational Cocoa Beach Community Church in 1940. The building still stands today.

It seems incredible today, but during World War II, Godke and other residents actually saw ships torpedoed off the coast of Cocoa Beach and even saw survivors brought to shore. Just before that time in 1942, the U.S. Navy built the Banana River Naval Air Station, which later became Patrick Air Force Base. The coming decades after the war would bring the eyes of the world to the area.

In 1950, the launch of a modified V-2 missile from nearby Cape Canaveral started a new era in history. However, it was not until the Soviet Union launched a satellite called *Sputnik* on October 4, 1957, that things really took off. People in the United States were shocked that the Russians were so far ahead in their technology, and the space race was on. Money, resources, and people would soon come to Brevard County, as the area of nearby Cape Canaveral was selected as the location to launch America's space program. The first seven astronauts were selected for NASA's Project Mercury in 1958, and over the next few years, Cocoa Beach would become a natural place for them to spend their time. Locations like the Holiday Inn on Highway A1A, Ramon's restaurant, Bernard's Surf restaurant, and of course, the beach, were common places to see astronauts, engineers, scientists, and their families.

Within a couple of years, the town that started with 49 people grew to almost 3,500. In 1961, Pres. John F. Kennedy announced the ambitious goal of sending Americans to the moon, and Cocoa Beach continued to grow along with the space program. The Cocoa Beach pier would be built in 1962, and in February of that year, 75,000 people would flood the beach to watch astronaut John Glenn as he went into space aboard his capsule called *Friendship 7*. The area could not be busier. Hotels, motels, apartments, homes, schools, and churches were sprouting to accommodate all the growth. NASA's Apollo moon program was just around the corner. In 1969, *Apollo 11* would deliver the first men to the moon.

During the 1960s, the popularity of Cocoa Beach was even evident by watching television. The NBC show *I Dream of Jeannie* premiered in 1965. The show, about an astronaut who lives in Cocoa Beach, ran until 1970. The city even created an I Dream of Jeannie Lane, located close to Lori Wilson Park near the beach. Barbara Eden, who played the character Jeannie in the show, can still be seen in local commercials—a testament to how recognizable the show still is to the area.

In the 1970s, the Apollo program was cancelled, and reports say that as many as 10,000 families left the area. With a nationwide recession came an unemployment rate of 12 percent in Brevard County. Cocoa Beach would survive, and tourists would still find themselves attracted to its beaches. It was not until the 1980s, though, and the coming of NASA's space shuttle program, that the area would see another real boom in its economy. Despite a nationwide real estate slow down in the last few years, Cocoa Beach has maintained its popularity.

Today tourists coming to Cocoa Beach find that the city Gus Edwards hoped for is a thriving, active, and just downright fun place to visit. The city still has a strong connection to the space program but at the same time has become known for its beaches, surfing, and culture. Pro surfer Kelly Slater, regarded by some as the greatest surfer in the sport, comes from Cocoa Beach. The number of condominiums has grown on the beach over the years, but the residents still welcome people like they are visiting a cozy beachside town.

# CHAPTER 1

# COCOA BEACH

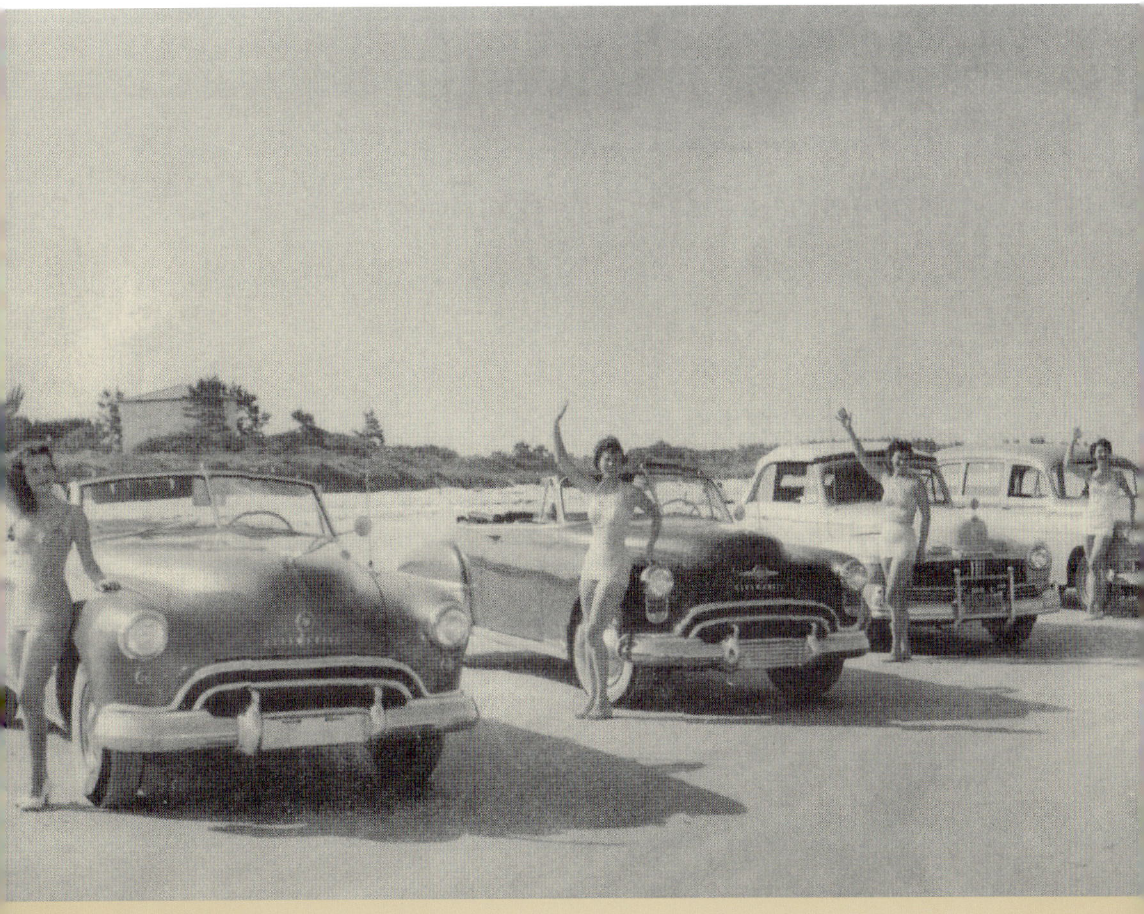

Cocoa Beach has always been a fun place for people to gather. In this classic photograph (probably taken in the 1940s), girls in bathing suits wait for planes to land on Cocoa Beach. Yes, cars used to drive on the beach, and planes used to land there, too. (Courtesy Florida Historical Society.)

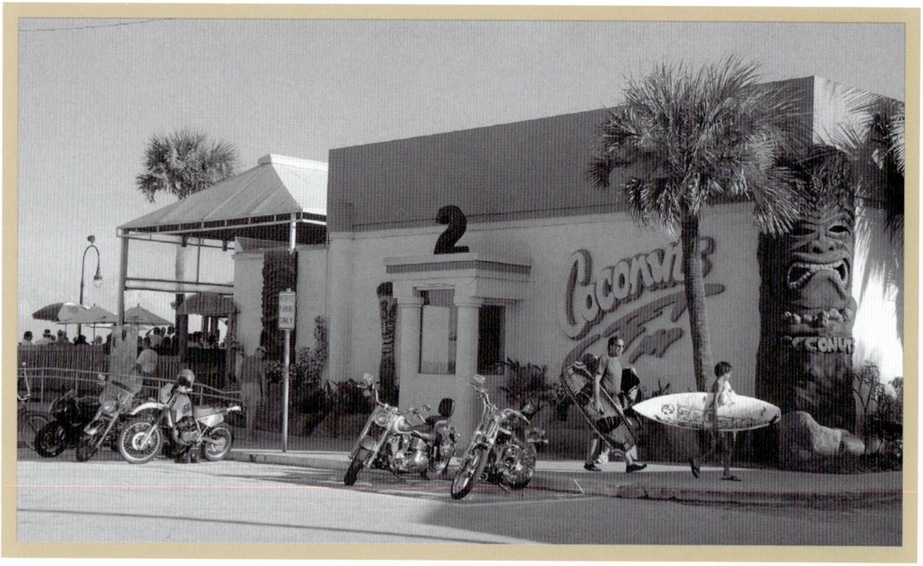


Pete Godke and his uncle stand next to the Ocean Lodge, once located at the end of Minutemen Causeway in Cocoa Beach. Early in its history, the location was home to a casino. The Godke family worked and lived at the lodge for a time, before later opening a gift shop. Today Coconuts on the Beach, a popular bar and restaurant for locals and tourists alike, stands at the beachfront location. (Courtesy Pete Godke.)

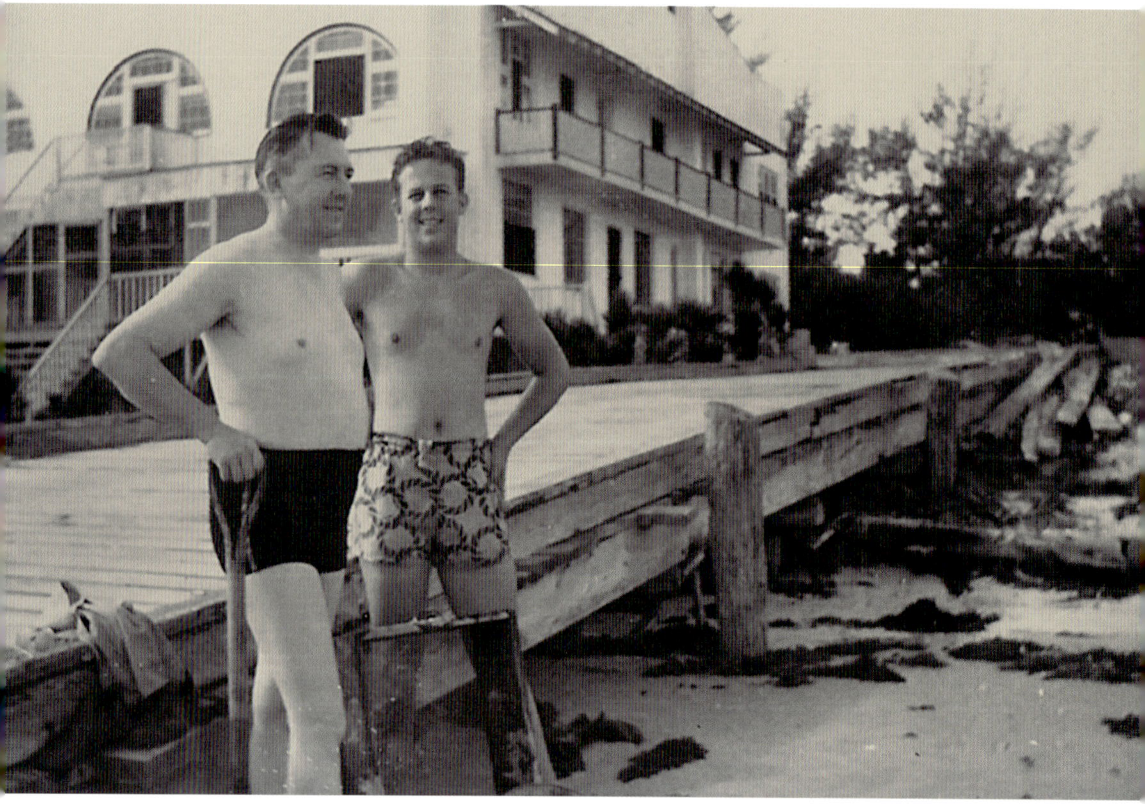

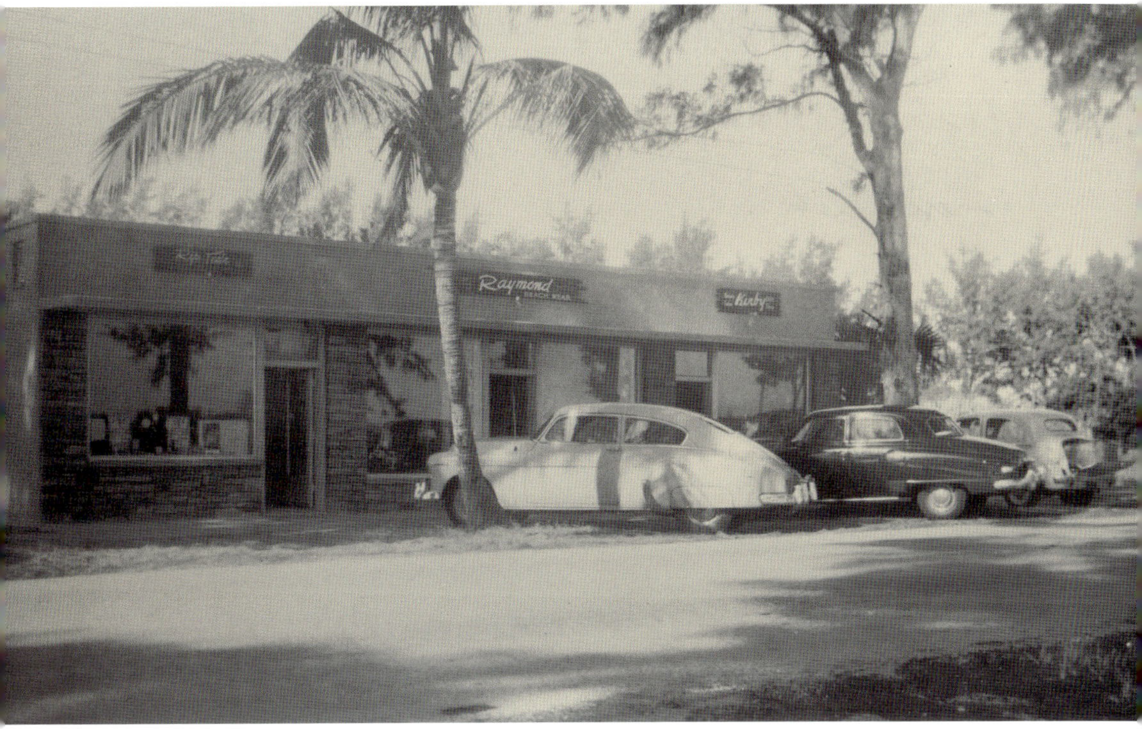


One of the original retail locations in Cocoa Beach, a small shopping center located near 62 South Atlantic Avenue, is shown in this 1940s photograph. The center included Raymond Beach Wear and Kirby Gifts. The building still exists as part of an air-conditioning business, but it is easy to miss today. Although the bricks look almost the same, a blue awning and additional construction on each side make it a little hard to find. (Courtesy Florida Historical Society.)

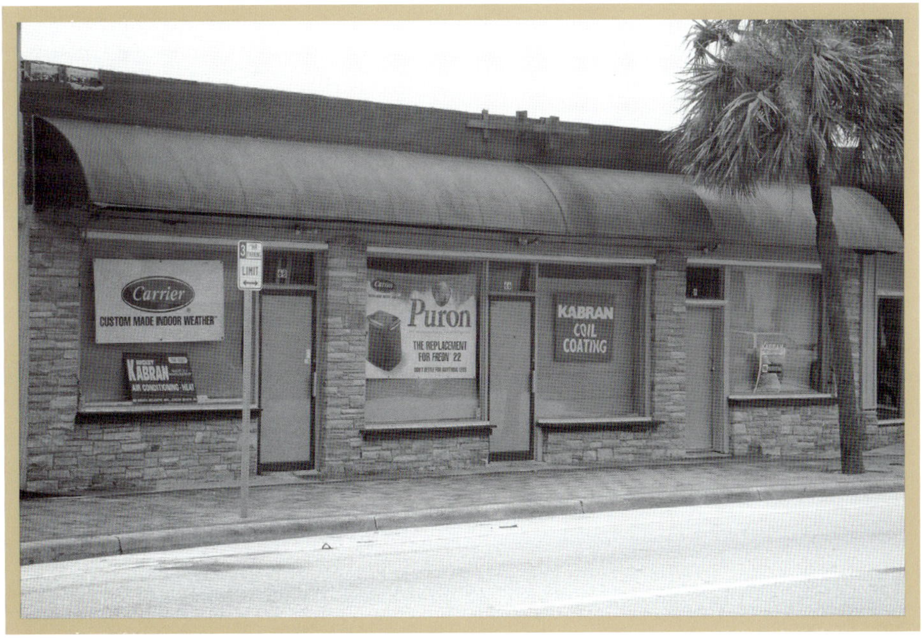

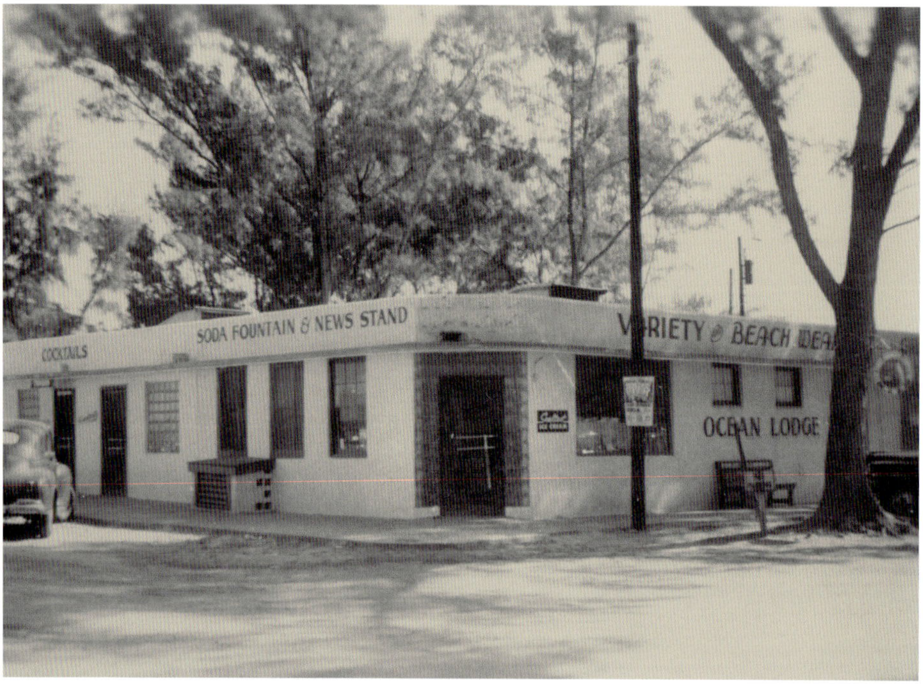


On the southeastern corner of North Atlantic Avenue and Minutemen Causeway sits one of the oldest buildings in Cocoa Beach, seen in this photograph that was probably taken in the 1940s. Originally it served beach-going customers with cocktails, sodas, and even ice cream. Today the same building still exists, and recent renovations have updated its appearance. Offering shells and other gifts, this longtime shop is still open for business. (Courtesy City of Cocoa Beach.)

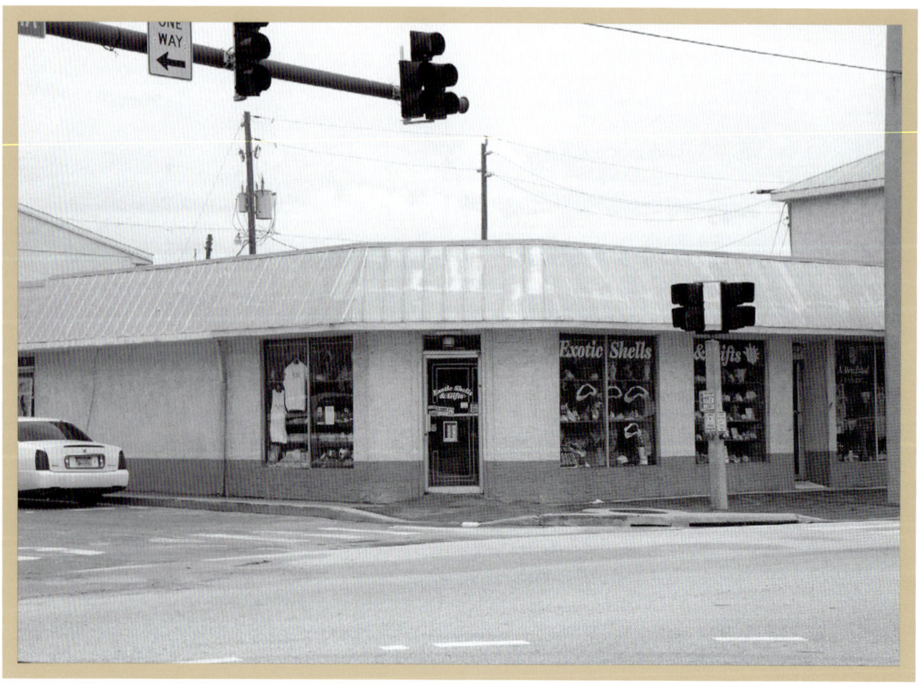

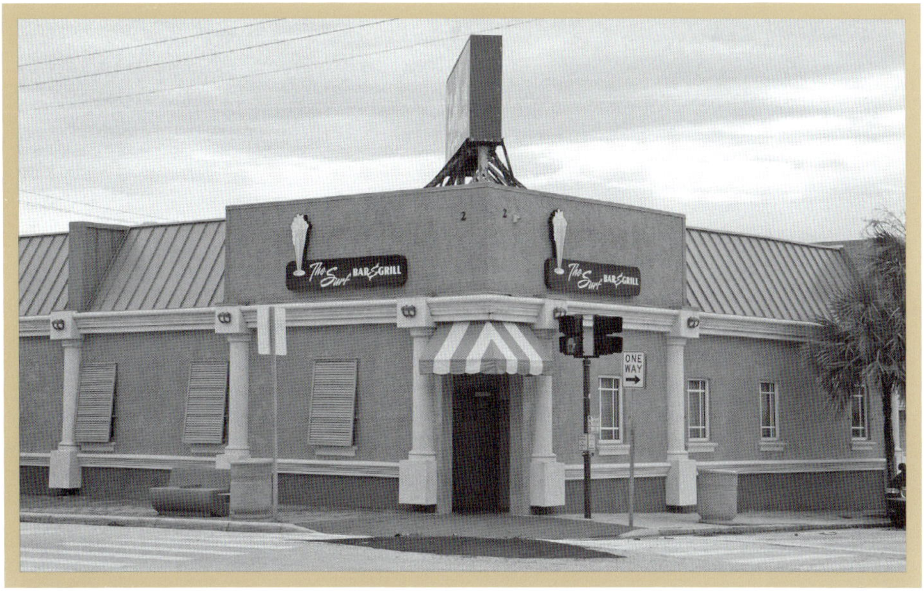


Bernard Fischer opened Bernard's Surf restaurant and cocktail lounge on October 30, 1948. Located at 2 South Atlantic Avenue at the intersection of Minutemen Causeway, the establishment still exists today as the Surf Bar and Grill. It has existed through many decades as a popular location for tourists and locals alike, although the Fischer family no longer owns the establishment. (Courtesy Rusty Fischer.)

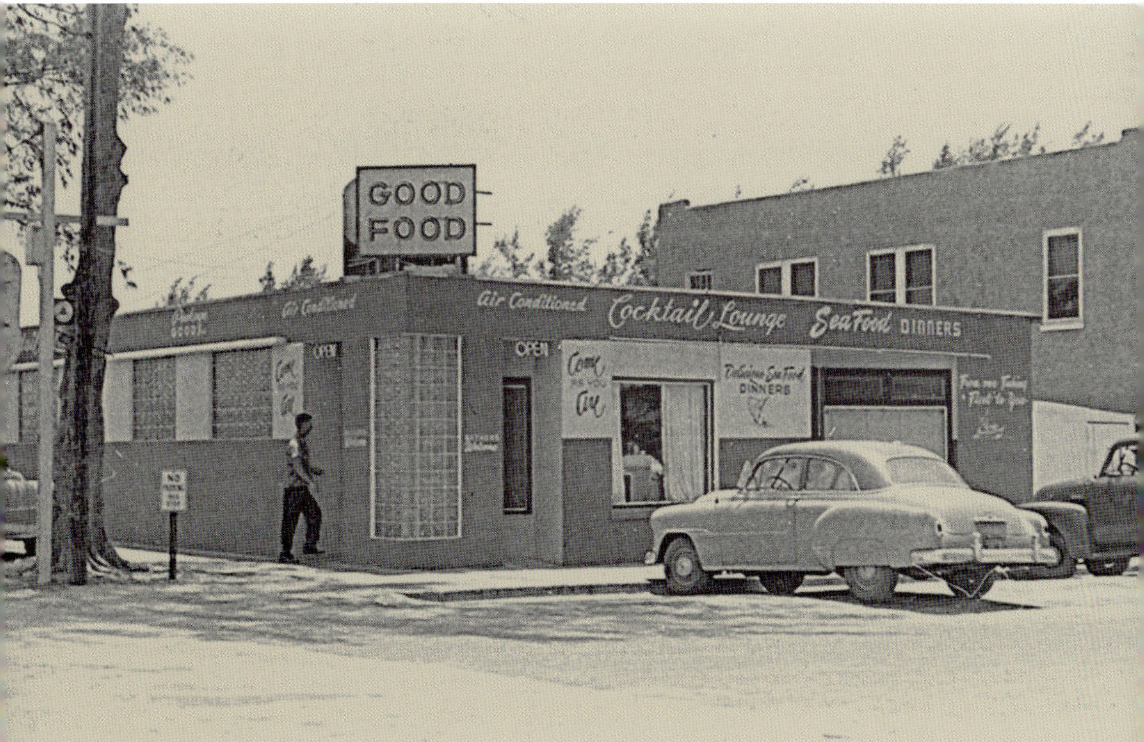

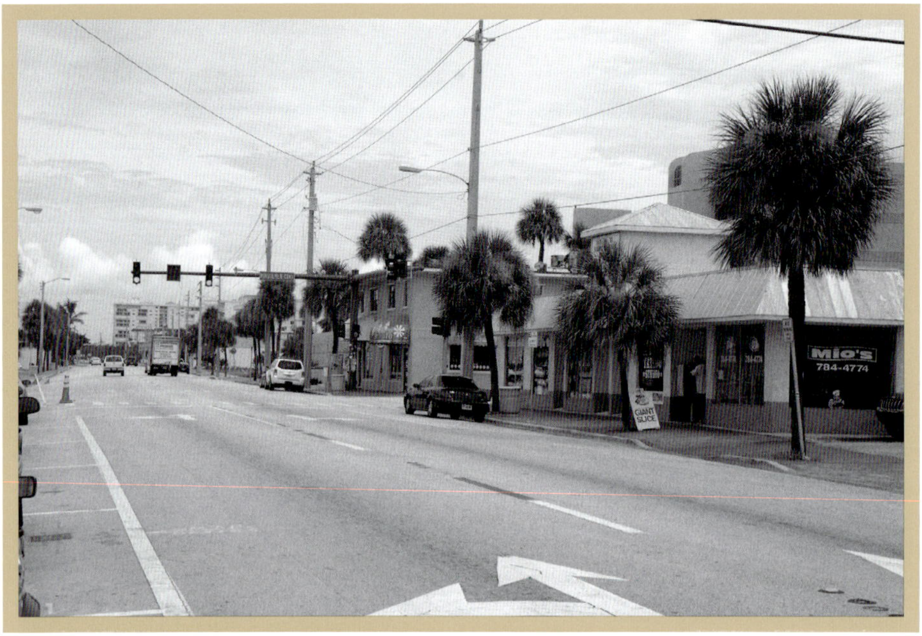

Looking north on Highway A1A, which is also known as Atlantic Avenue, this 1940s postcard shows a dramatically different view of what exists today at the intersection of Minutemen Causeway. The buildings on the right are still around, though, as is the Surf restaurant, which can be seen on the left in its early heyday. (Courtesy Florida Historical Society.)

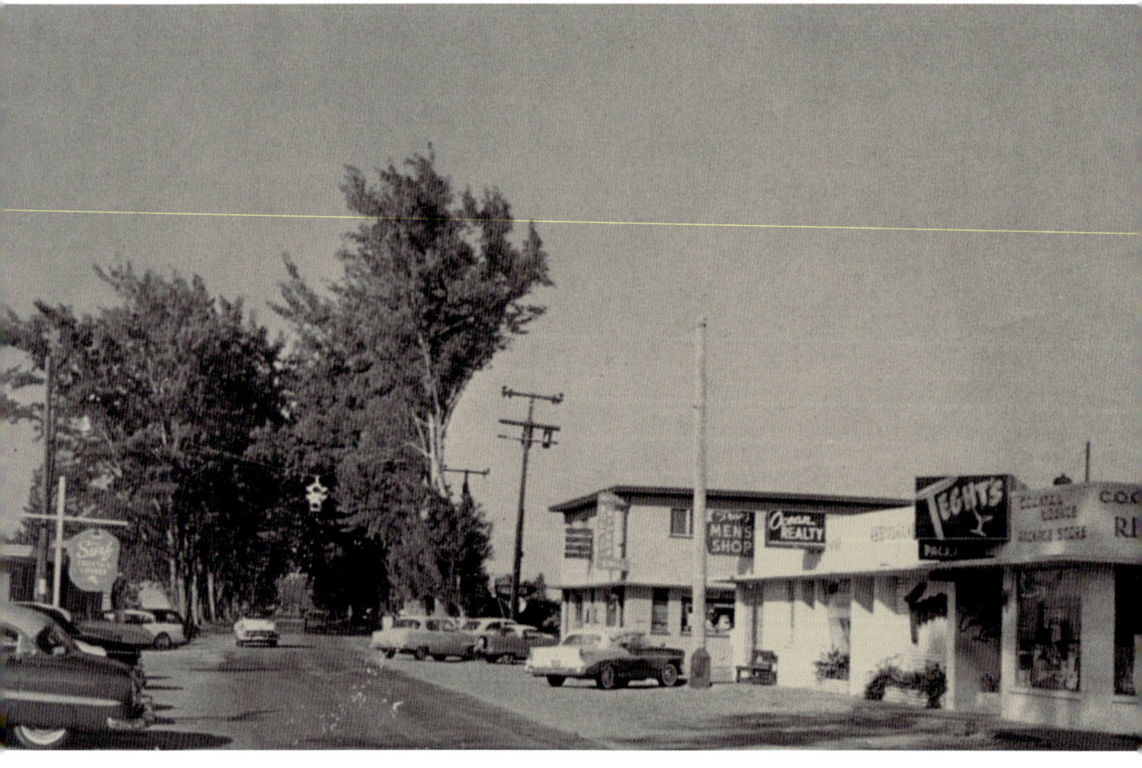

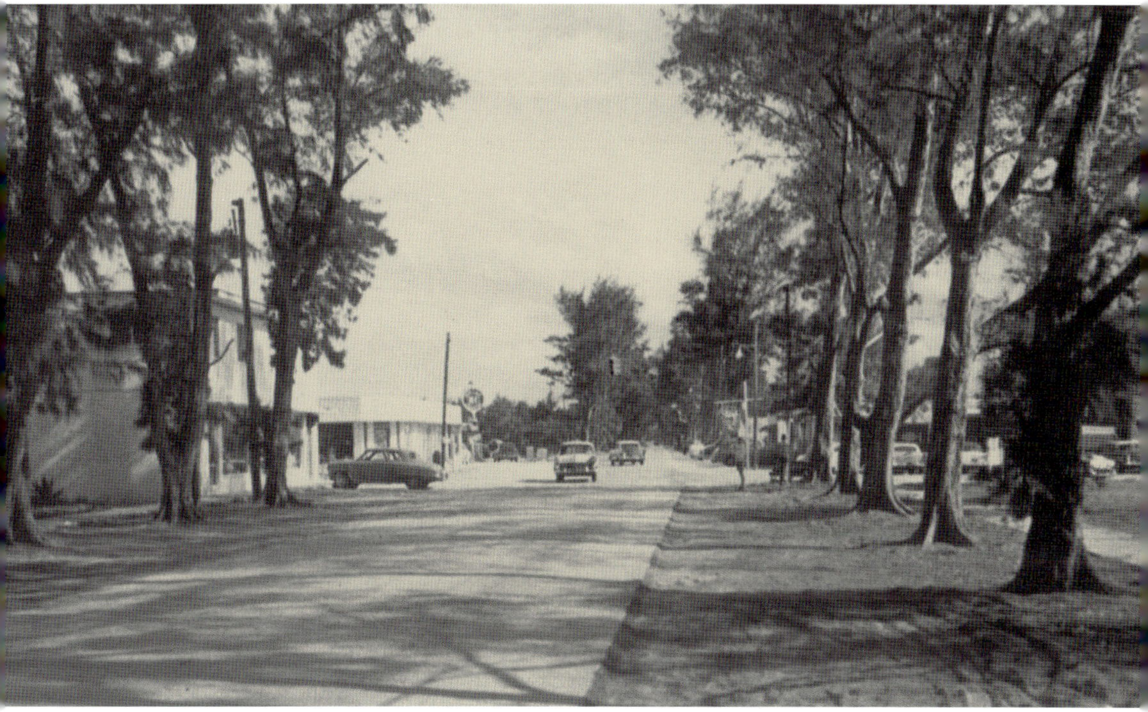

It would seem incredible today that trees lined Atlantic Avenue, also known as Highway A1A, at one time in the 1940s. This view shows how life looked just before the space race would transform the entire area. The trees were likely planted by real estate pioneer Gus Edwards but would eventually be uprooted to make way for Cocoa Beach's expansion during the 1950s and 1960s. (Courtesy City of Cocoa Beach.)

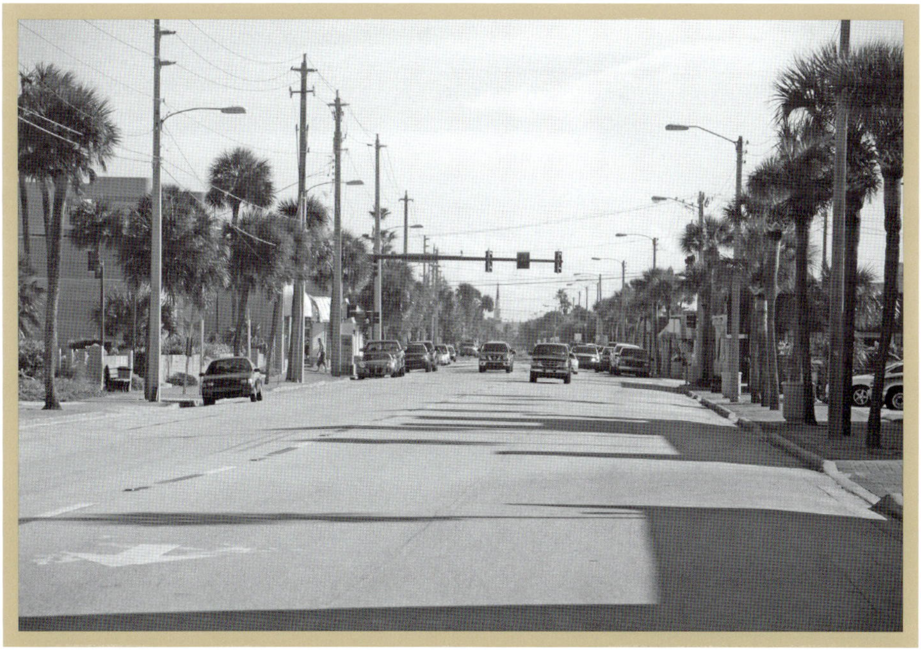

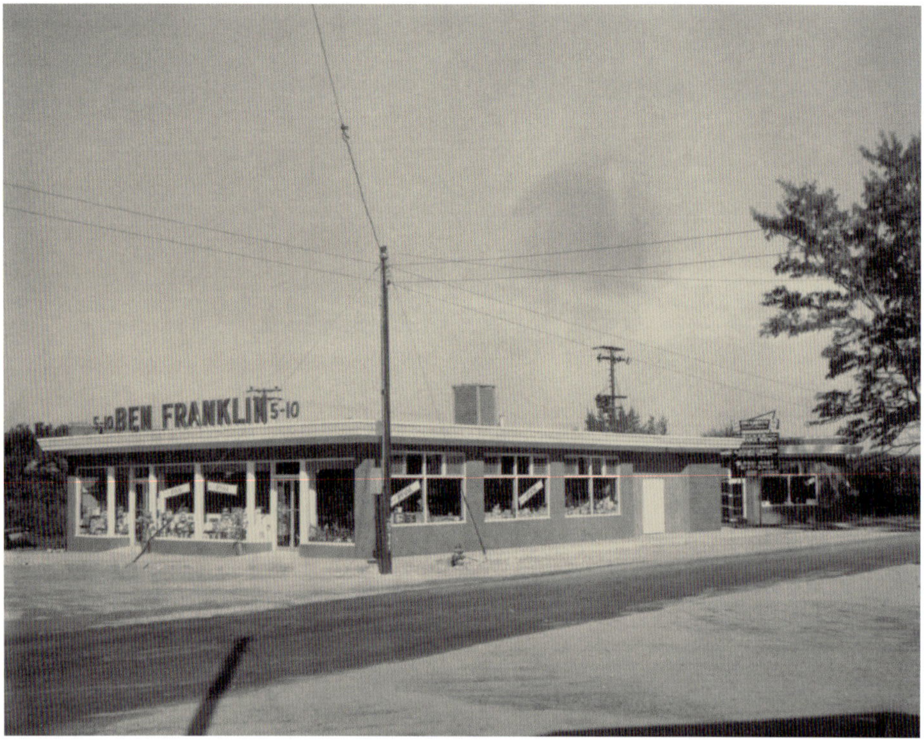


When this Ben Franklin store opened its doors at 2 North Atlantic Avenue in the 1950s, some local shop owners were worried that a major chain establishment might take away their business. The store did not last, and years later the location was home to the Prince of Wales restaurant. In 1992, it was renovated to become the Yen Yen Chinese Cuisine restaurant, which still exists today. (Courtesy City of Cocoa Beach.)

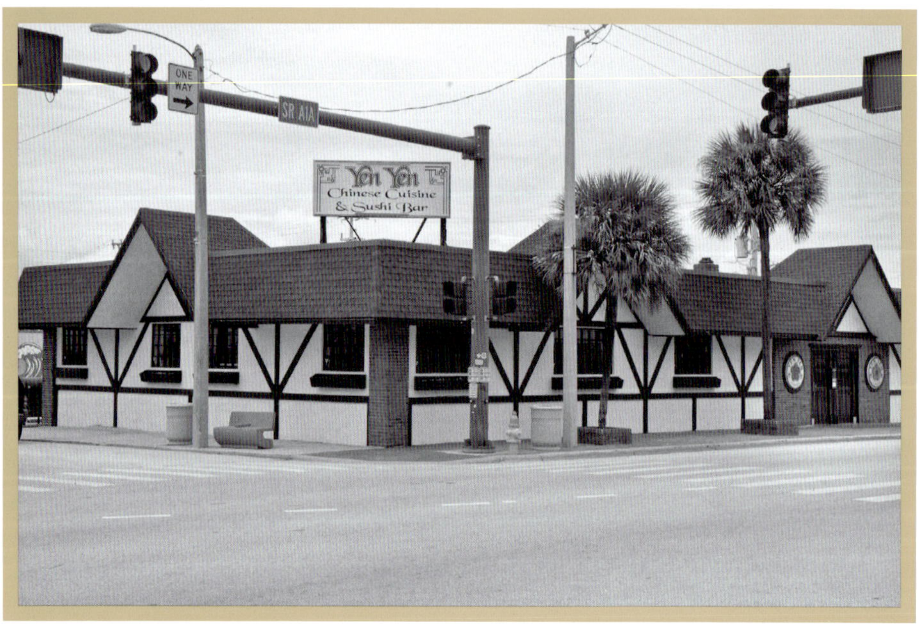

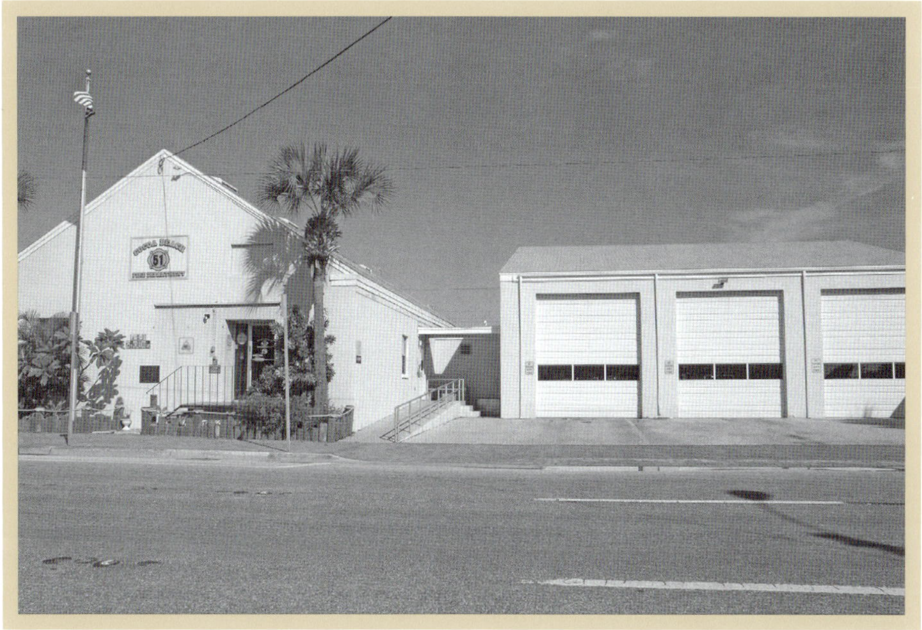

The first fire station in Cocoa Beach housed a U.S. Army surplus 1942 Chevy fire truck and started its service to the community in 1949. Today the fire department operates 24 hours a day and seven days a week to protect the citizens of Cocoa Beach. It has over 30 employees, one fire station at 25 South Orlando Avenue, and another on Volusia Lane, one block north of Highway 520. (Courtesy City of Cocoa Beach.)

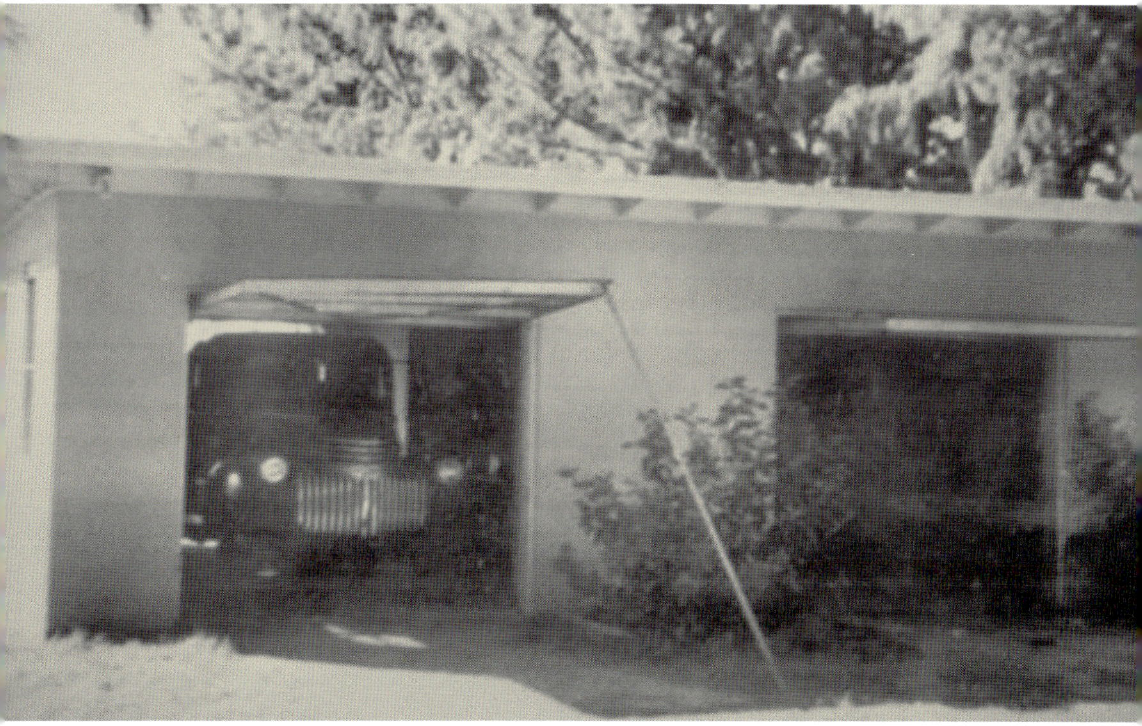

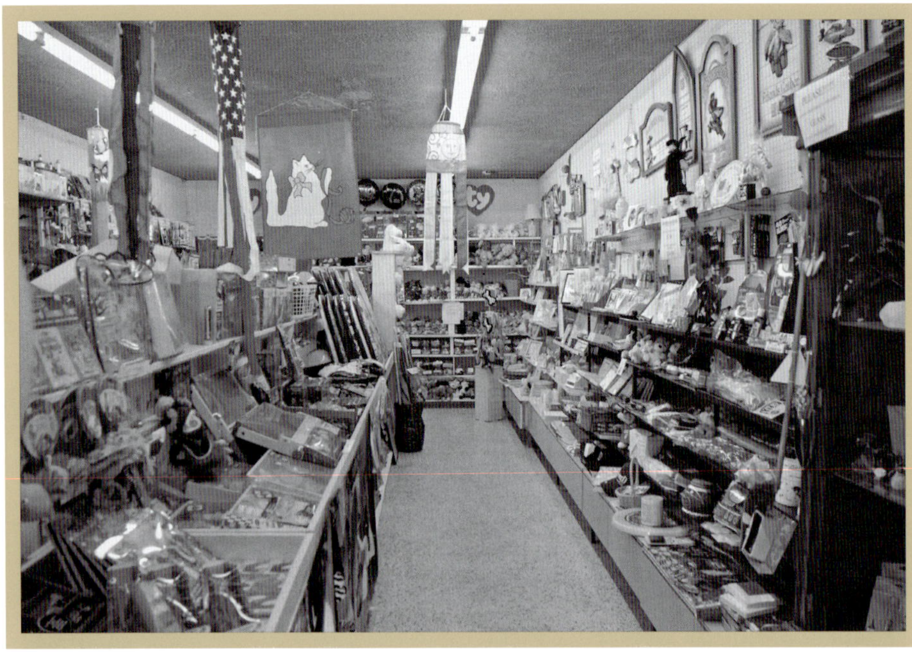

Ann and Pete Godke owned Ann Lia's gift shop located at 38 South Atlantic Avenue in Cocoa Beach. It opened around 1953 and is one of the longest-running businesses in the area. In the 1970s, their son Pete Godke took over as owner of the shop after retiring from the military. Under new ownership, the inside of the shop today looks much like it did years ago and is still a popular destination for tourists. (Courtesy Pete Godke.)

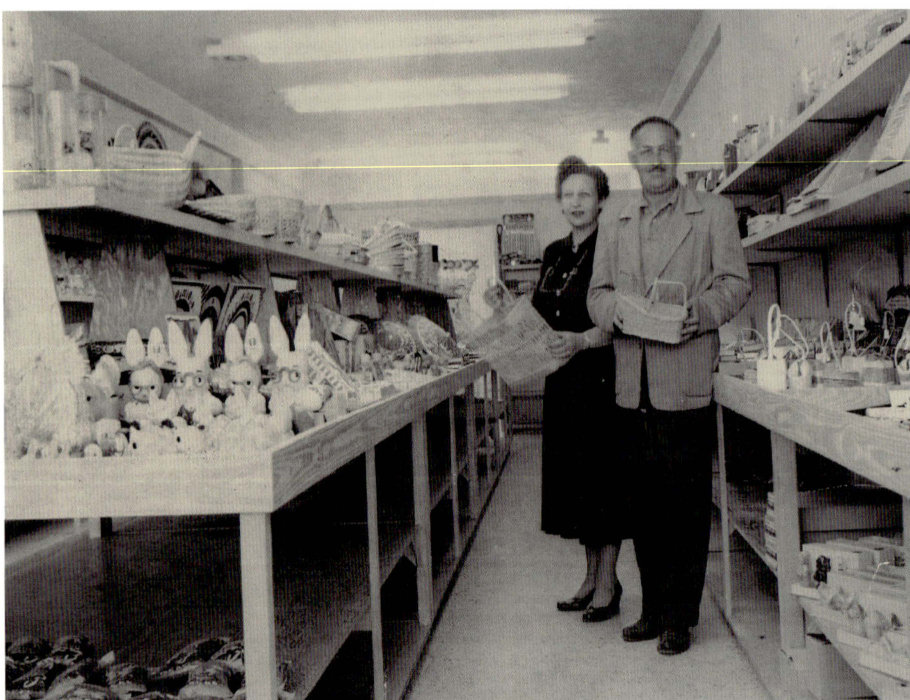

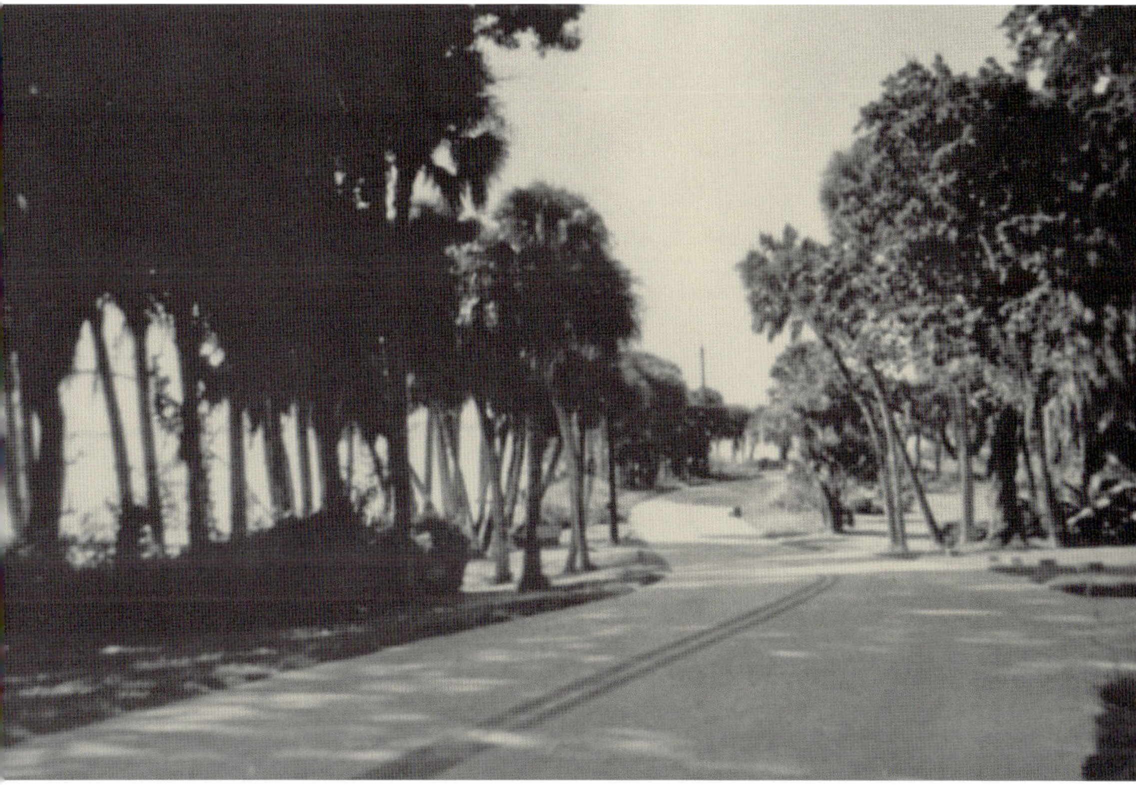

Highway A1A splits in two at this unidentified section of the road. Notice how many trees lined the road before much else existed in the area. At one time, the only development that existed in Cocoa Beach was between South First and South Third Streets, but today it is a very different place. Highway A1A now has traffic, plenty of condominiums, homes, and businesses of all types. (Courtesy City of Cocoa Beach.)

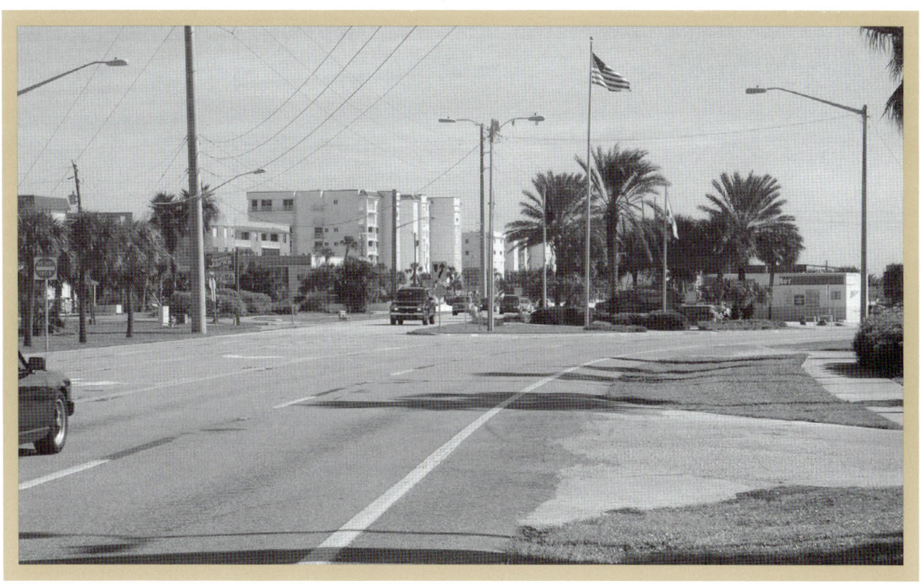

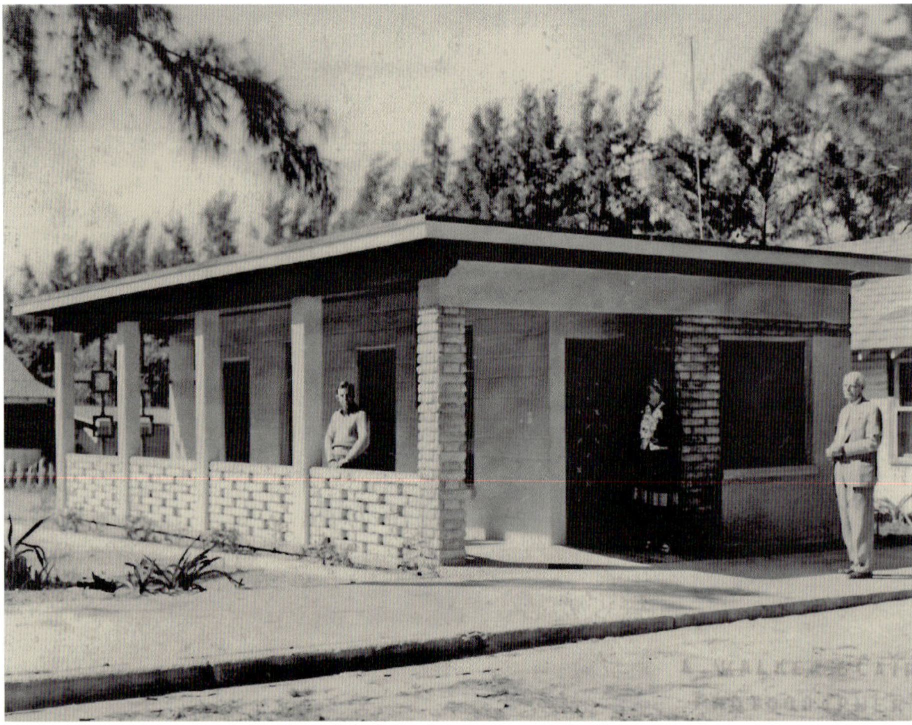

Some buildings in Cocoa Beach that still exist today look similar yet are very different from how they were years ago. This building, at 142 Minutemen Causeway, was probably used as a post office during the 1940s. Today the renovated building is called Big Licks Cigar Lounge, and the fanciful exterior paint hides what it once was. It took a personal visit with the current owner to confirm that this was the same building. (Courtesy City of Cocoa Beach.)

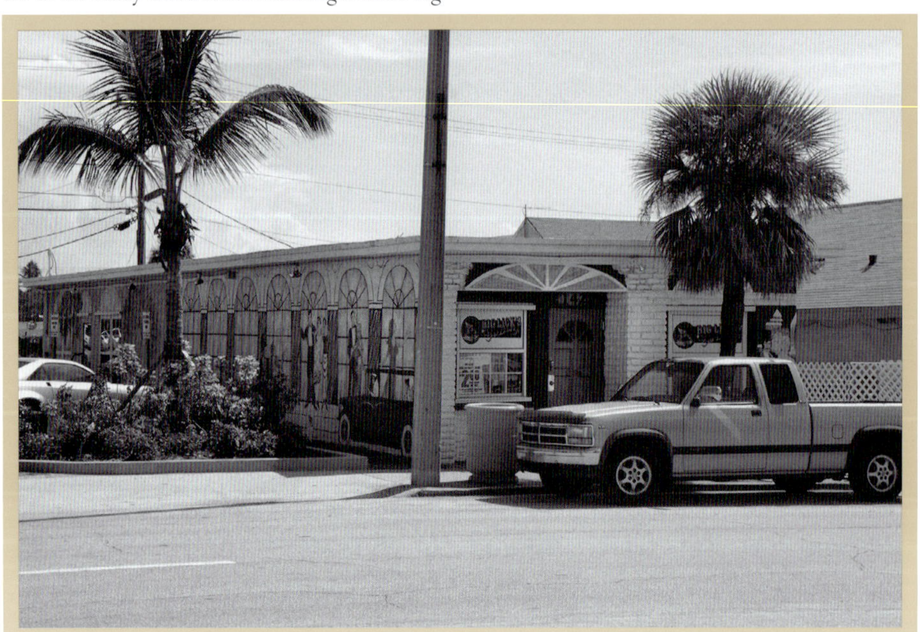

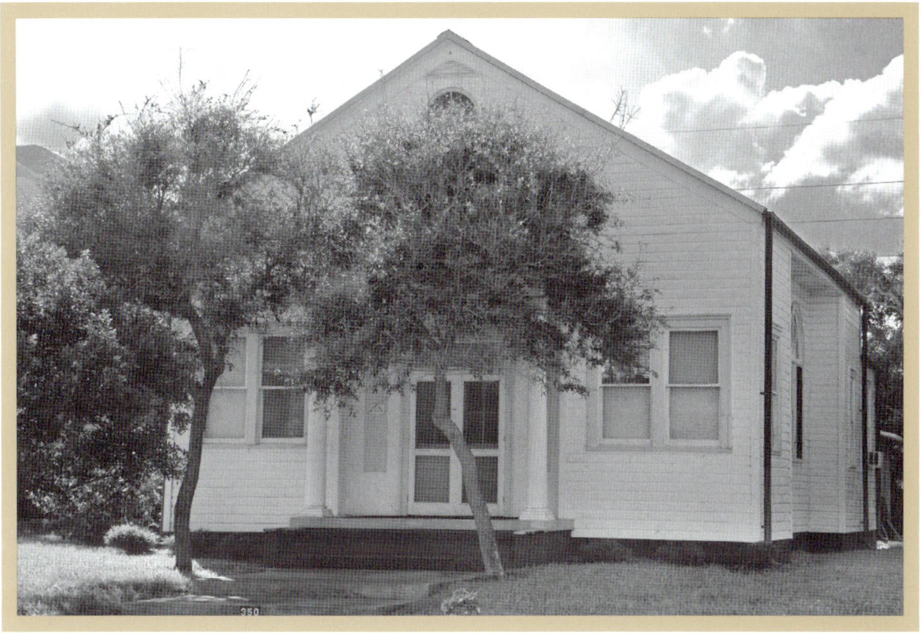

Around 1927, pioneer real estate developer and community icon Gus Edwards built the Cocoa Beach Community Church. Located on Third Street until the 1950s, it was later moved to its current location at 350 South Orlando Avenue. The church has been home to many different congregations and, although it is hard to see behind the surrounding trees, it is in excellent condition today. (Courtesy City of Cocoa Beach.)

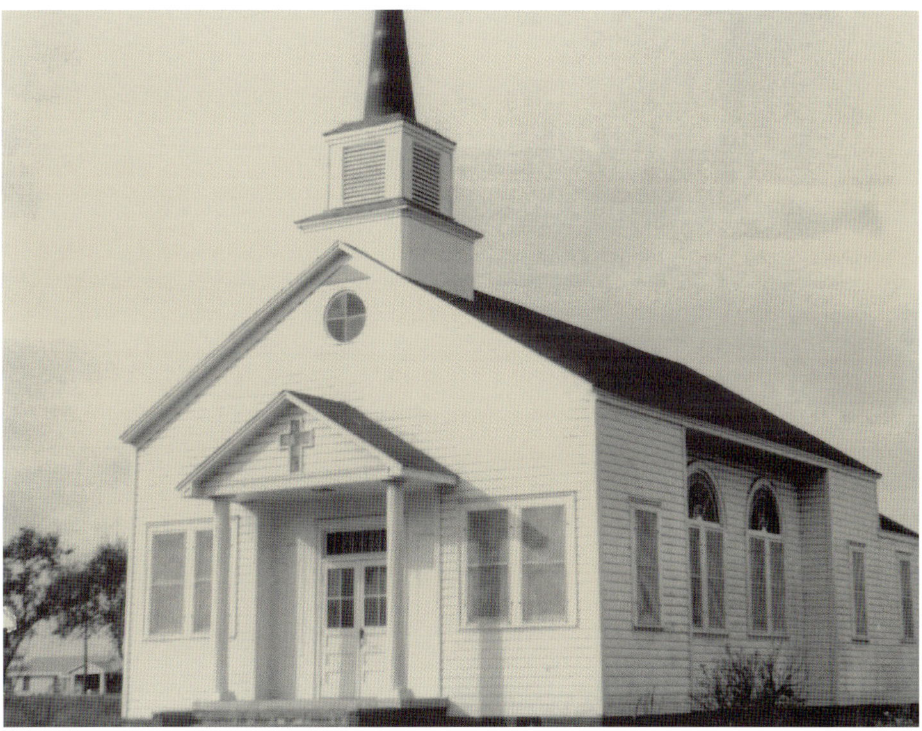

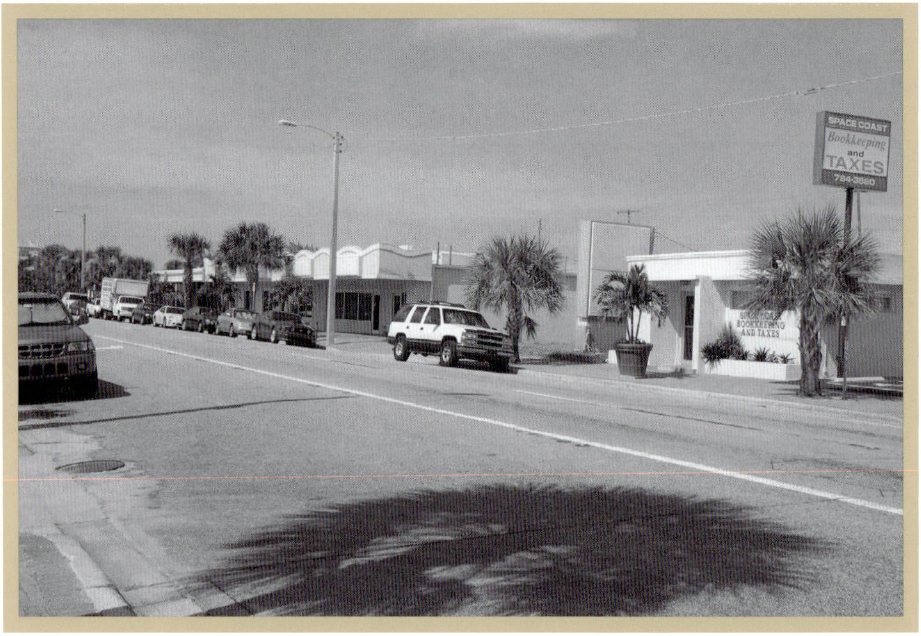


In this 1950s photograph of downtown Cocoa Beach, workers take measurements for a new sewer line to be installed. The medical building on the right still exists almost unchanged today, except a tax business is now run from that location. Note the Gus Edwards real estate sign in the background. Edwards was a pioneer real estate developer and one of the first city commissioners. Today the downtown area includes restaurants, retail establishments, and other businesses. (Courtesy City of Cocoa Beach.)

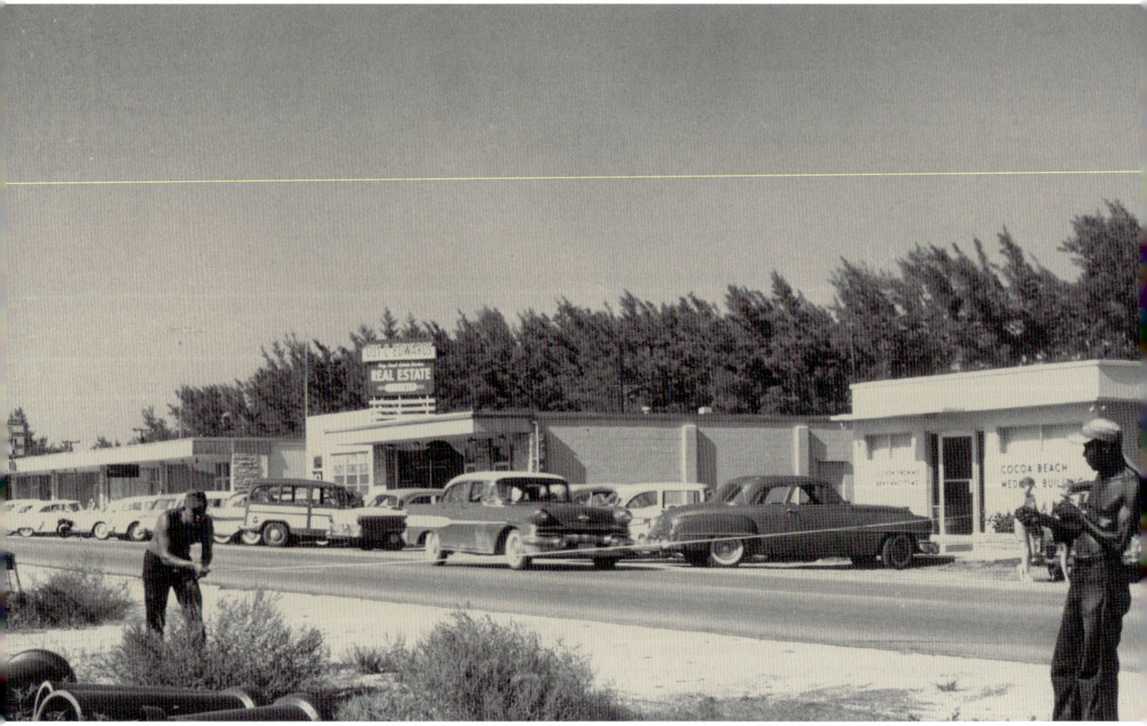

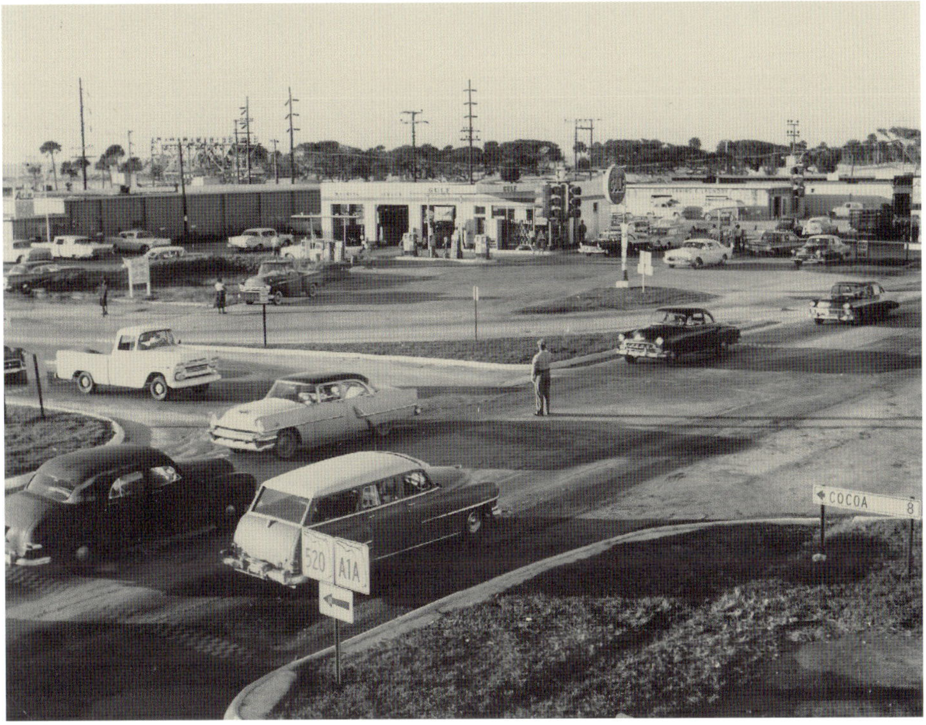


The intersection of Highway 520 and Highway A1A in Cocoa Beach looks almost as busy in the past as it does today. To the right of the photograph is the beach. Note that a police officer directs traffic because no traffic light existed at the location yet. The Gulf gas station on the corner sat next to Jake's Bowling Alley. Today both of those locations house retail shops that sell beach gifts to tourists. (Courtesy City of Cocoa Beach.)

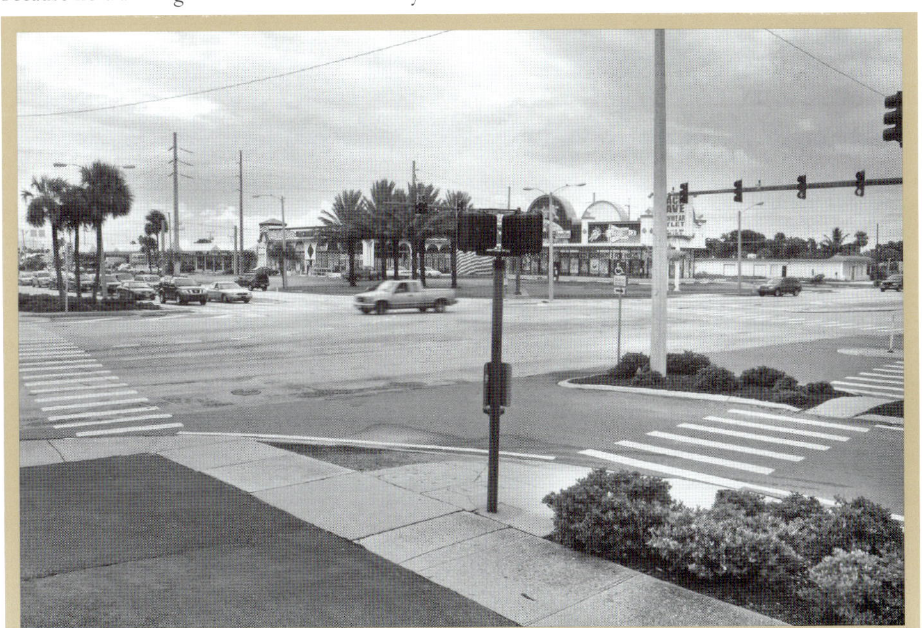

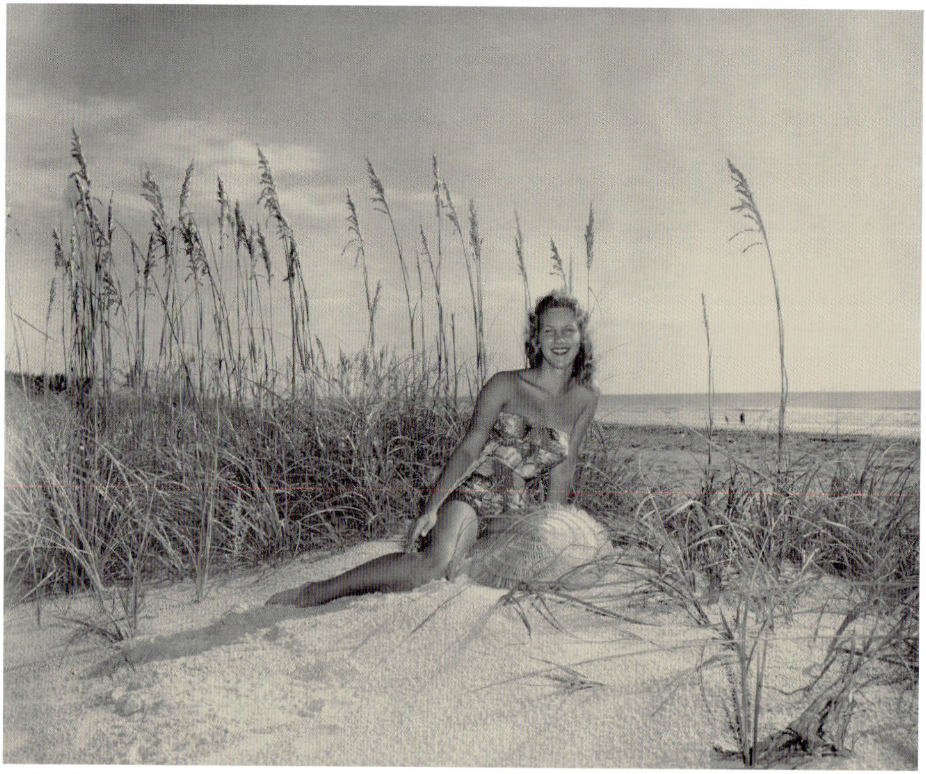

Cocoa Beach attracts millions of visitors each year, who come for the sunshine, smooth sand, and ocean waves. The area's small-town atmosphere is still the same as it was in the 1940s and 1950s. (Courtesy City of Cocoa Beach.)

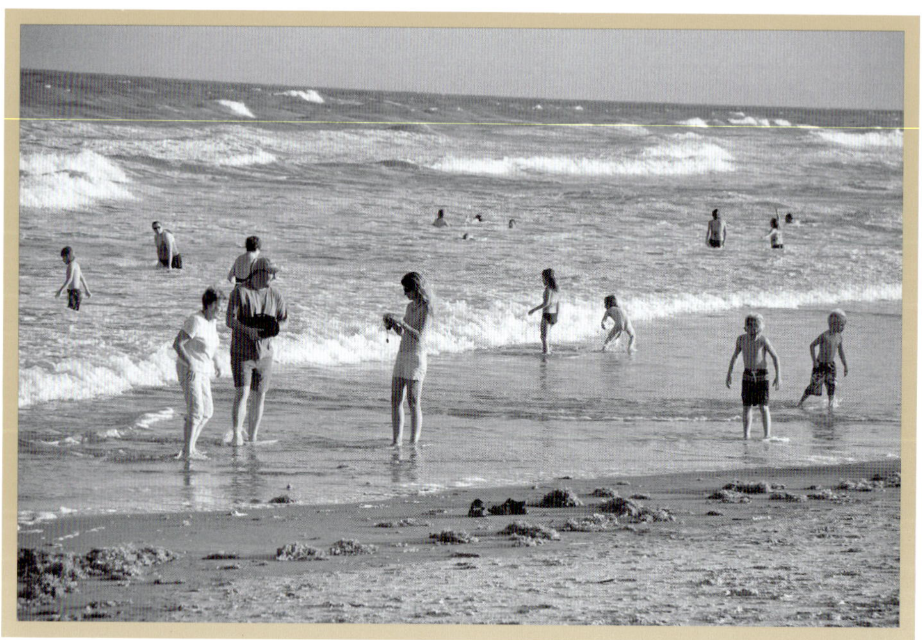

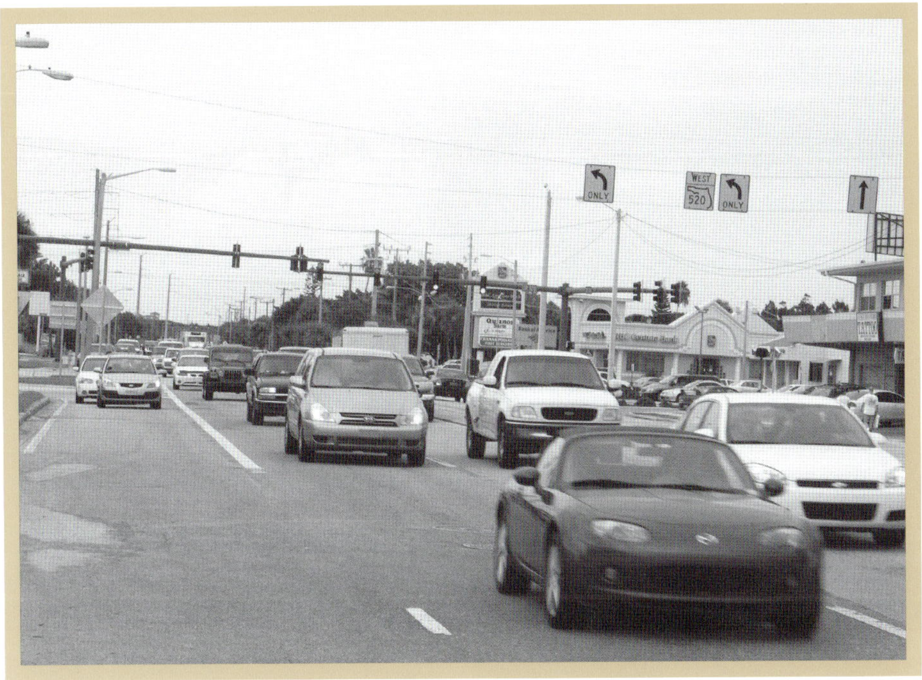


Looking toward the intersection of Highway A1A and Highway 520 in the 1950s showed much less development than what exists today. Sidewalks have replaced the sand, and the missile sign seen in the background is gone as well. One thing that has not changed is the traffic. Highway A1A today is four lanes, which still gets backed up by cars filled with people going to the beach. The building on the right still exists today. (Courtesy City of Cocoa Beach.)

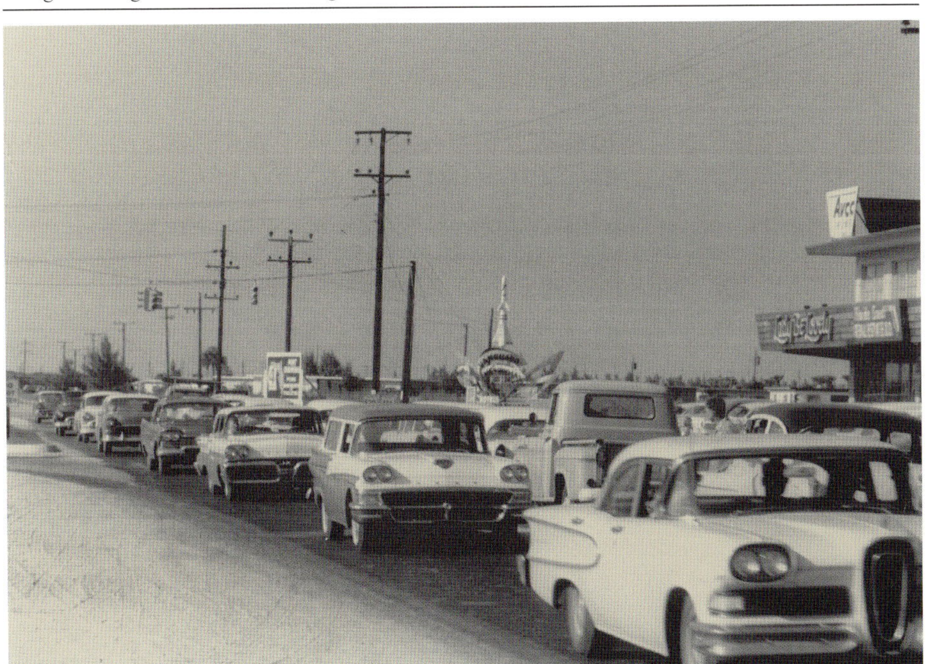

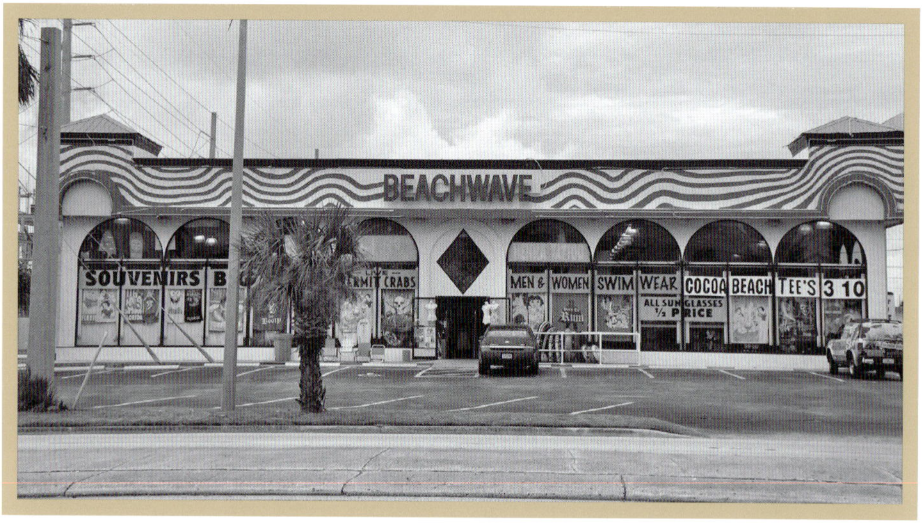


One of the places to visit in Cocoa Beach was Jake's Bowling Alley, located near 175 West Cocoa Beach Causeway, which is also near the intersection of Highway 520 and Highway A1A. Across the street was Ramon's restaurant. Within walking distance of the beach, today it is a retail gift shop called Beachwave that caters to the millions of tourists that come to the area every year. (Courtesy City of Cocoa Beach.)

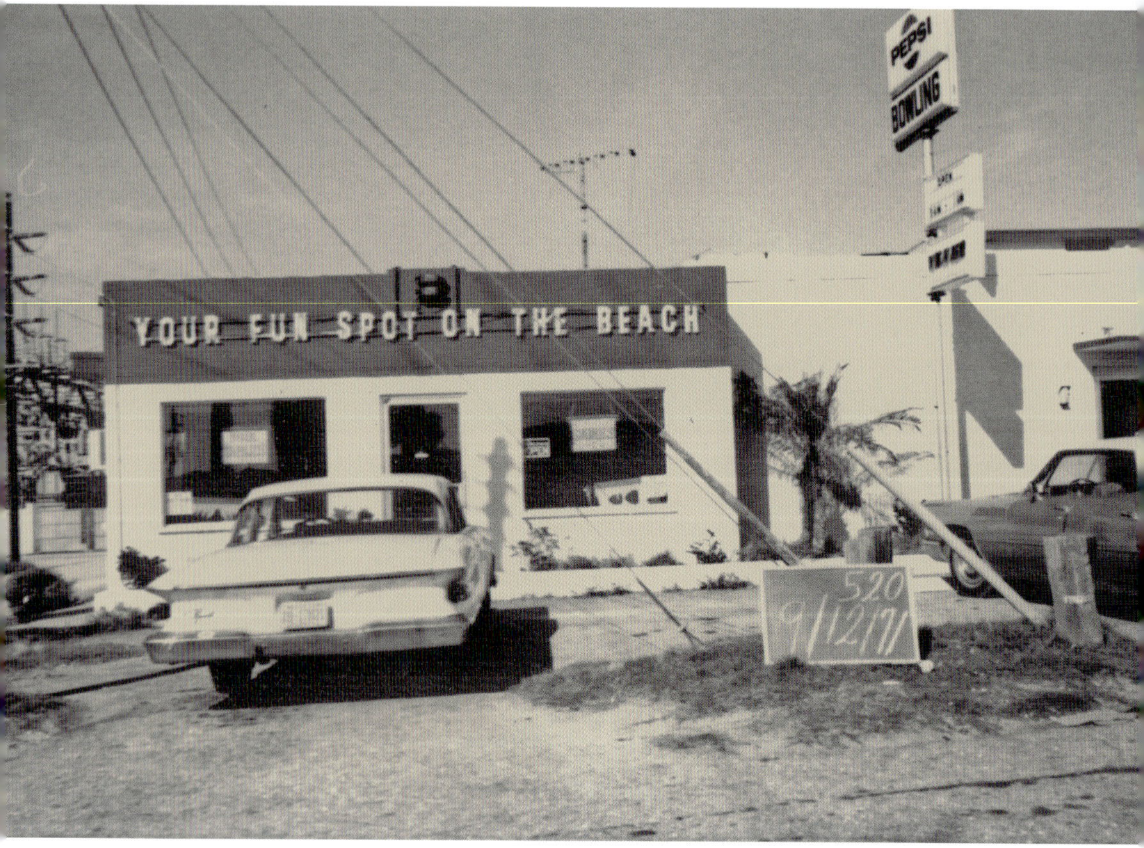

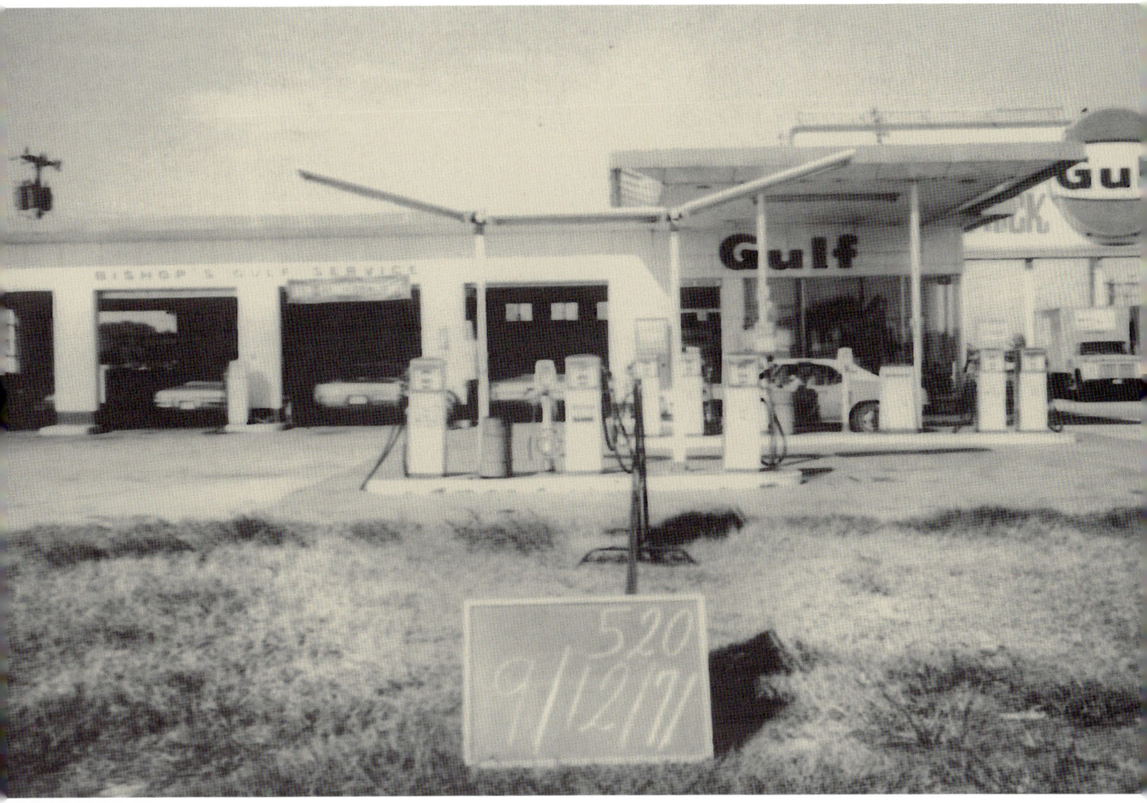


This Gulf gas station existed at the intersection of Highway A1A and Highway 520. It was one of the first gas stations in Cocoa Beach and probably got a lot of business due to its location. Right next door, just out of sight and to the left, was Jake's Bowling Alley. Today it is a business that offers beach souvenirs to the millions of tourists that come to Cocoa Beach each year. (Courtesy City of Cocoa Beach.)

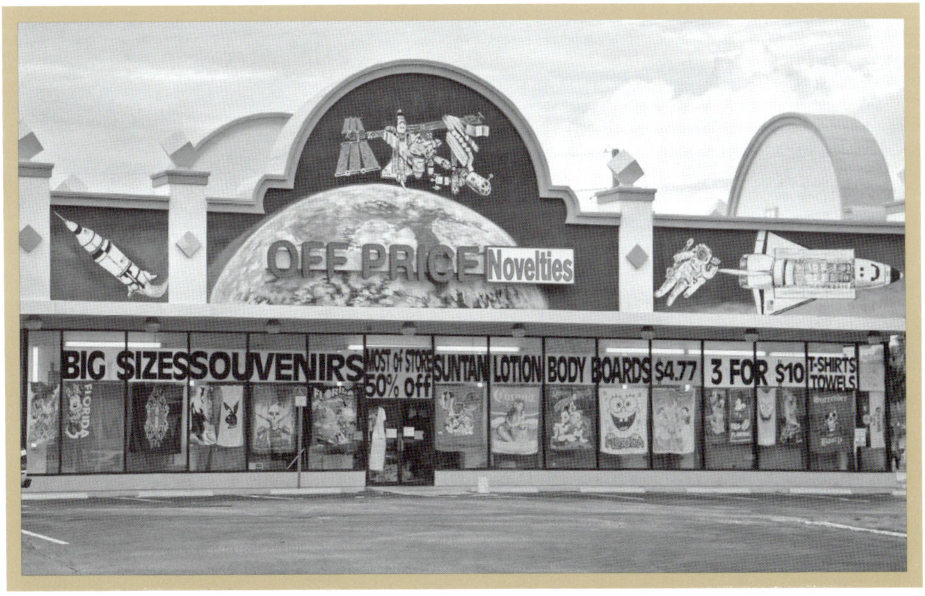

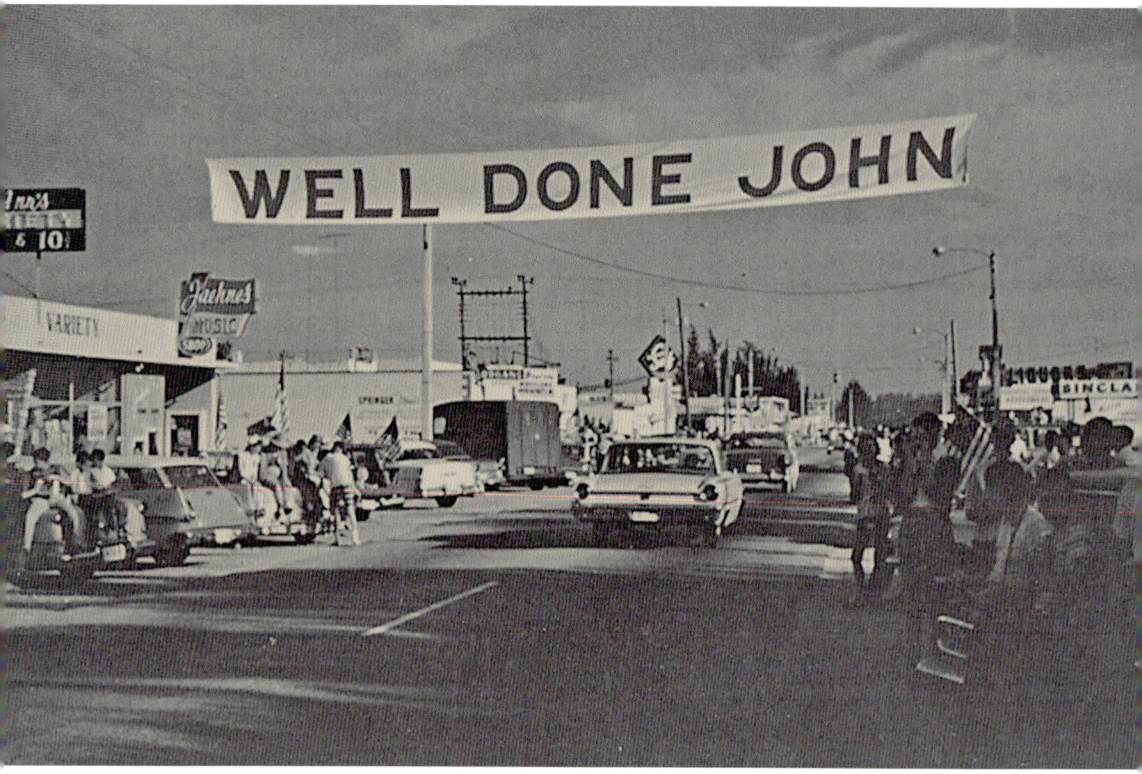


In this image, probably taken in 1962, Mercury astronaut John Glenn is honored in a parade that celebrates his successful launch and return to Earth as the first American to orbit the planet. The parade went right through Cocoa Beach. Glenn called his space capsule *Friendship 7*, and the country had a new hero. The Godke family's variety shop can be seen on the left. Ann Lia's gift shop, which was next to the variety shop, still exists. (Courtesy Pete Godke.)

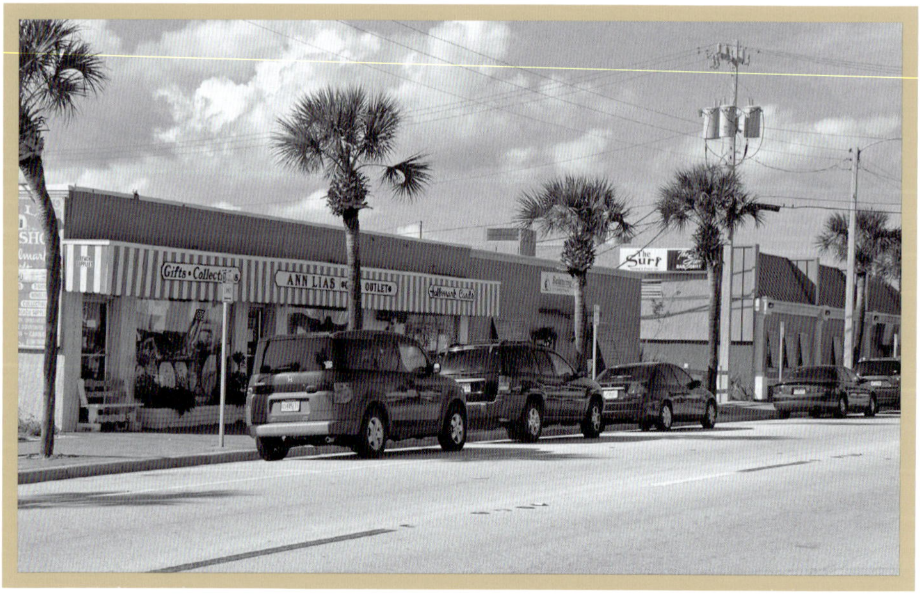

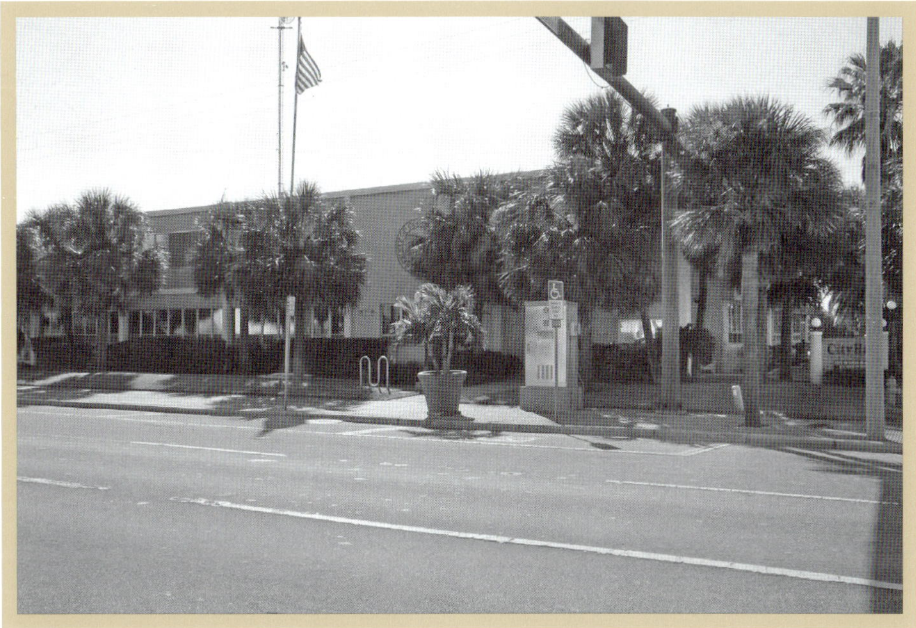

Today the City of Cocoa Beach city hall building looks similar to how it appeared in 1963. Built in 1962, the structure has gone through many renovations. The fire department was once housed in this building as well, but moved in 1984. The Cocoa Beach Police Department operates from a building that was later connected to city hall. (Courtesy City of Cocoa Beach.)

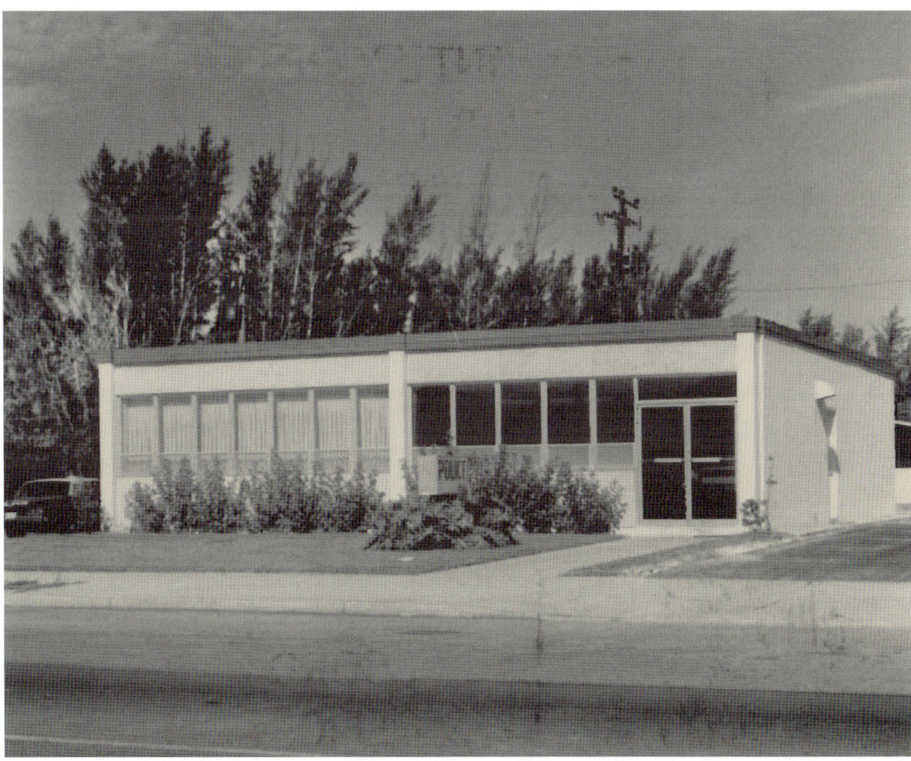

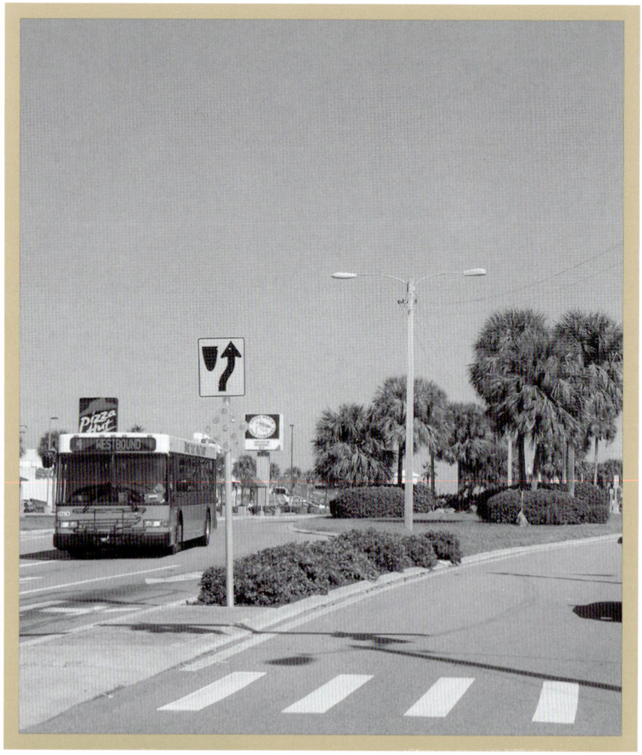


A famous sign advertising motels in the 1960s stood just east of the intersection of Highway 520 and A1A, near where a Bank of America stands today. During the space race of the era, many motels' names and designs were based on the space program. Unfortunately the sign is long gone, and all that remains is the end of Highway 520 to the beach. (Courtesy City of Cocoa Beach.)

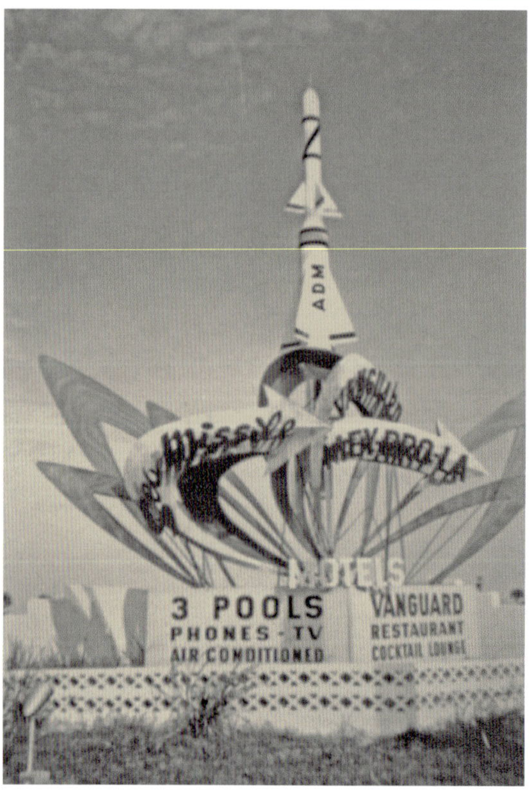

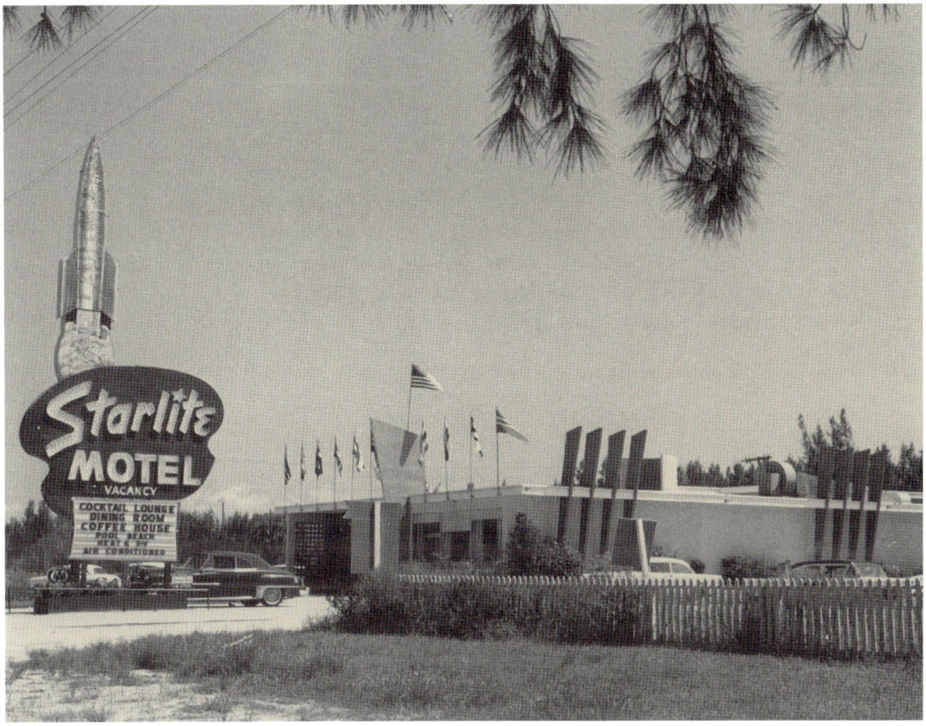


The Starlite Motel was located at 900 North Atlantic Avenue in Cocoa Beach. The establishment was one of many that added a unique charm to Cocoa Beach and served the area's growing population and tourists during the 1960s. A cocktail lounge, dining room, and coffeehouse were all located at the motel. Today the motel is gone, replaced by the Ocean's Landing Resort. Also at the location is a restaurant and popular nightclub. (Courtesy City of Cocoa Beach.)

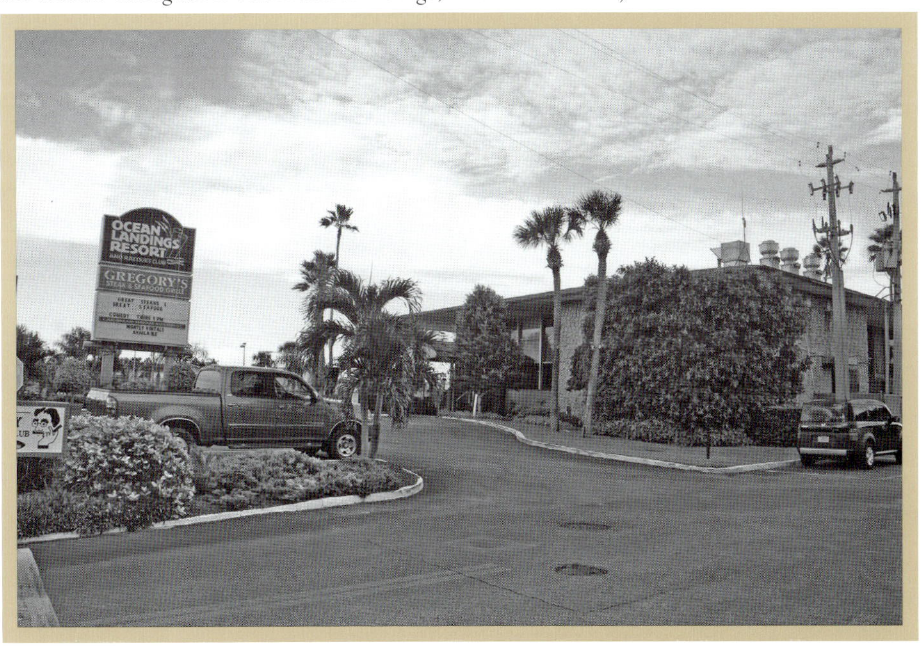

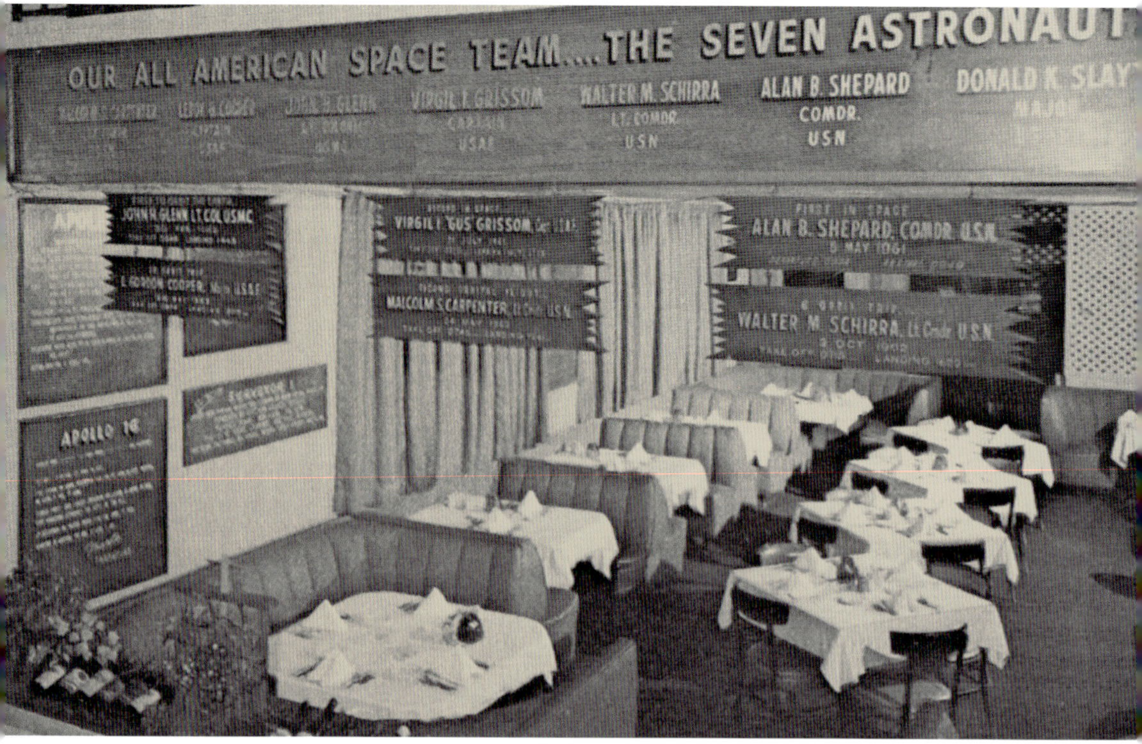


Ramon's restaurant was operated by Don and Allene Holt and was located somewhere near 204 West Cocoa Beach Causeway, across from the White Shopping Center in Cocoa Beach. The restaurant was a popular destination in the 1960s, but the only piece of the restaurant that remains is a large sign commemorating the original seven NASA astronauts. The sign can be found inside the Cocoa Beach Country Club lounge, located off of Minutemen Causeway. (Courtesy Joe Morgan.)

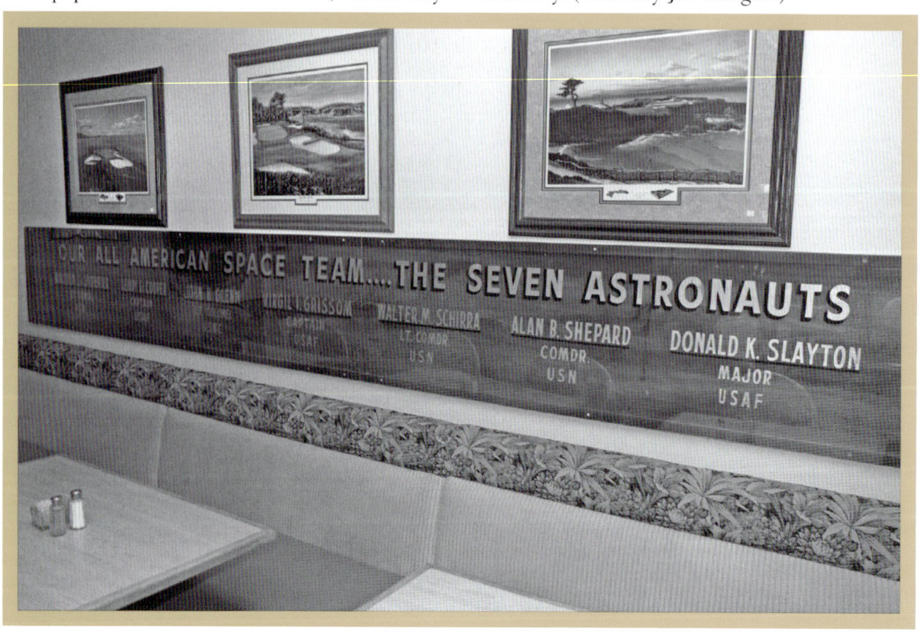

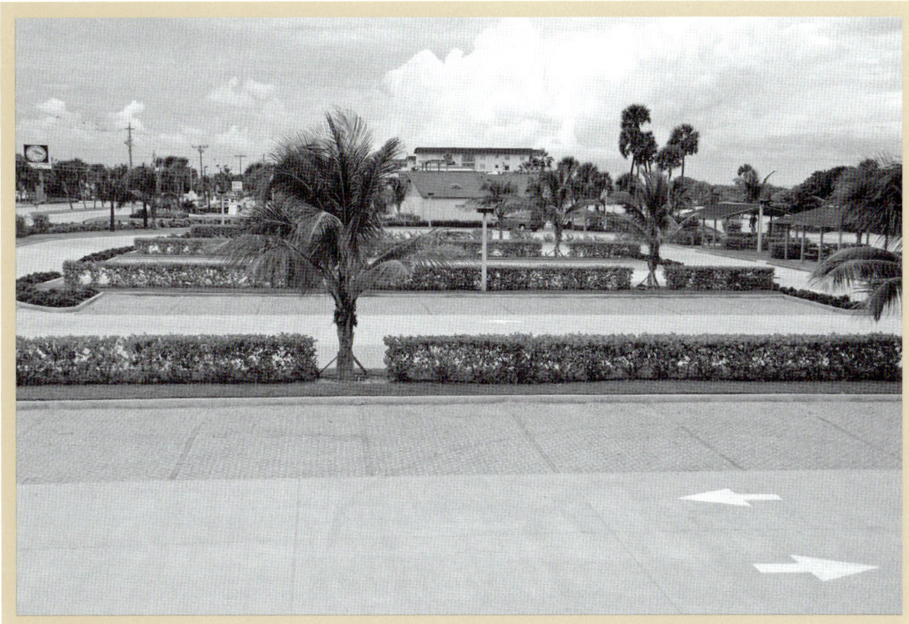

The Shepard Park of the 1970s was probably just as busy as it is today. Located at the east end of Highway 520 and Ocean Beach Boulevard, it was named after the famous astronaut Alan Shepard. Retail shops, food, lodging, entertainment, and of course the beach are literally all a stone's throw away from the popular park. Today it is a classic location known for viewing NASA shuttle launches and for holding surfing contests. (Courtesy City of Cocoa Beach.)

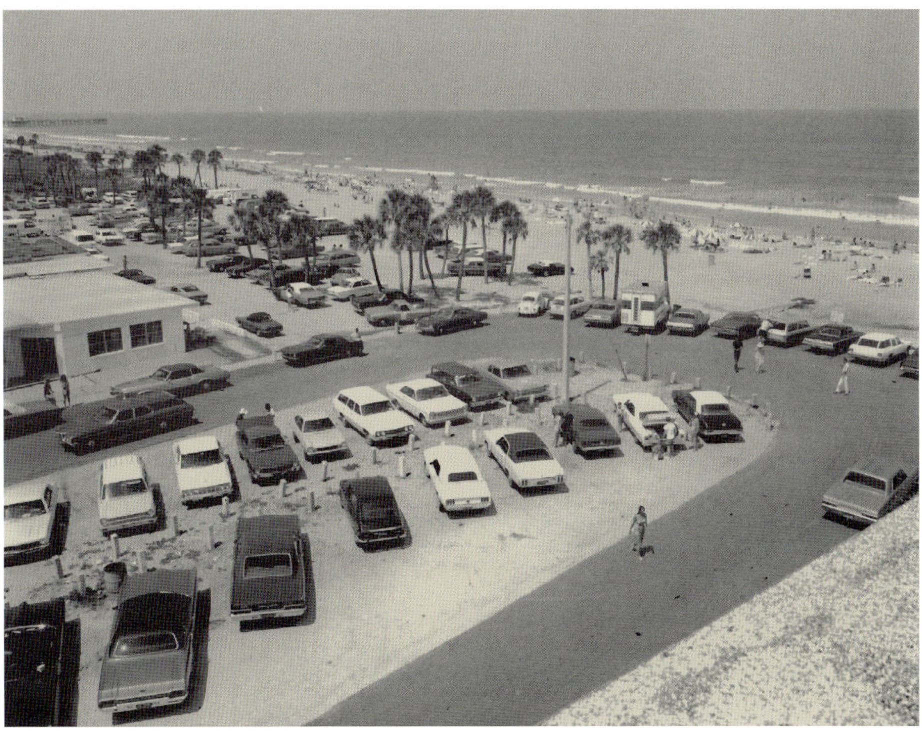

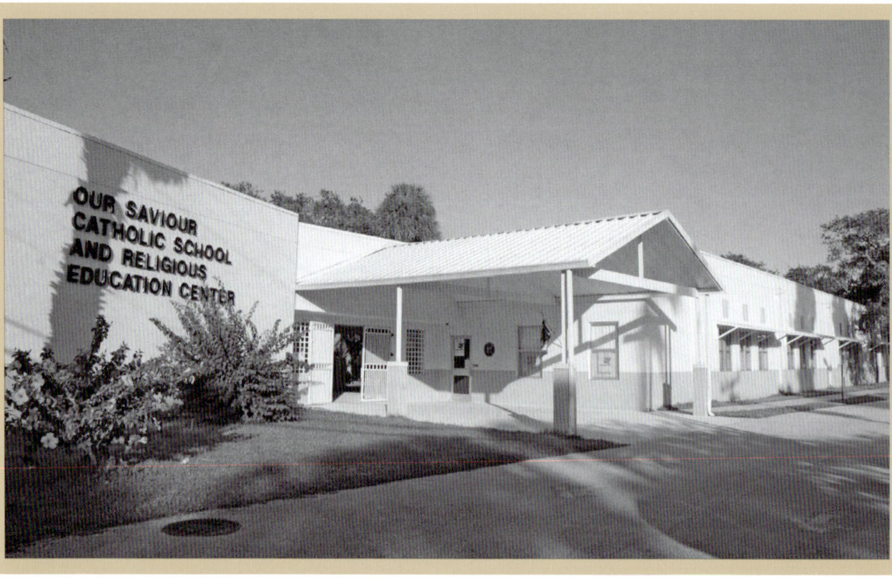


Our Saviour Catholic School is located at 5301 North Atlantic Avenue in Cocoa Beach. This first-grade class from the 1960s would have attended school in a building that largely no longer exists. Today just a part of it remains, and there is now a parking lot where the rest of the building stood. A new school was built in its place to offer more classroom space for additional students. (Courtesy Our Saviour Catholic School.)

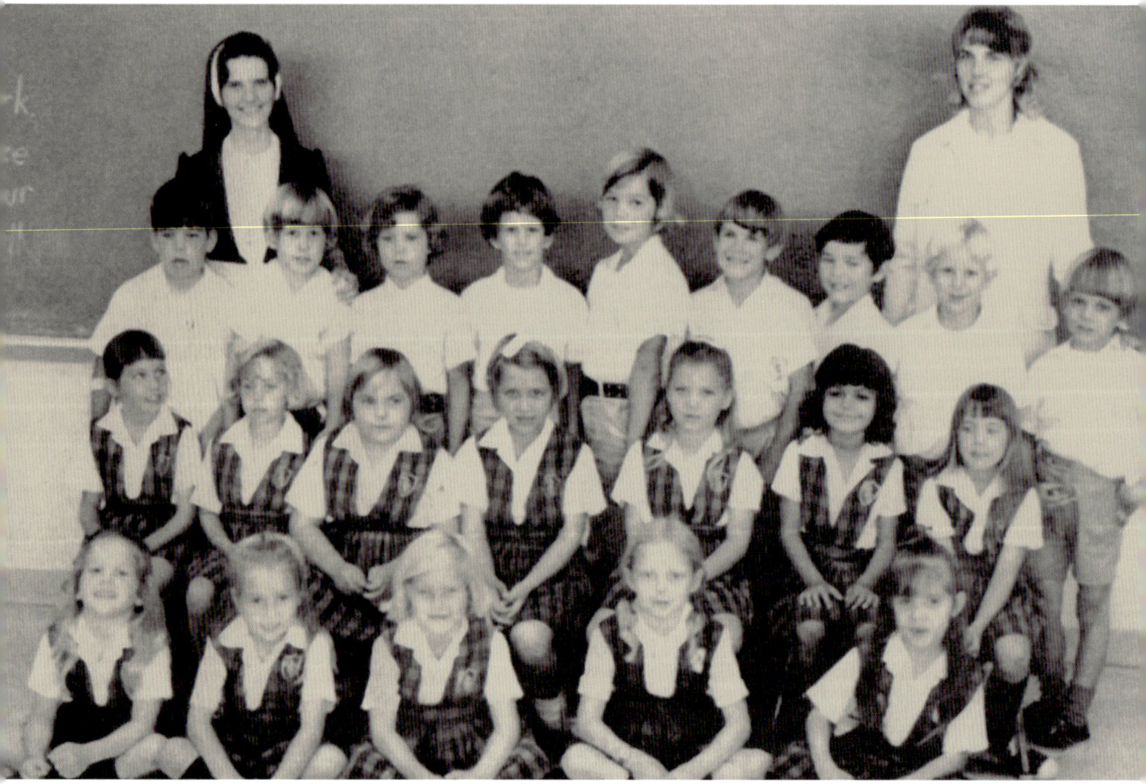

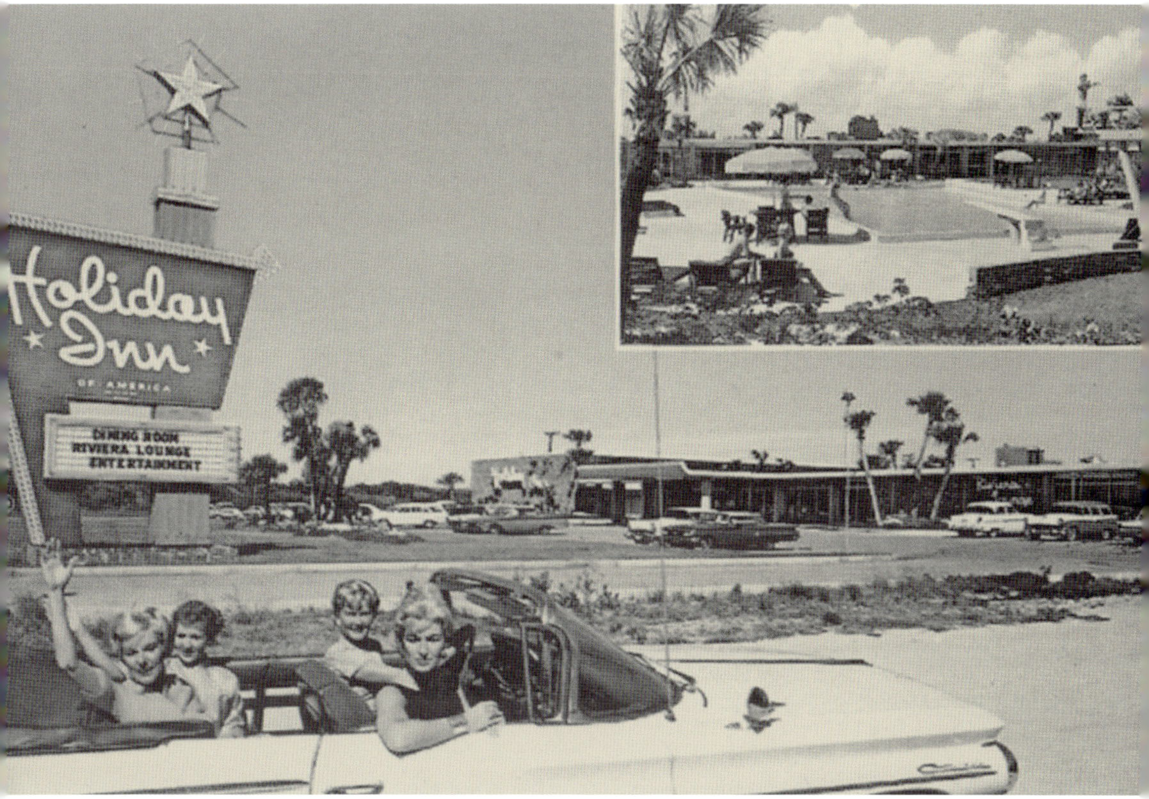


The Holiday Inn of the 1960s was located at 1300 North Atlantic Avenue, one of the most popular locations for tourists and astronauts of the time. Some say that a few wild stories can be told about the fun the astronauts had while staying there. Today the location is still a Holiday Inn, but it has expanded dramatically to accommodate the many visitors to Cocoa Beach. (Courtesy Holiday Inn Cocoa Beach Oceanfront Resort.)

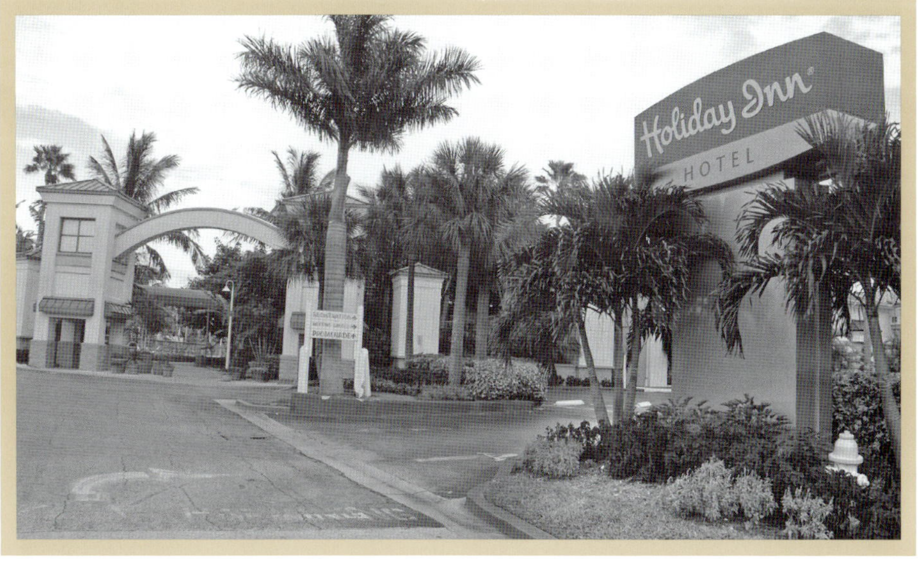

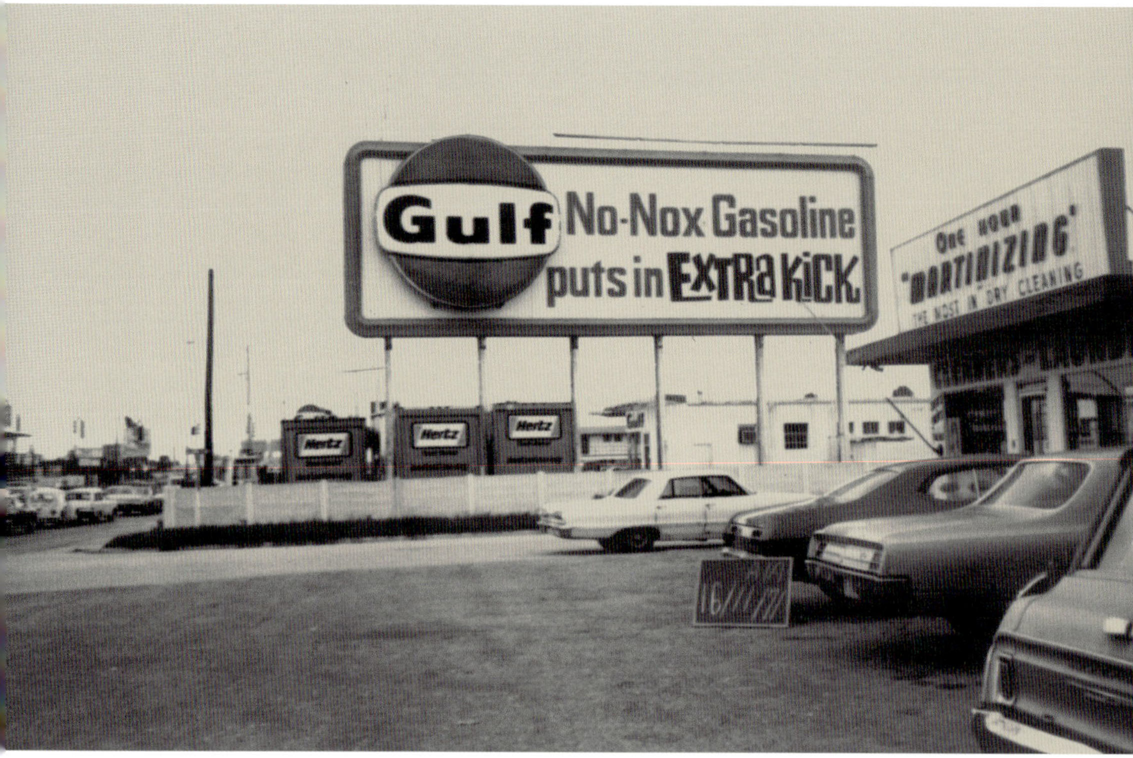


The One Hour Martinizing Cleaners and Laundry, located at 300 West Cocoa Beach Causeway, is seen in this 1971 photograph. Although the exterior of the building has changed, it still exists today. Now known as the 60 Minute Cleaners, it is owned by Central Florida Drycleaning. The company runs six locations in Brevard County and has been in operation since 1968. (Courtesy City of Cocoa Beach.)

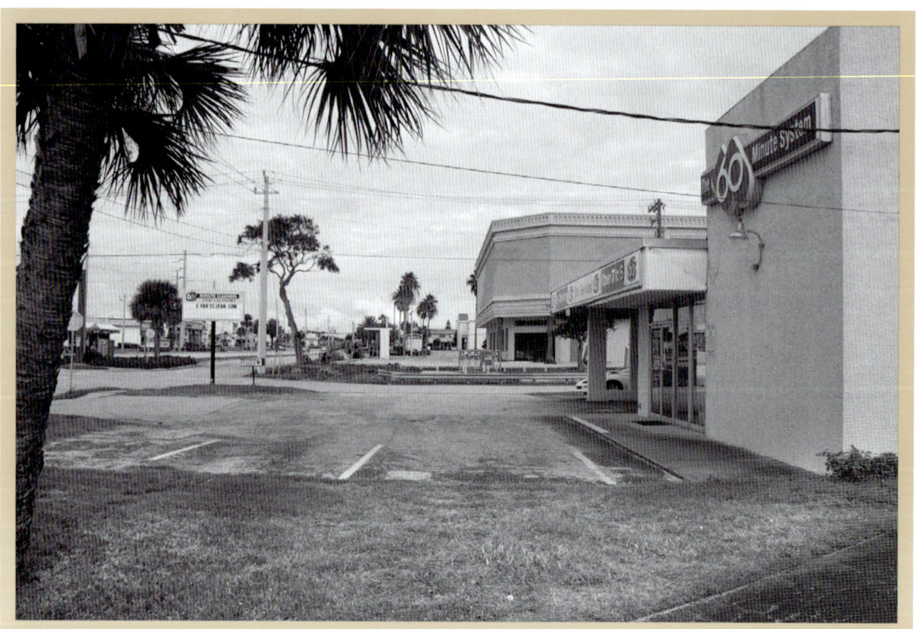

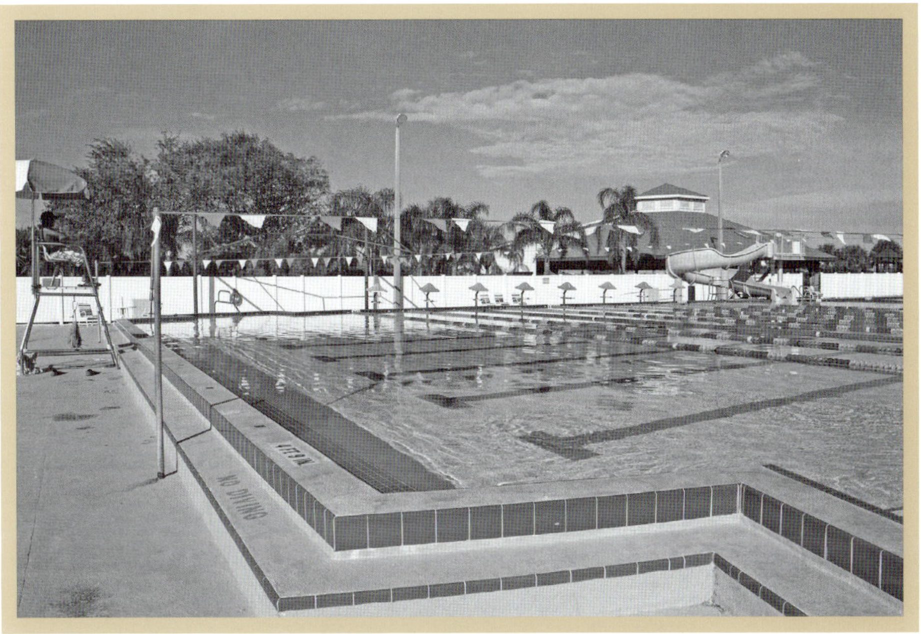

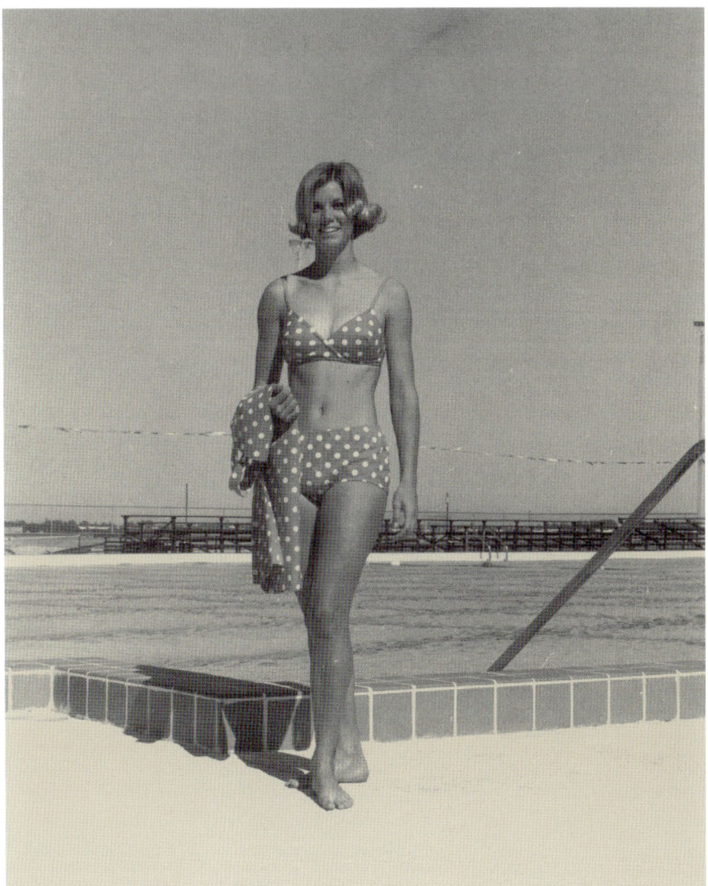

A 1960s swimmer shows off her polka-dotted bikini at the Cocoa Beach Country Club swimming pool, located on Tom Warriner Boulevard, just off of Minutemen Causeway. The pool and club still exist today and are surrounded by the Banana River Lagoon. The Olympic-sized pool is a public facility owned by the City of Cocoa Beach and is also known as the Aquatic Center. (Courtesy City of Cocoa Beach.)

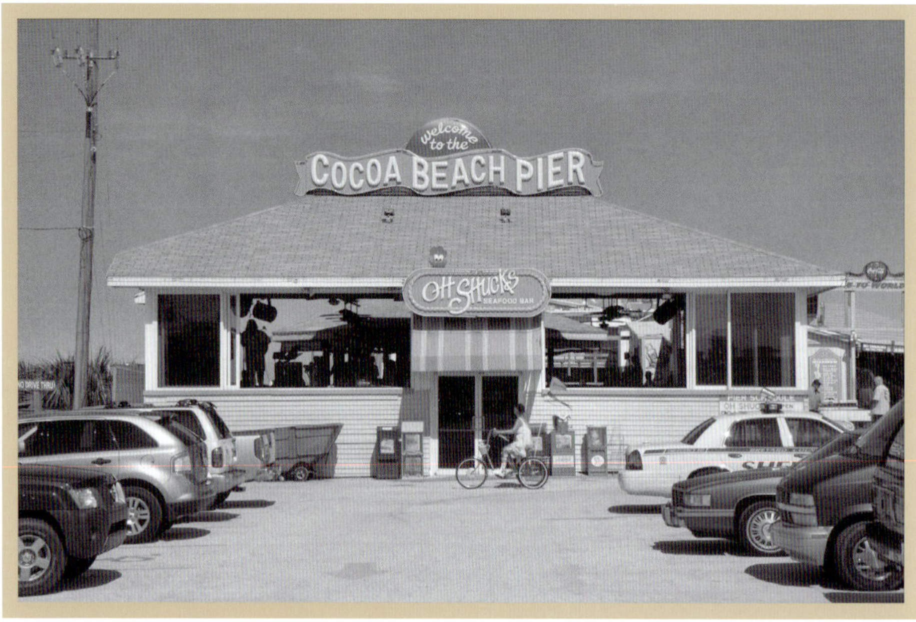


Still known to many surfers as Canaveral Pier, the 800-foot-long structure was built in 1962 at 401 Meade Avenue in Cocoa Beach. Ron Jon Surf Shop originally sold surfboards from the pier, and over the years, it has become a prime destination for surfers and tourists alike. Confused by the pier's name?Years after it was built, the named was changed to Cocoa Beach Pier, which reflects its actual location within city limits. (Courtesy Ron Jon Surf Shop.)

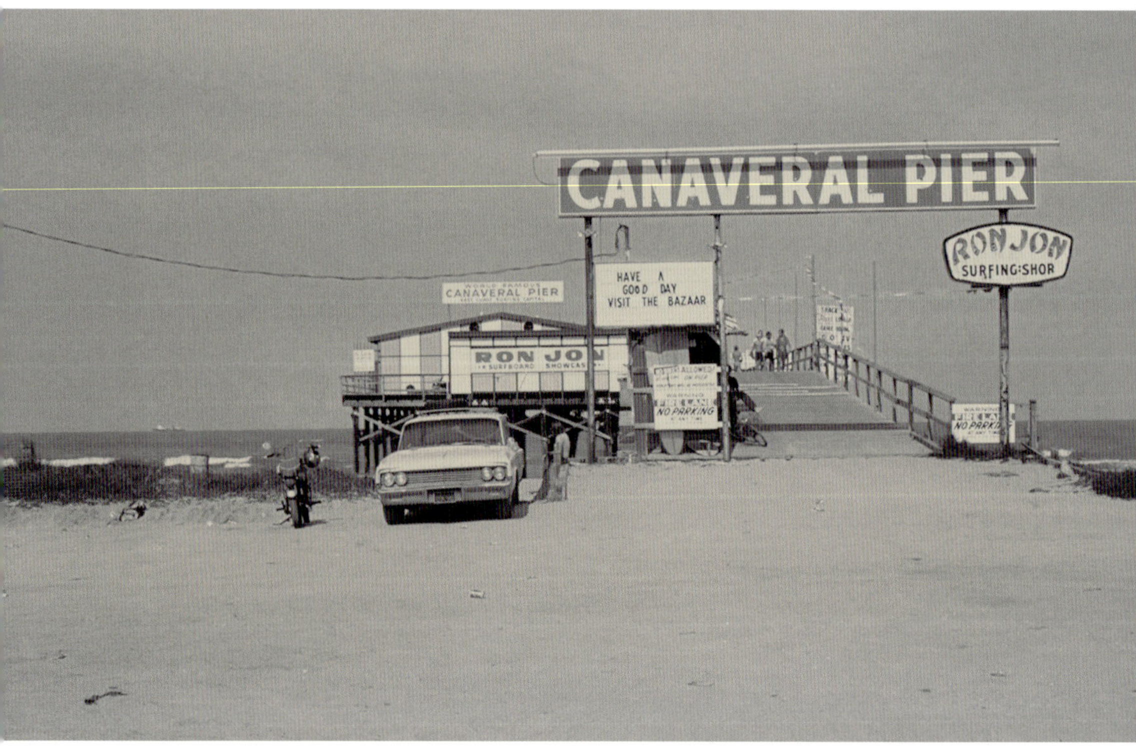

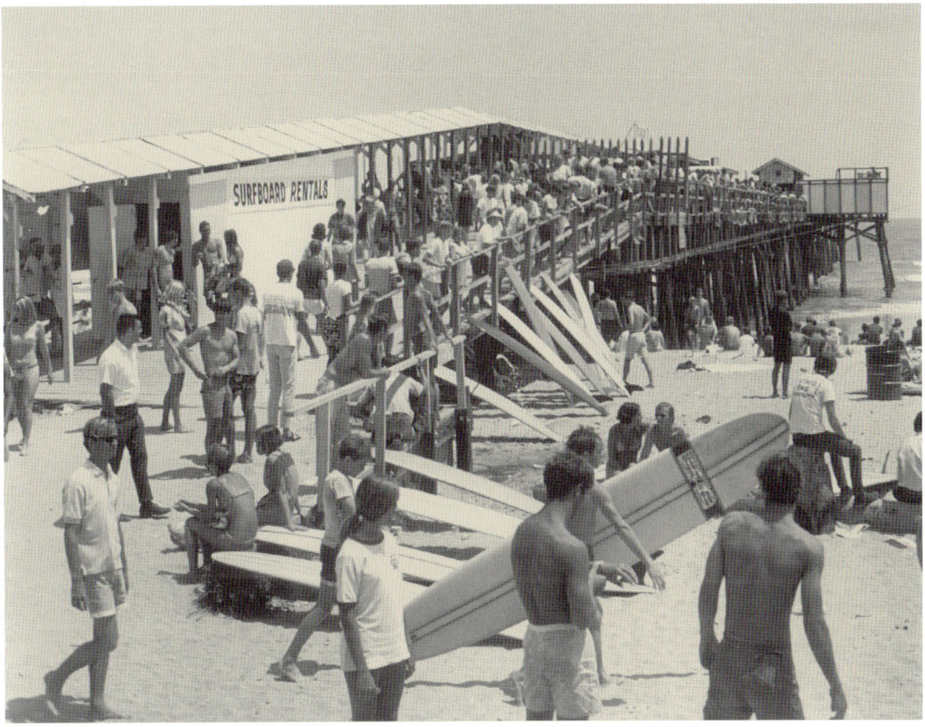


Surfers line their longboards on Canaveral Pier, now called Cocoa Beach Pier, which was built in 1962. The Cocoa Beach area has developed its own surfing culture over the years, and today is the home of Ron Jon's Surf Shop. It also has its own surfing museum. Professional surfer Kelly Slater, considered by many to be the best surfer in the world, was born and raised in Cocoa Beach. (Courtesy City of Cocoa Beach.)

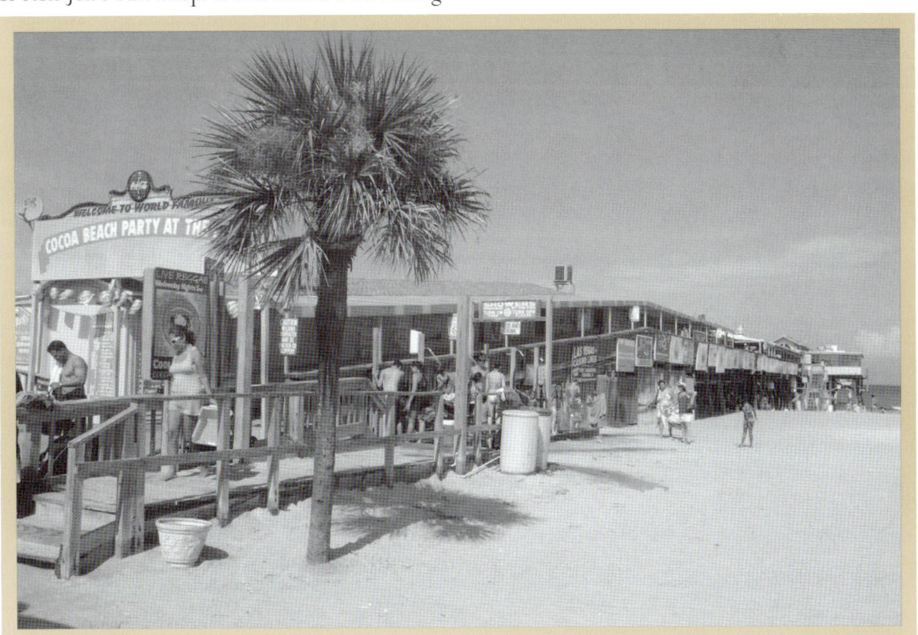

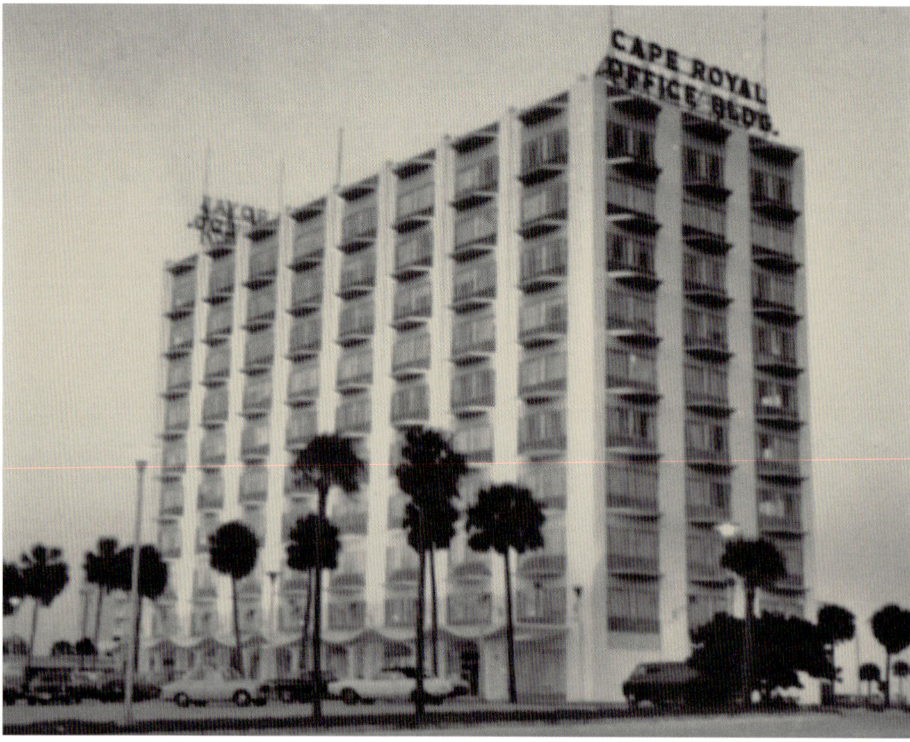


Opened sometime in the 1960s, the Cape Royal Building is a familiar part of the Cocoa Beach skyline and is the only high-rise business structure that still operates in the city today. Located at 1980 North Atlantic Avenue, the building was a popular destination for fans of NASA to watch launches into space as America headed for the landing on the moon. (Courtesy Florida State Archives.)

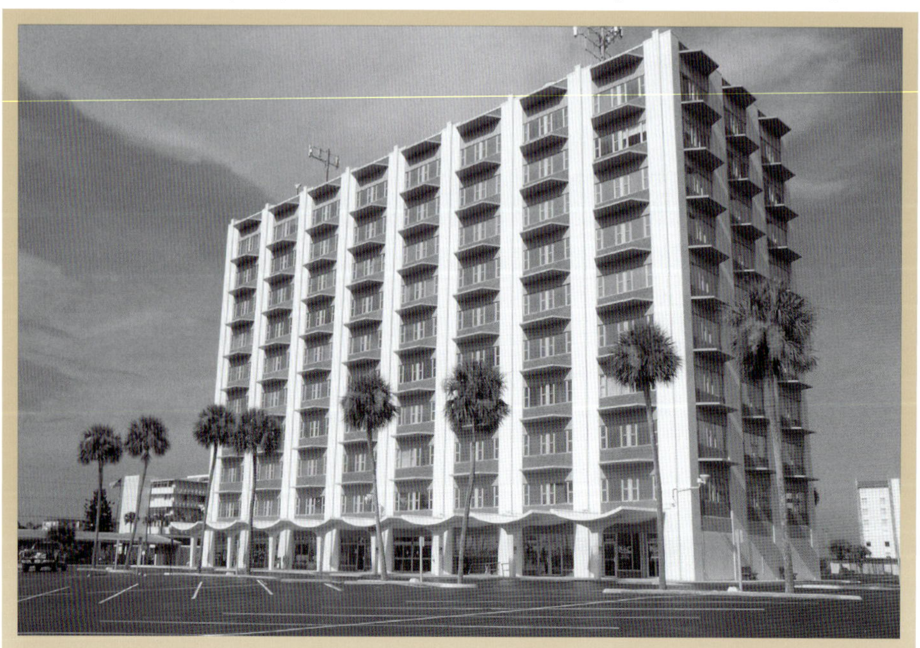

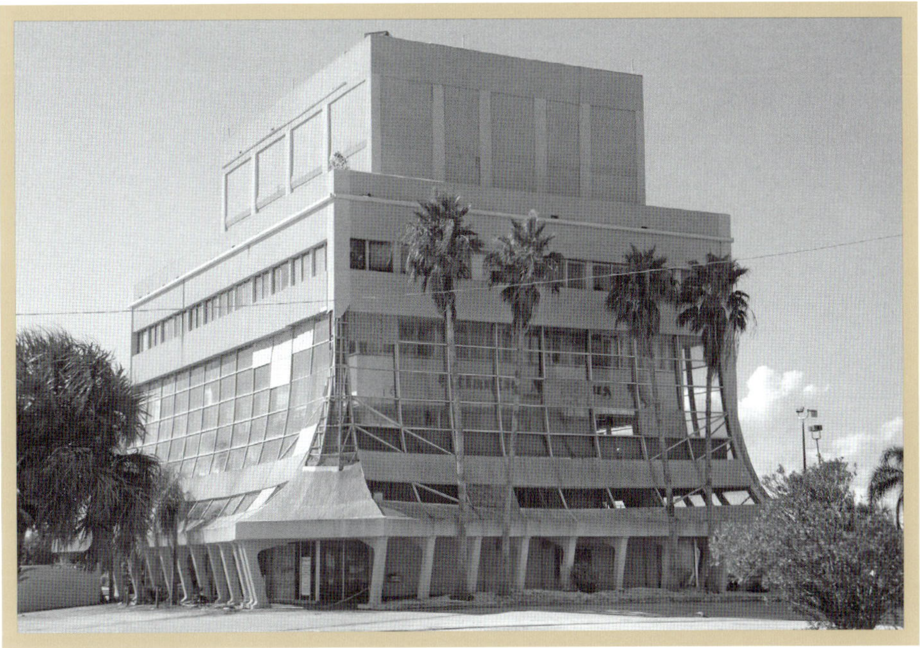

Considered by many to be a Cocoa Beach landmark, the First Federal Savings and Loan building was constructed in the 1960s, giving the city's skyline a modern look for the time. Locally the building was nicknamed "the Glass Bank," because originally the structure boasted glass windows on its entire exterior. Today the building still exists but is largely unoccupied by any businesses and is in need of repair and renovation. (Courtesy Florida Historical Society.)

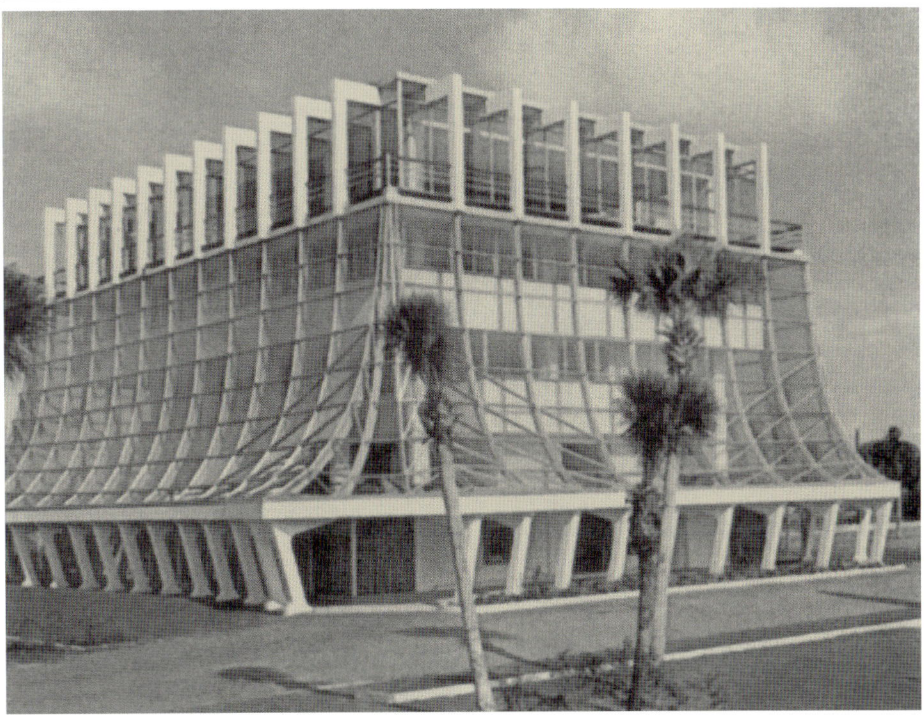

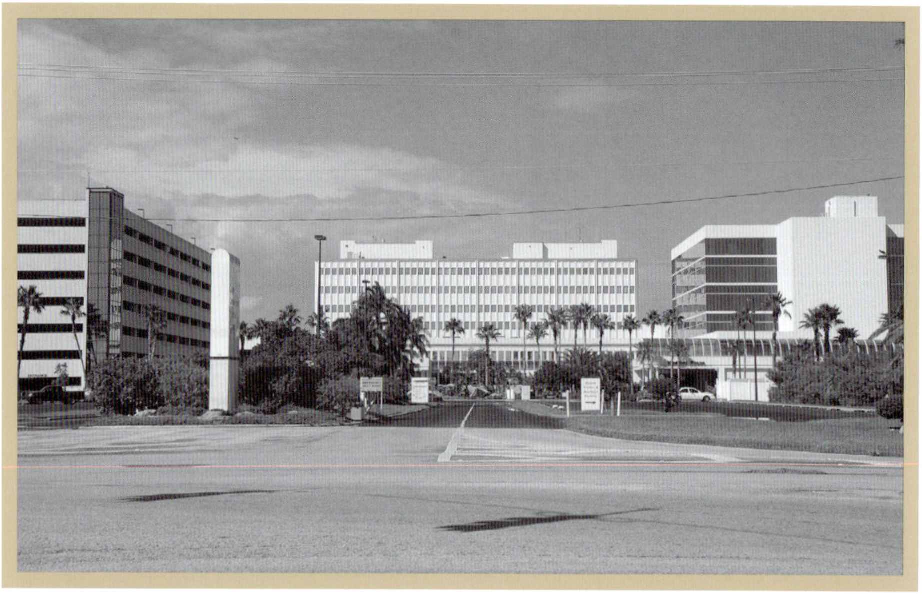

Built on filled-in land, Cape Canaveral Hospital, located at 701 West Cocoa Beach Causeway, opened in 1962. Despite its name, the hospital is actually located in Cocoa Beach. Today it operates as a full-service, nonprofit hospital that includes a 21-bed emergency department, a baby unit, a cancer care program, and many other health services for the community. Over the years, it has expanded greatly from its original size. (Courtesy Florida Historical Society.)

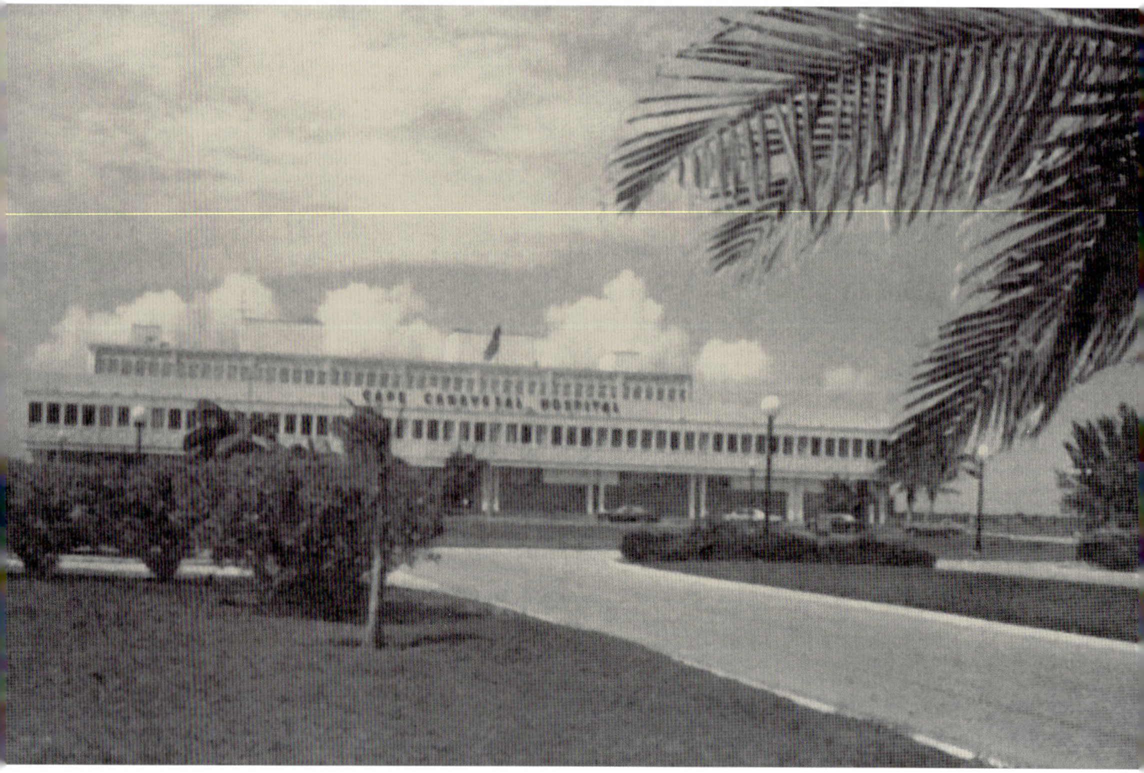

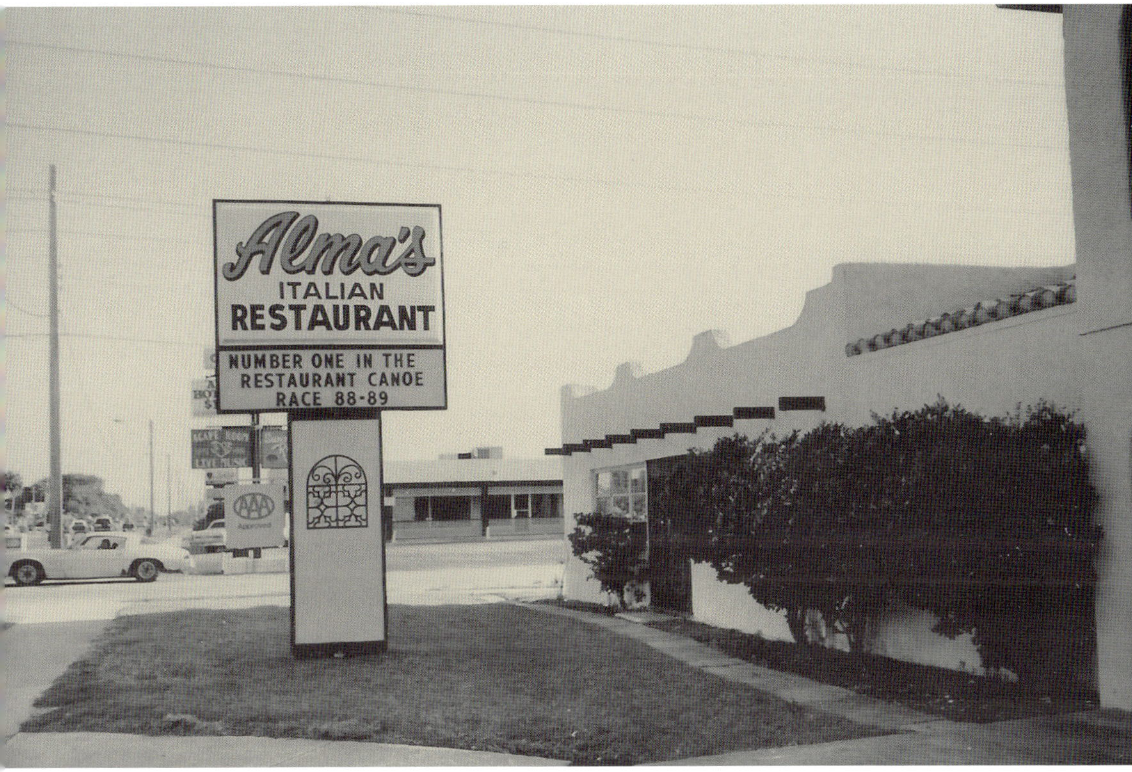


Alma's Italian Restaurant was opened in 1963 by a brother of former Cocoa Beach mayor Joe Morgan. The restaurant operated for over 40 years at 306 North Atlantic Avenue in Cocoa Beach. In September 2004, one day before a hurricane hit the area, the Slow and Low Bar-B-Que restaurant opened at that location and still serves customers today. (Courtesy Joe Morgan.)

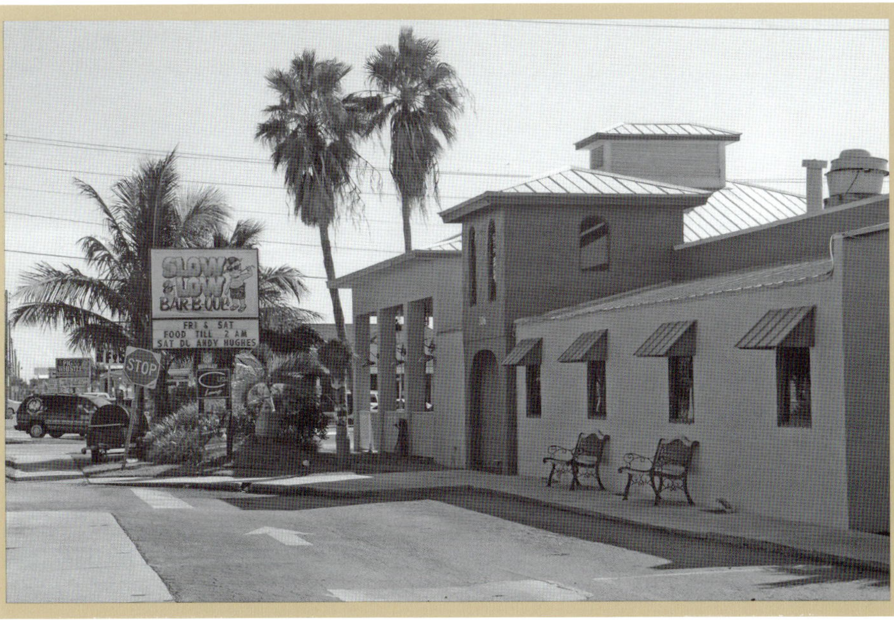

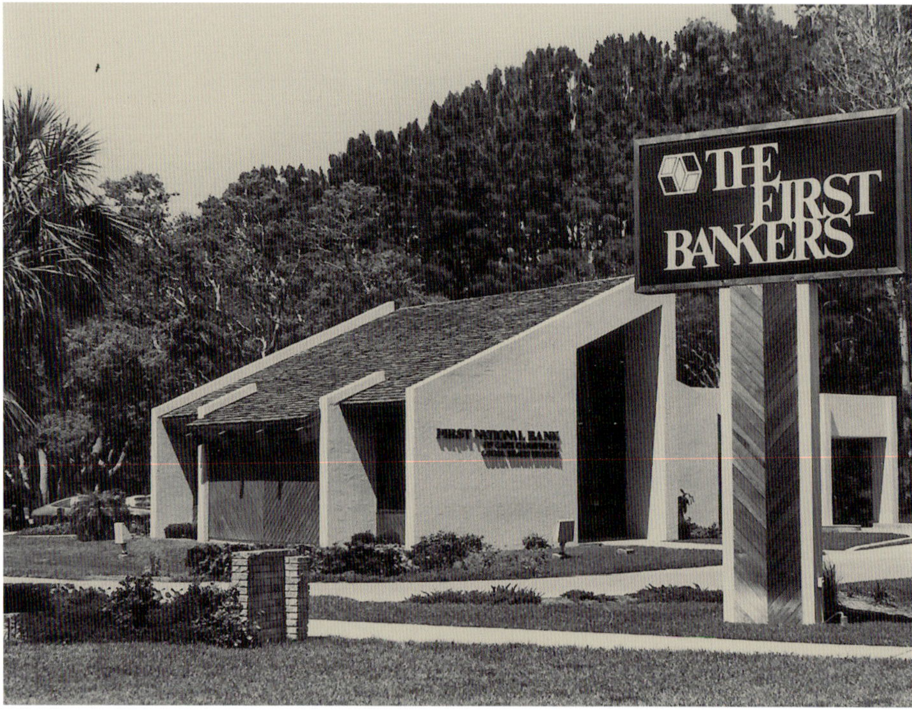


Around 1980, Cocoa Beach's former mayor, Joe Morgan, helped to open the First Bankers bank, located at 1205 Atlantic Avenue, also known as Highway A1A, in Cocoa Beach. Morgan served as mayor from 1973 to 1999. Today the bank location is part of the Space Coast Credit Union, which has been around since 1951. The credit union has many locations and serves 145,000 members throughout Brevard County. (Courtesy Joe Morgan.)

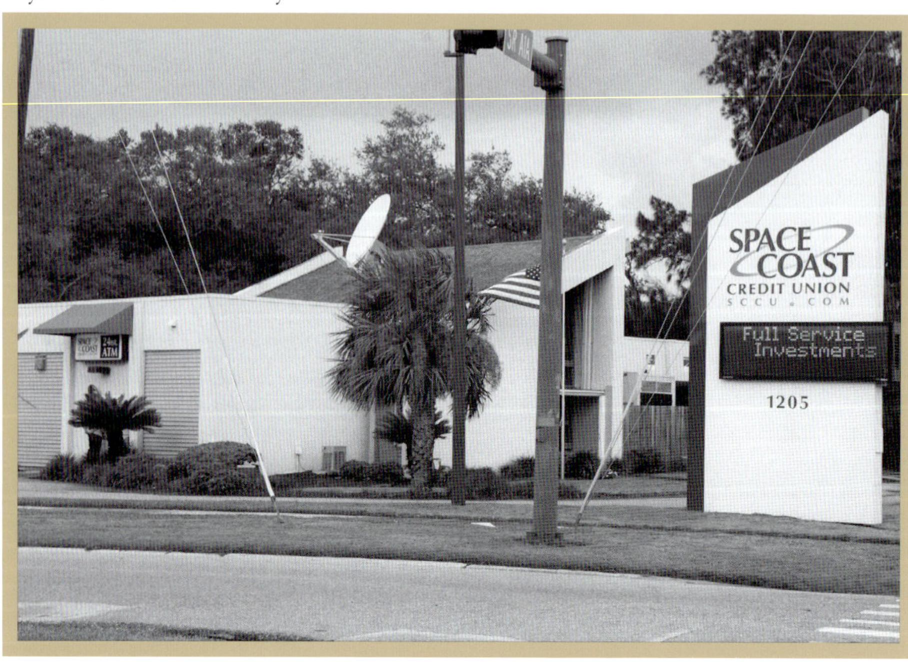

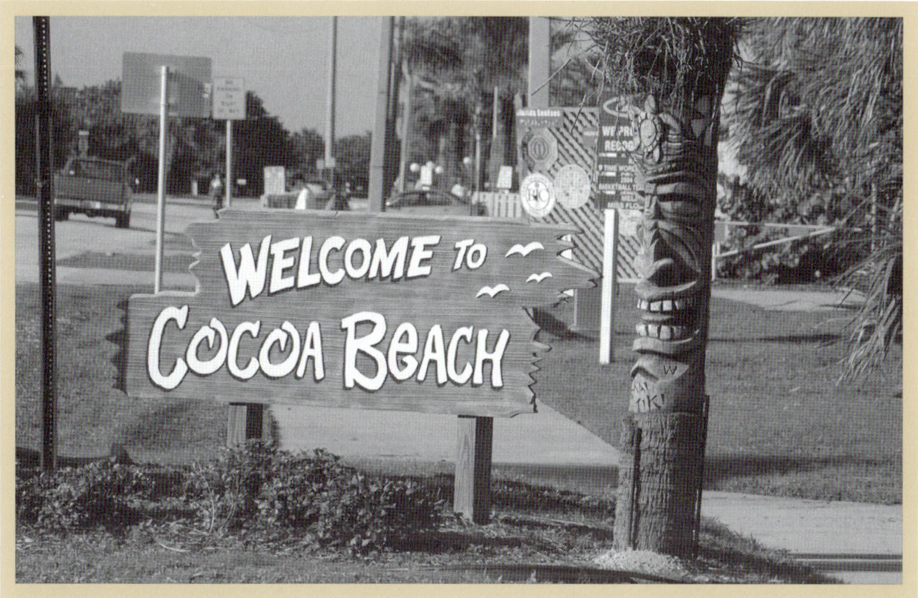


Over the years, the City of Cocoa Beach has had a few different designs for its welcome signs. The signs welcome visitors to the area, and today they really reflect the city's connection to the beach. Designed by longtime resident Wayne Coombs, who owns the Mai Tiki gallery, the current signs feature a jovial tiki statue. (Courtesy City of Cocoa Beach.)

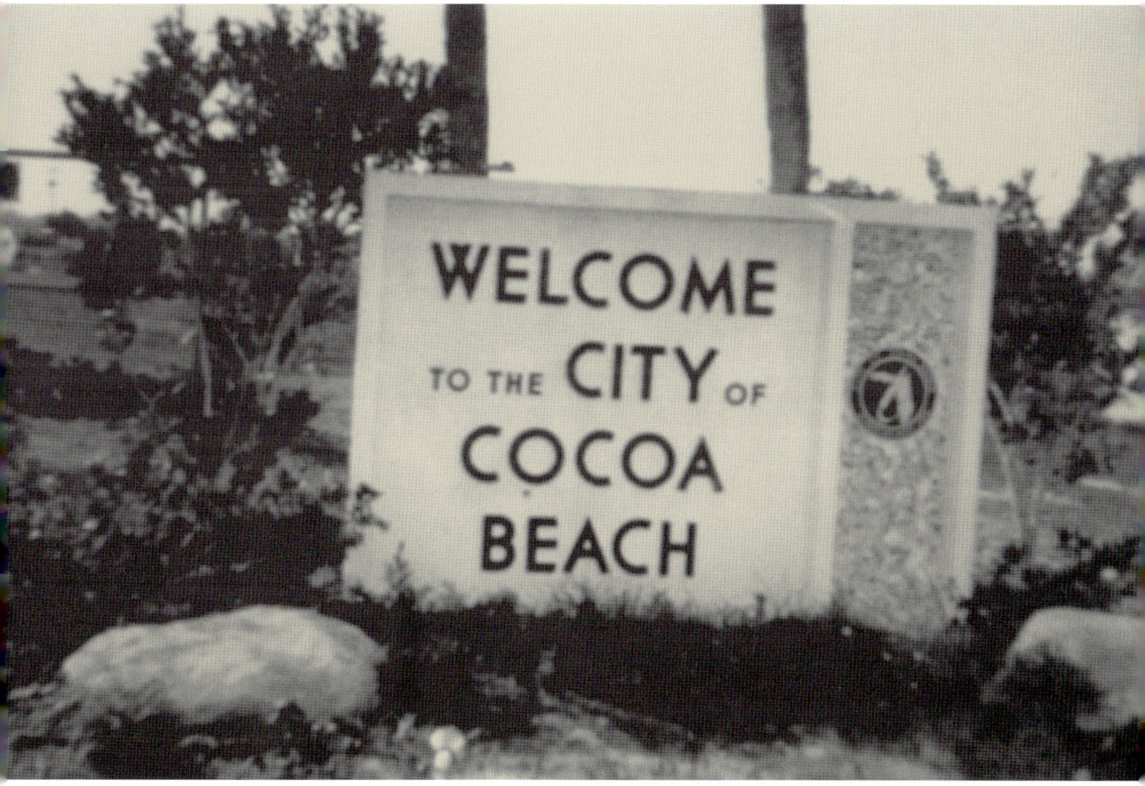

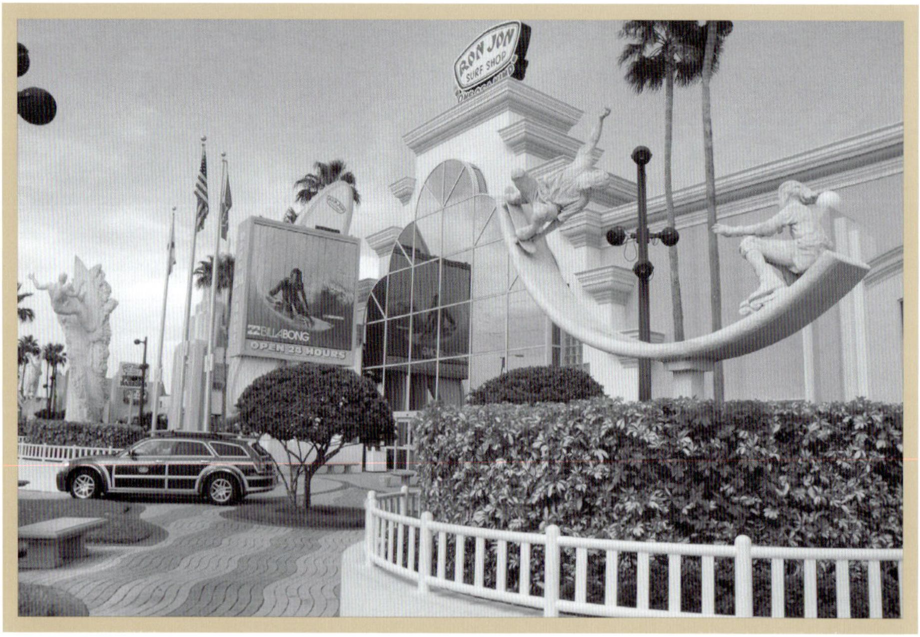


The "One of a Kind" Ron Jon Surf Shop has served customers in Cocoa Beach since the early 1960s. The shop's sign might have seemed large in the 1980s, but it was nothing when compared to the huge presence the establishment has today. It is truly an icon that many consider synonymous with Cocoa Beach. Ron DiMenna opened his shop after moving to the area from New Jersey. Today it is located at 4151 North Atlantic Avenue. (Courtesy City of Cocoa Beach.)

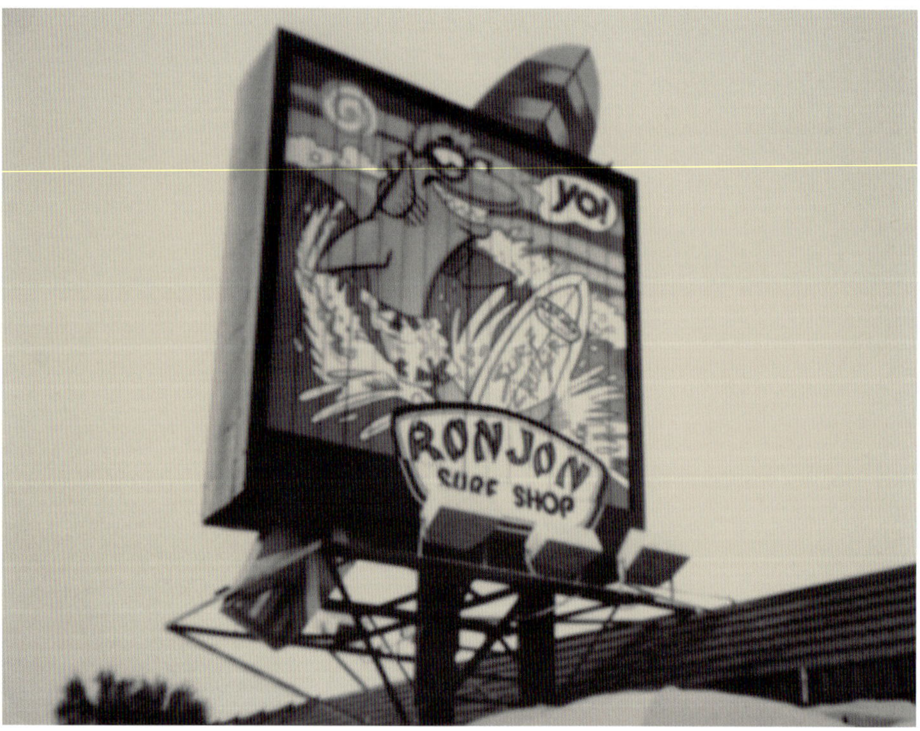

CHAPTER 2

# The Space Race

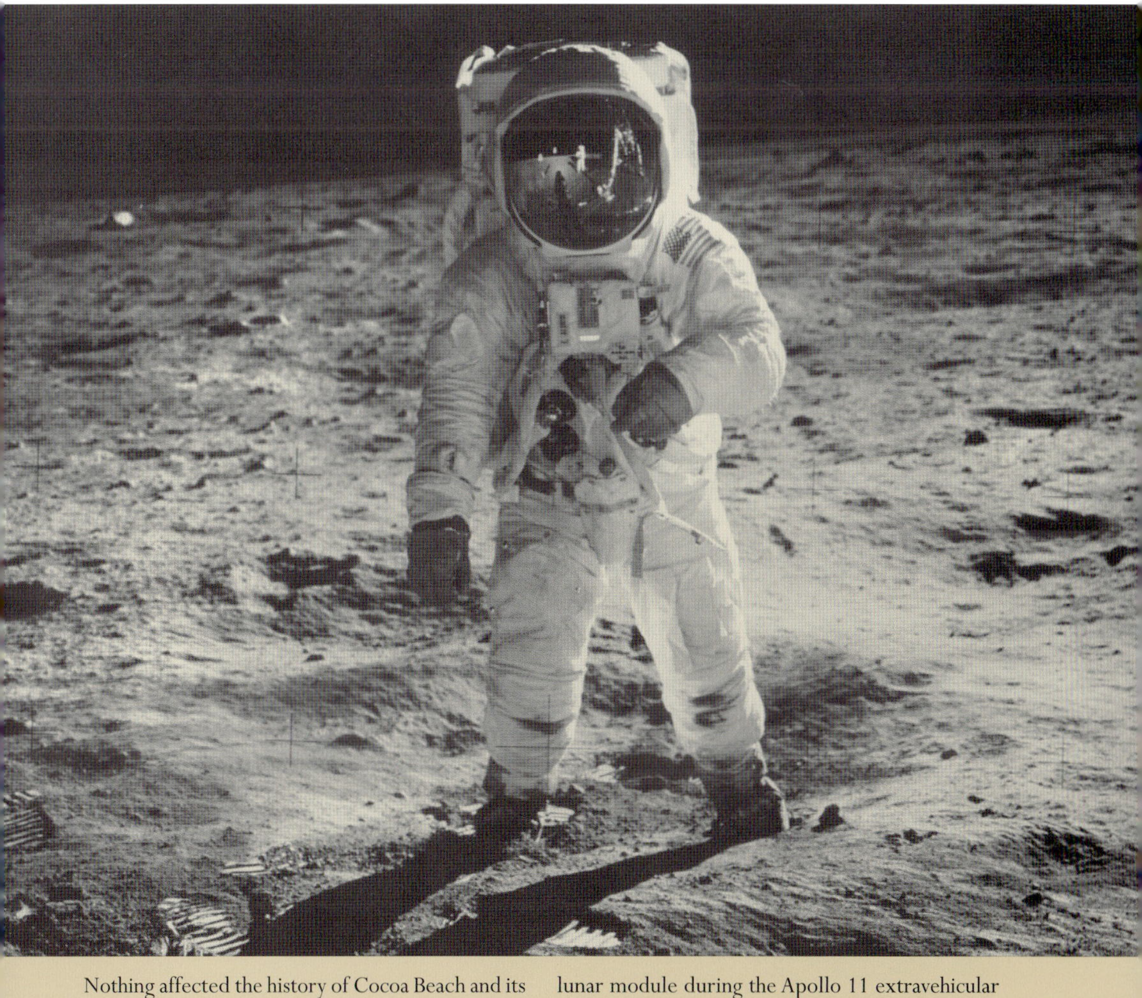

Nothing affected the history of Cocoa Beach and its neighboring communities like the 1960s space race. In this photograph, astronaut Edwin E. Aldrin Jr., a lunar module pilot, is photographed walking near the lunar module during the Apollo 11 extravehicular activity. This picture was taken by astronaut Neil A. Armstrong, commander, with a 70-mm lunar surface camera. (Courtesy NASA.)

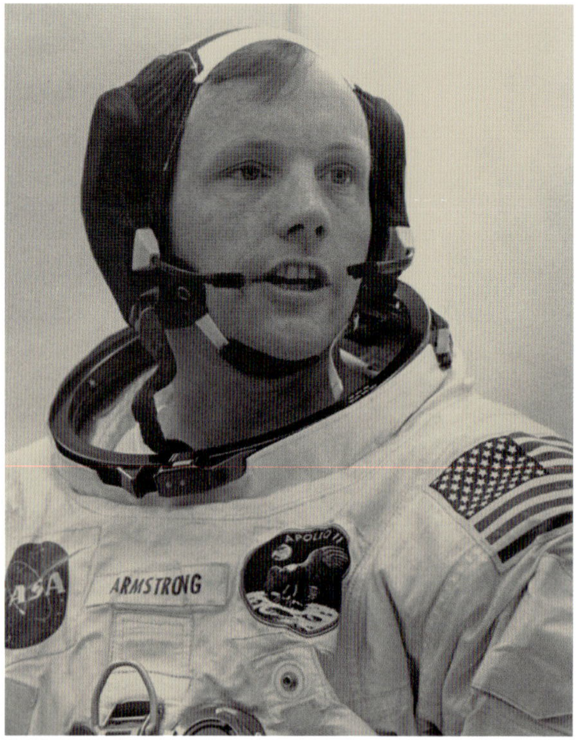


Neil A. Armstrong suits up for NASA's Apollo 11 mission in July 1969. The first man to walk on the moon, he would become an American hero. Today NASA astronauts train, prepare, and perform their missions with the same dedication. STS-125 pilot Gregory C. Johnson prepares for an upcoming space shuttle launch after taking part in a simulated launch countdown aboard space shuttle *Atlantis*. Crews participate in various launch activities, including emergency training. (Courtesy NASA/Kim Shiflett.)

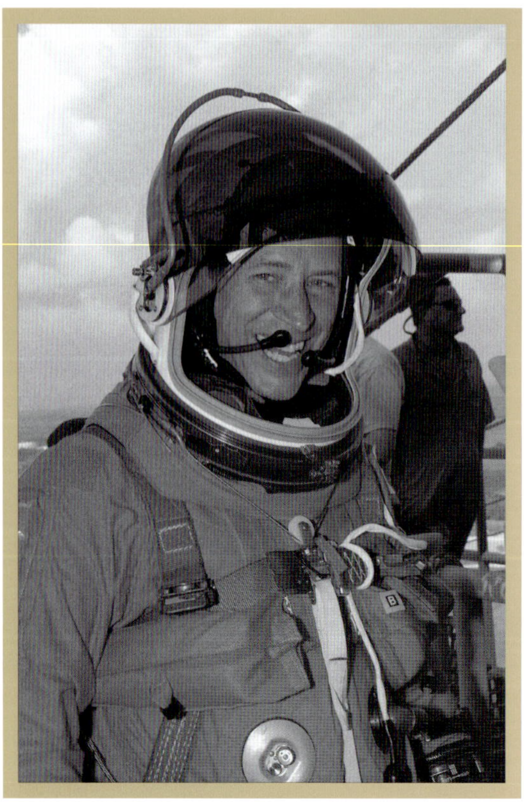

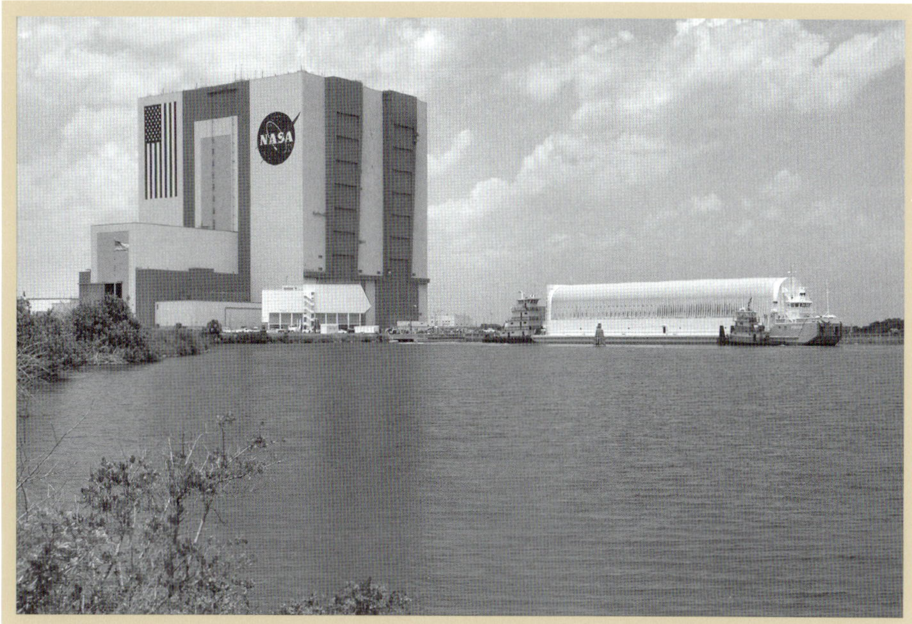


NASA's Vehicle Assembly Building, located at Kennedy Space Center, was constructed in the 1960s in order to accomplish the task of building each Apollo mission rocket. Later the building, known simply as the VAB to NASA insiders, was modified to accommodate space shuttle missions. In the present-day photograph, two tugboats maneuver a barge that carries the space shuttle's external fuel tank. The tank will be off-loaded and transported to the VAB. (Courtesy NASA/Kim Shiflett.)

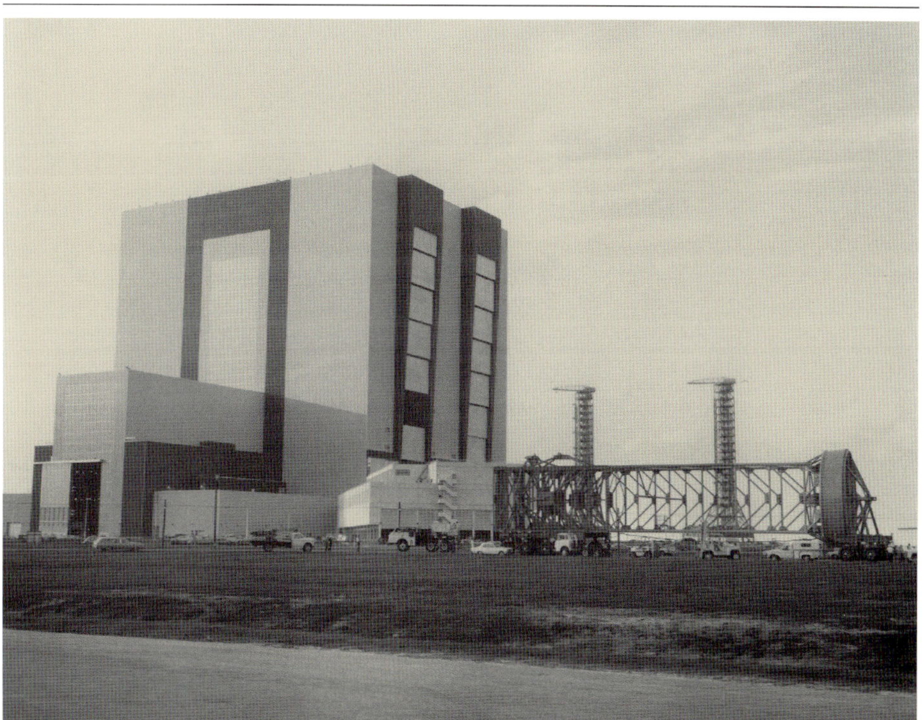

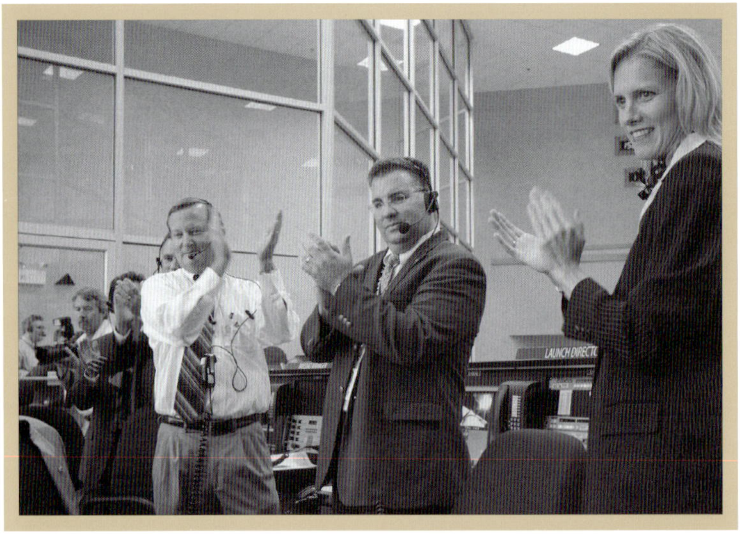

In 1969, Apollo 11 mission officials relax in the Launch Control Center, located at Kennedy Space Center, following a successful Apollo mission liftoff. Included in the photograph is famous engineer and physicist Dr. Wernher von Braun (below, wearing binoculars). Officials today still wait anxiously in the Launch Control Center during each shuttle liftoff and celebrate after each successful launch. Pictured from left to right are NASA shuttle launch director Michael Leinbach, STS-124 assistant launch director Ed Mango, and flow director for space shuttle *Discovery* Stephanie Stilson. (Courtesy NASA/ Bill Ingalls.)

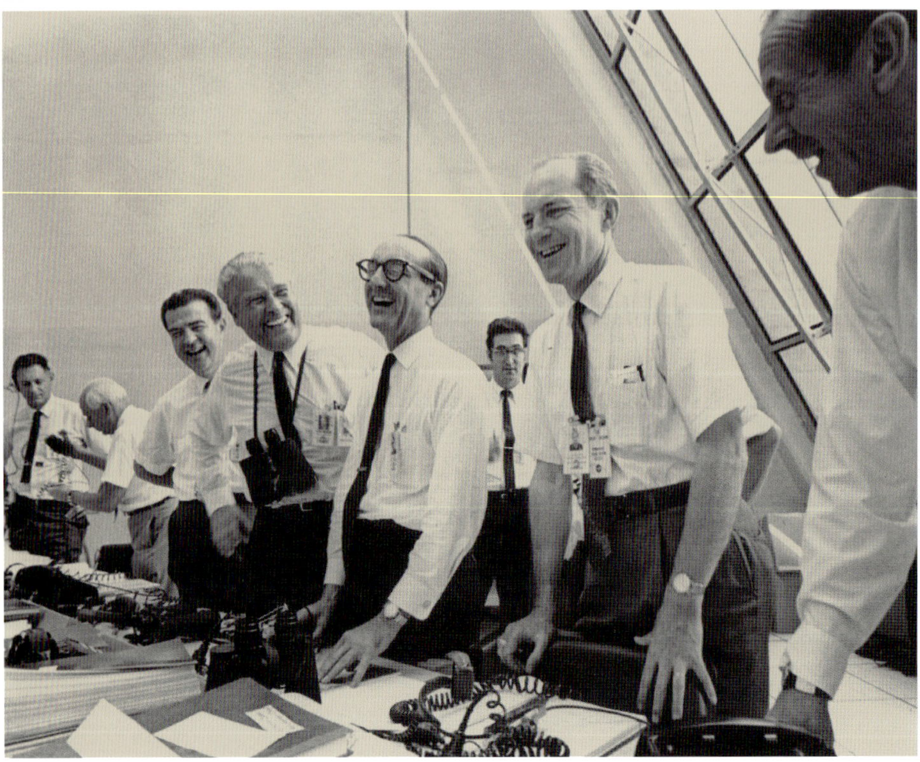

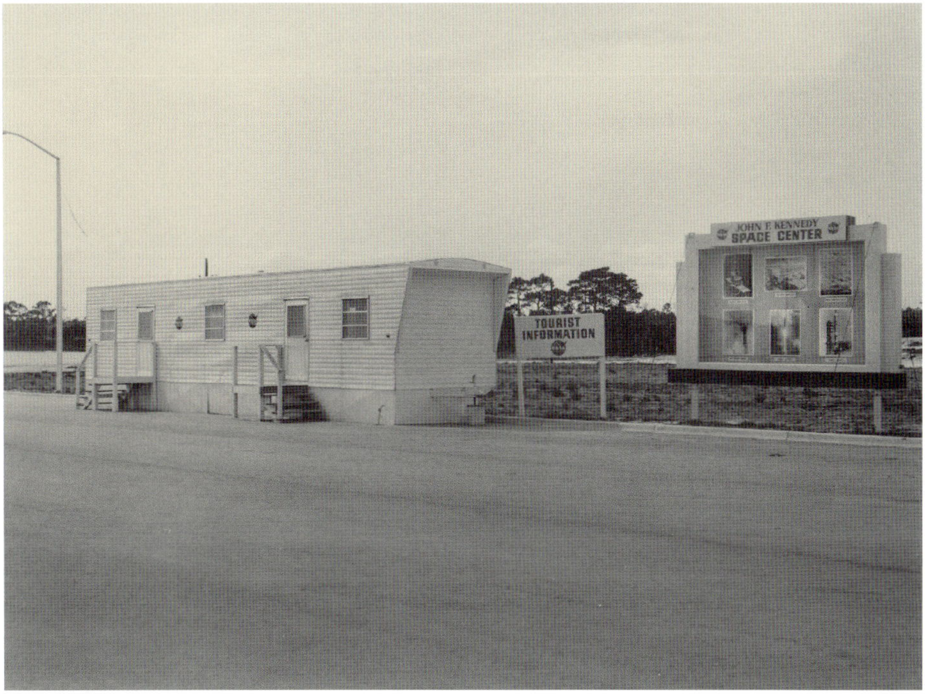


In 1965, a small trailer welcomes tourists with information about Kennedy Space Center. Millions of people have visited Kennedy Space Center and its surrounding communities to learn about America's space program since the 1960s. Today the visitor complex is a sprawling facility that welcomes tourists with rides, an IMAX theater, and other activities. In the background of this aerial photograph can be seen the Rocket Garden, which exhibits rockets from throughout the space program. (Courtesy NASA.)

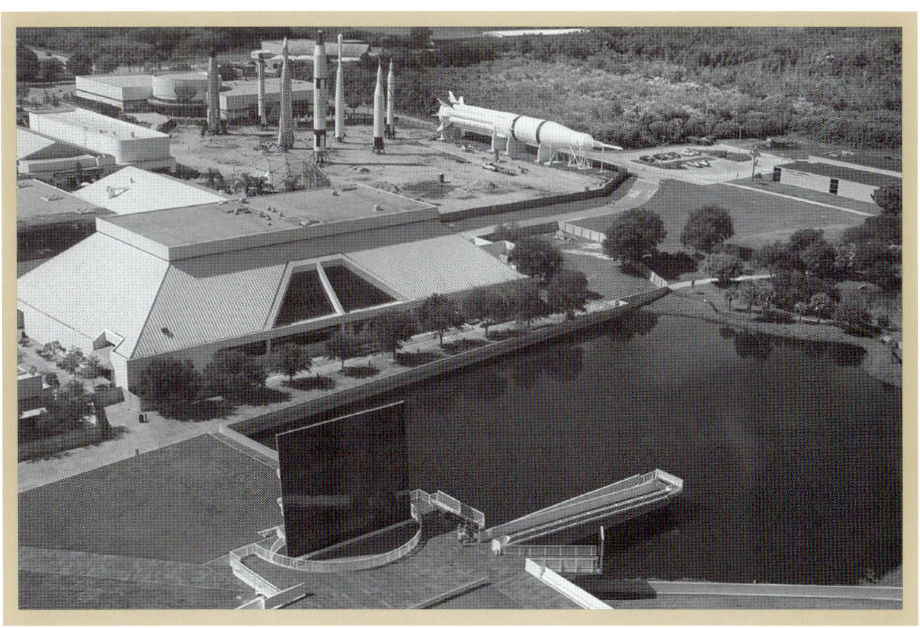

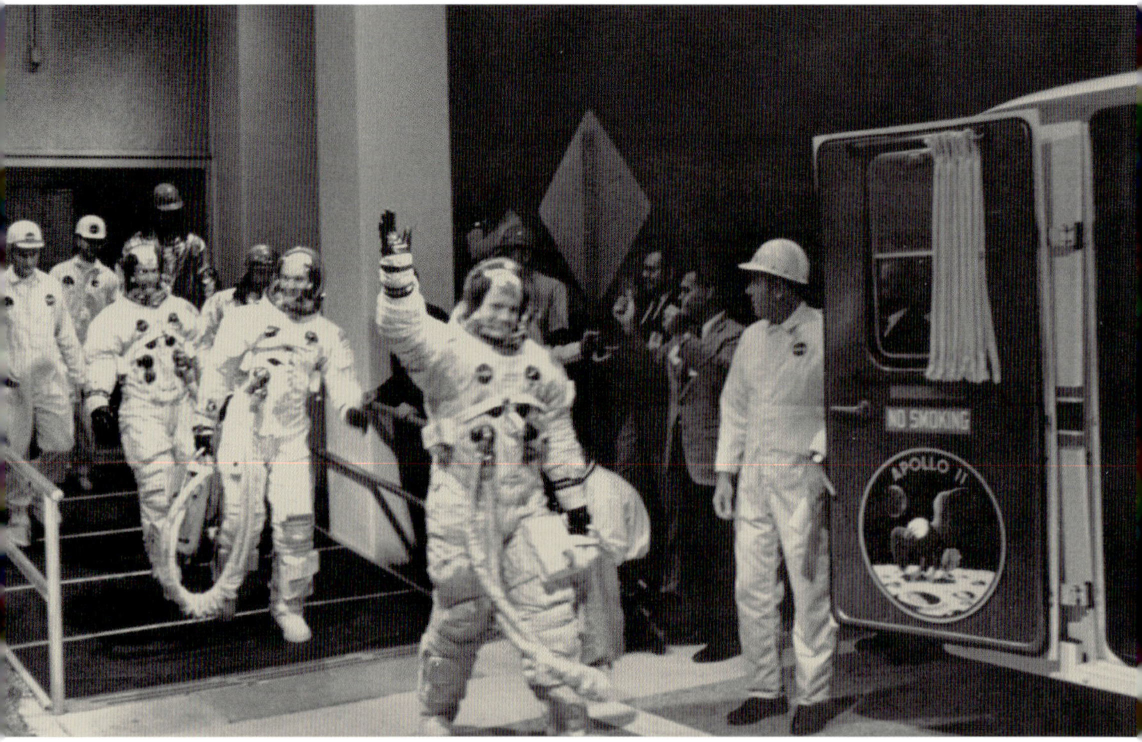


Apollo 11 commander Neil A. Armstrong waves as he leads astronauts Michael Collins and Edwin E. Aldrin Jr. at Kennedy Space Center to what is now called the Astrovan for an 8-mile trip to Pad 39A. Apollo 11 would be man's first lunar-landing mission. Mirroring the astronauts of years ago, the entire space shuttle *Atlantis* STS-125 crew heads for the Astrovan after suiting up. The crew will also go to Launch Pad 39A. (Courtesy NASA.)

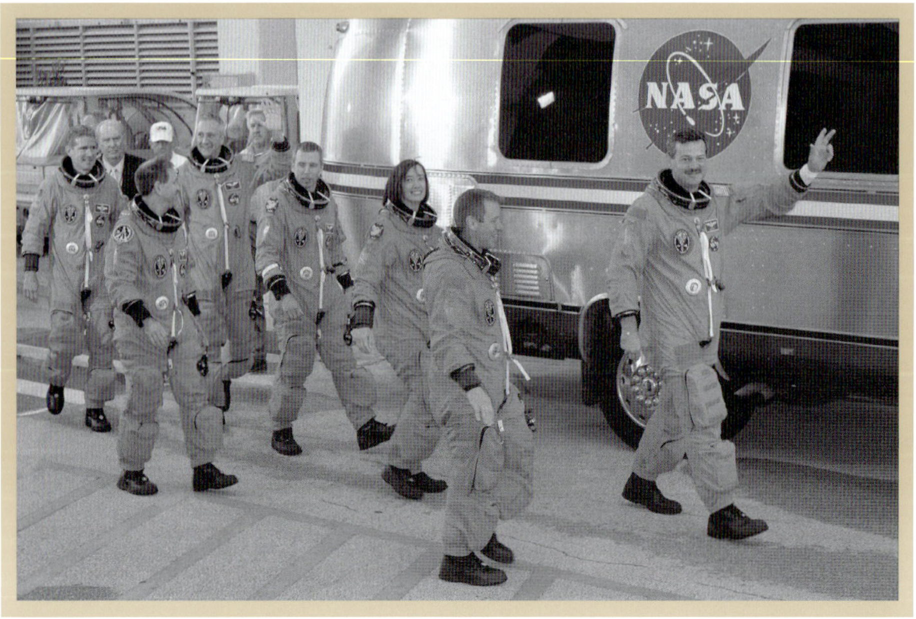

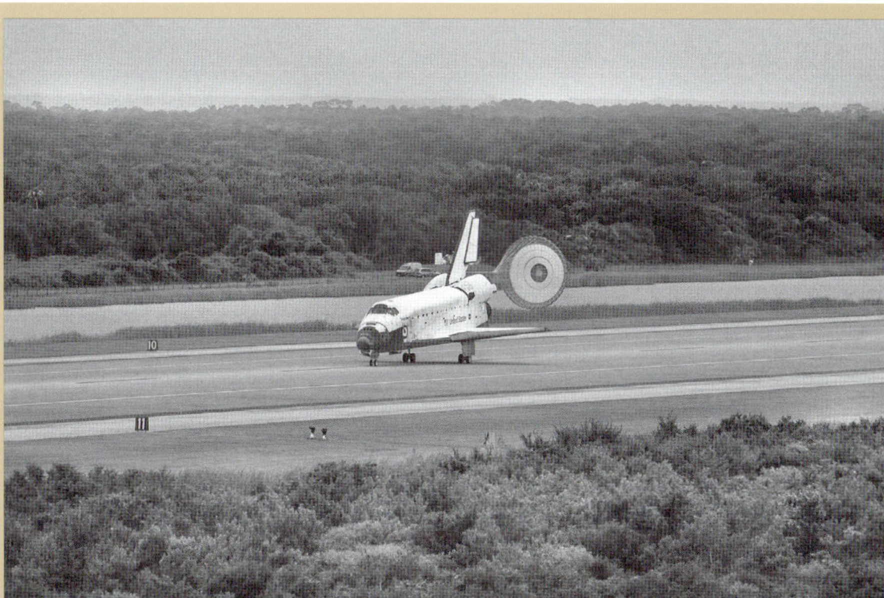

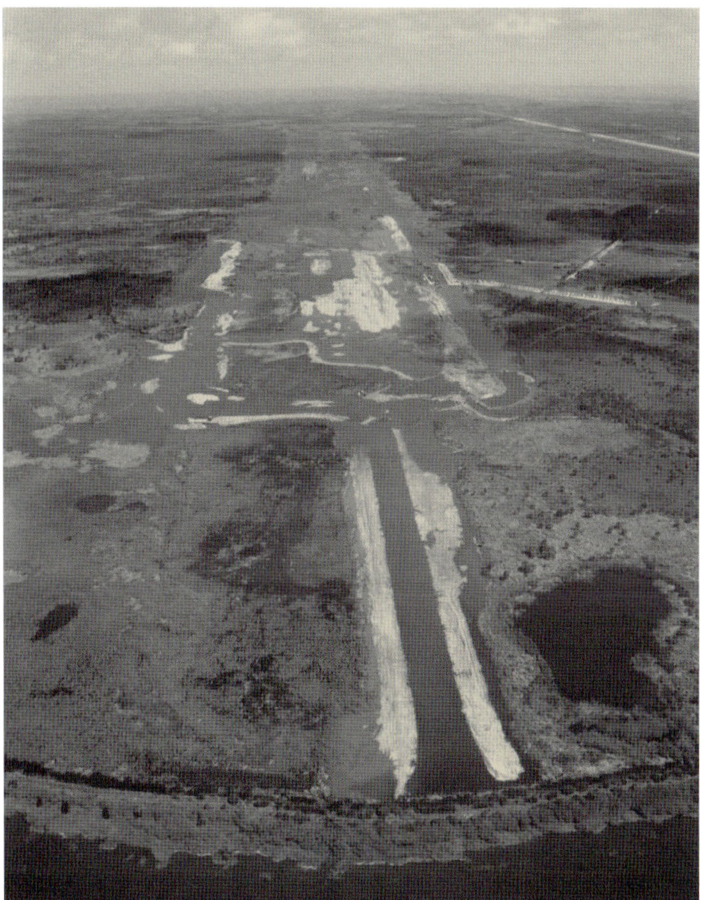

In 1974, dredging began on land owned by Kennedy Space Center to prepare for the building of NASA's Shuttle Landing Facility. The facility would include a 15,000-foot runway with a 1,000-foot overrun on each end specifically designed for returning space shuttles. It opened in 1976. After a recent mission, the orbiter *Discovery* slows to a stop after landing on Runway 15 at NASA's Shuttle Landing Facility. (Courtesy NASA.)

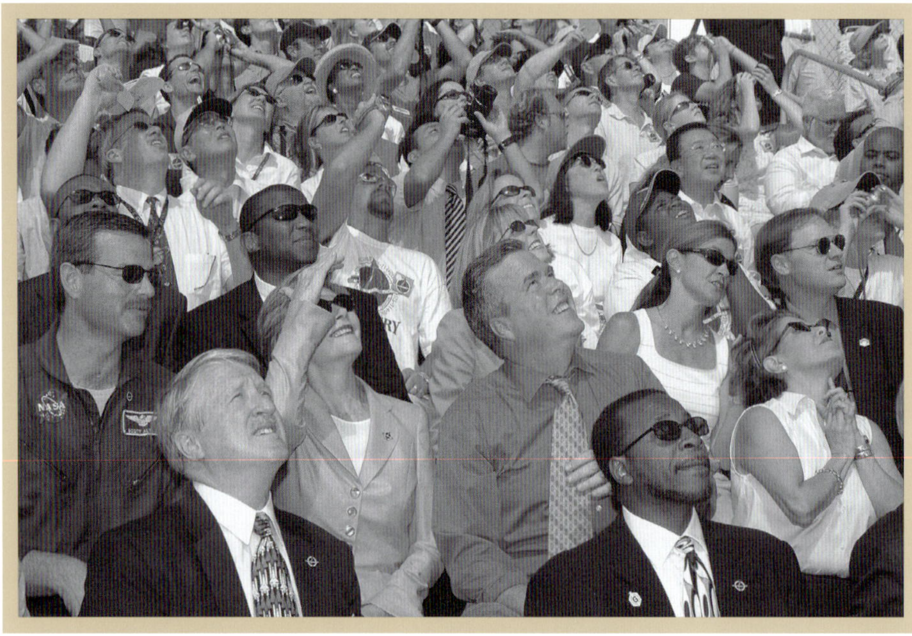

Launches into space are viewed today in much the same way as they were years ago. In 1969, Vice Pres. Spiro Agnew and Pres. Lyndon Johnson view the liftoff of *Apollo 11* at the Kennedy Space Center viewing site. This recent photograph shows the stands at NASA Kennedy Space Center's Banana Creek viewing site, where first lady Laura Bush, former Florida governor Jeb Bush, and other guests follow the path of space shuttle *Discovery* as it successfully launches. (Courtesy NASA.)

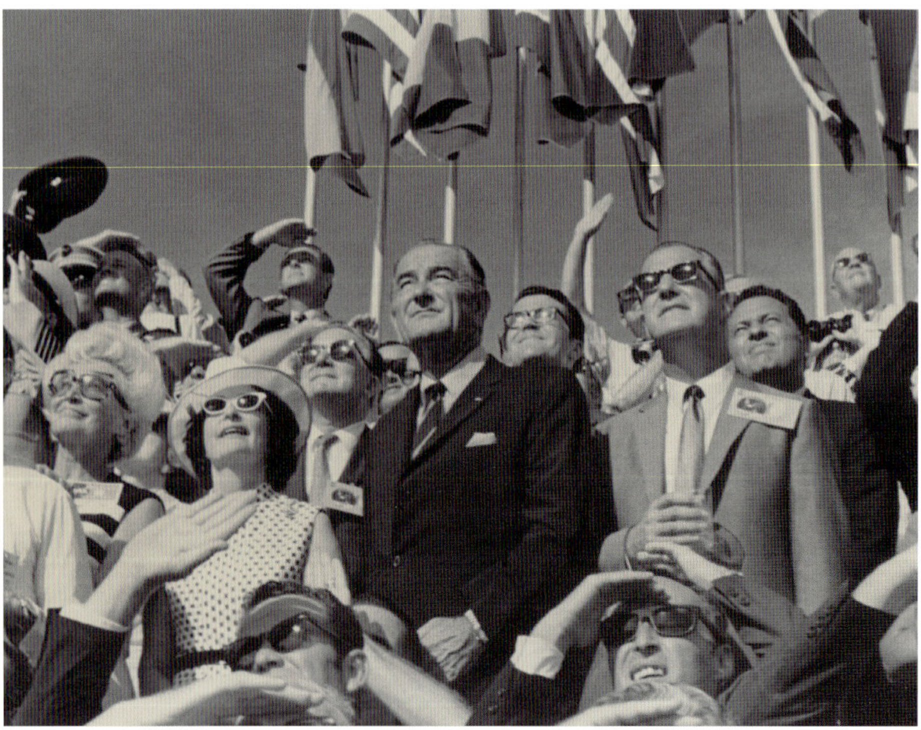

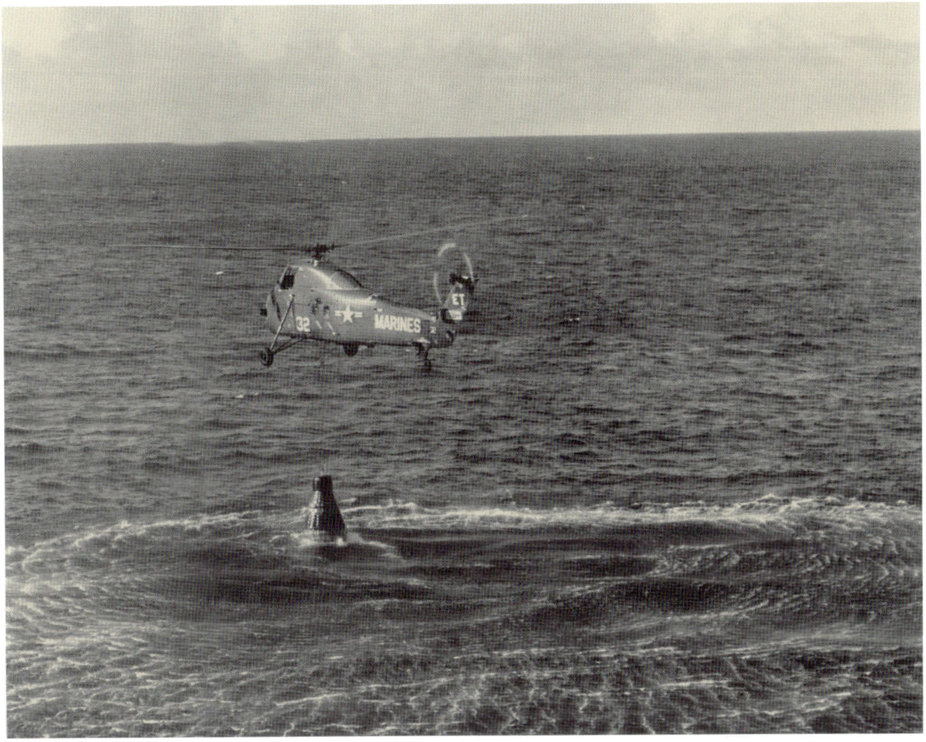


In 1961, a Marine helicopter appears to have *Liberty Bell 7* in tow after astronaut Virgil "Gus" Grissom's successful launch and return to Earth. Minutes after Gus Grissom got out of the spacecraft, it sank. Today the U.S. Air Force Reserve 920th Rescue Wing provides emergency and medical support to every NASA space shuttle and rocket launch with their Pavehawk helicopters. The aircraft here are shown during a recent demonstration flight. (Courtesy NASA.)

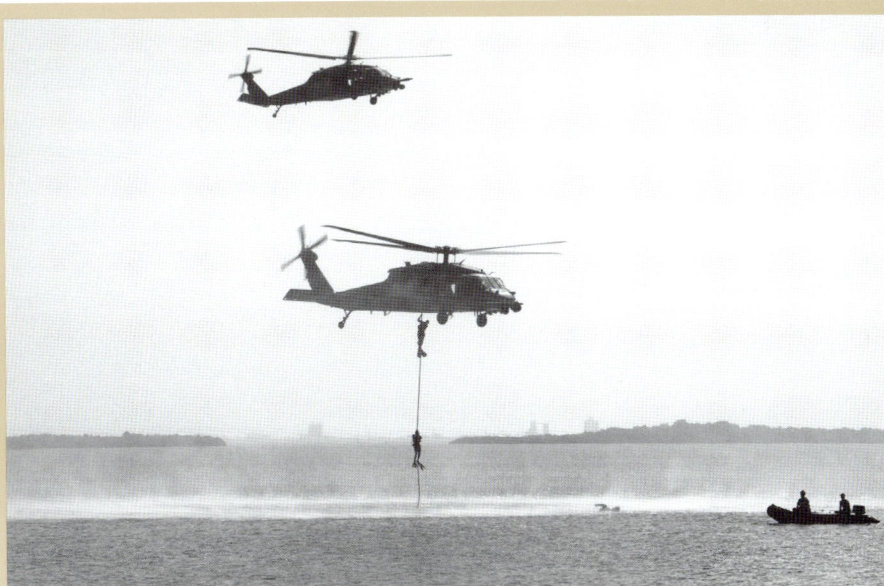

The Apollo 11 Saturn V space vehicle lifts off with astronauts Neil A. Armstrong, Michael Collins, and Edwin E. Aldrin Jr. on July 16, 1969. Armstrong and Aldrin would become the first men on the moon. Today watching a launch is just as exciting as it was during the Apollo days. During a recent launch, clouds of smoke and steam billow around space shuttle *Discovery* as it leaps off Launch Pad 39B. (Courtesy NASA.)

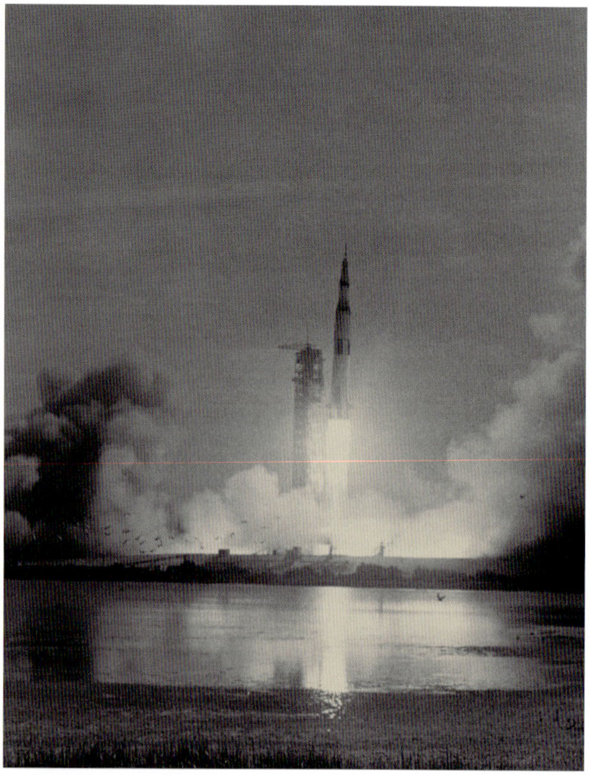

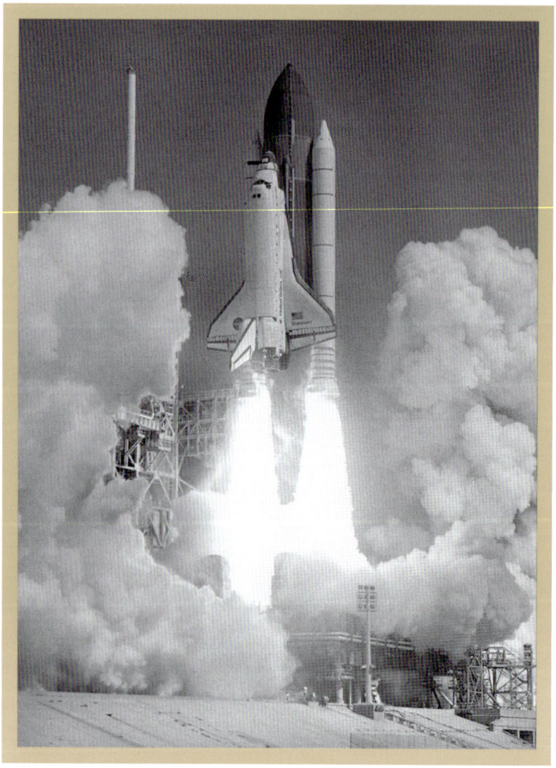

CHAPTER 3

# Cape Canaveral

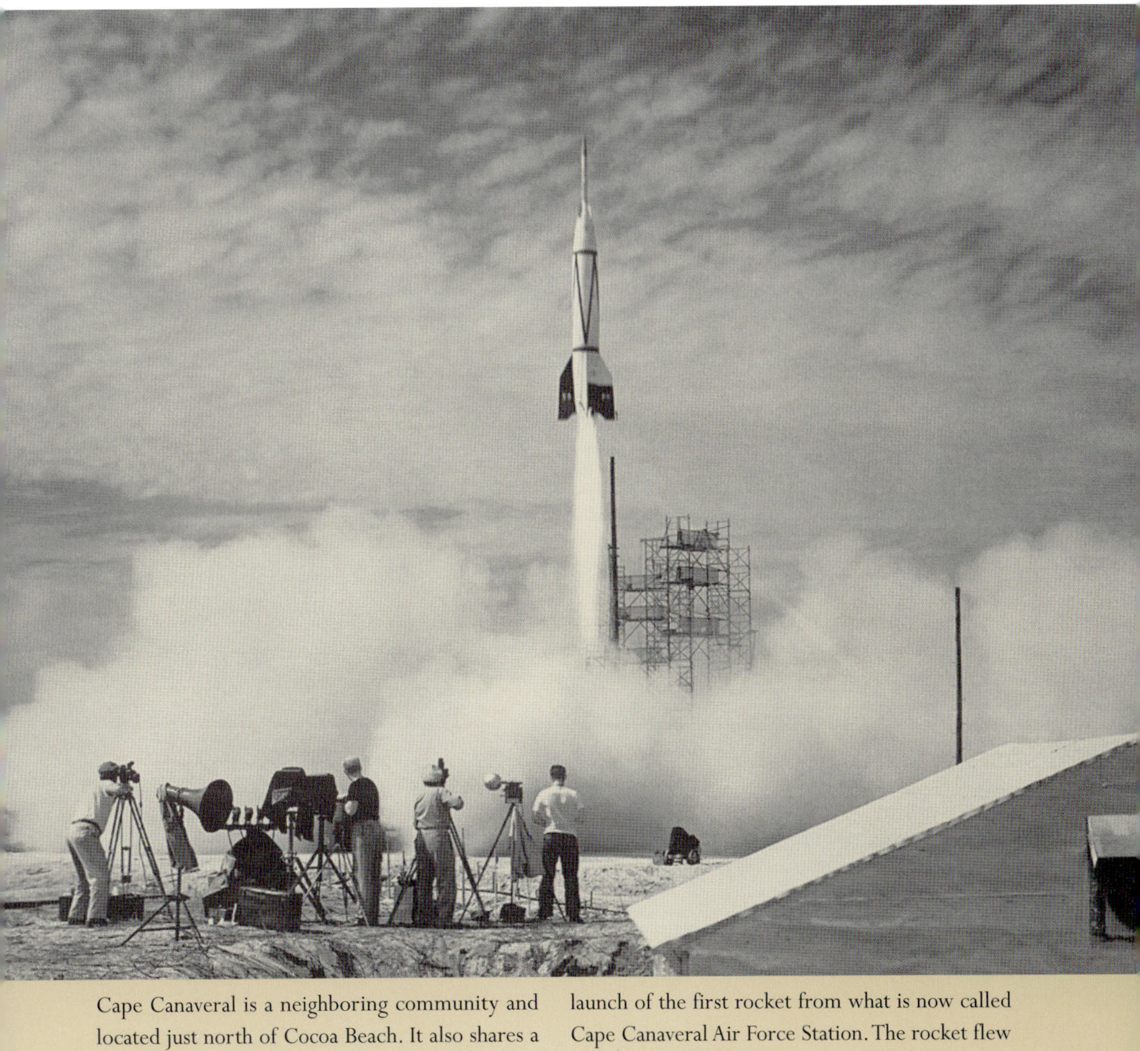

Cape Canaveral is a neighboring community and located just north of Cocoa Beach. It also shares a strong connection with the space program. A new chapter in space flight began in July 1950 with the launch of the first rocket from what is now called Cape Canaveral Air Force Station. The rocket flew higher than even modern space shuttles fly today. (Courtesy NASA.)

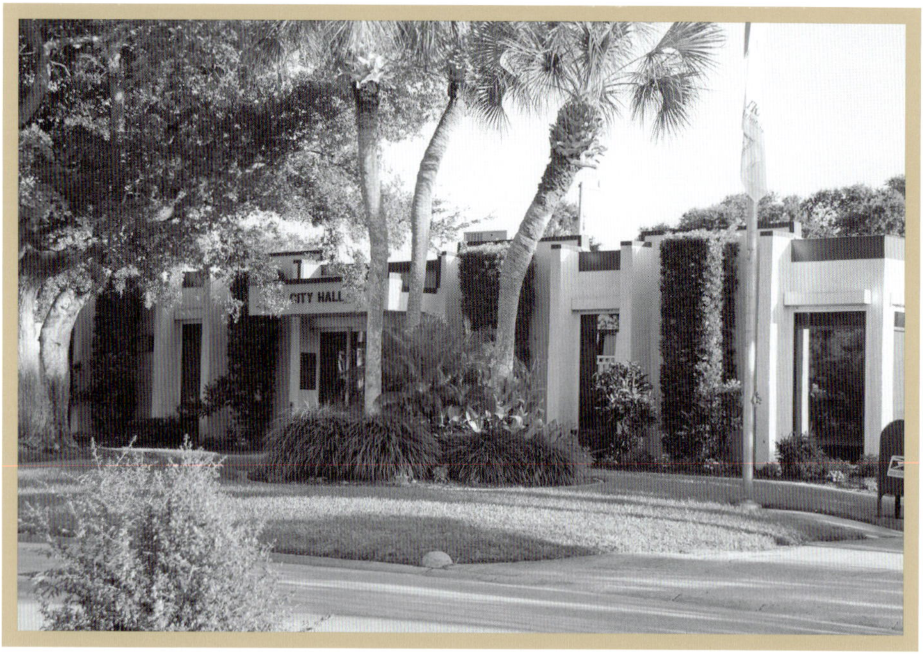


Cape Canaveral was incorporated in 1962 with a meeting of 200 property owners. For many old-timers, the city's name conjures memories of America's space race to the moon. In fact, just north is Cape Canaveral Air Force Station, where the first American rockets were launched into space. This 1974 photograph of Cape Canaveral City Hall shows the building much unchanged from how it looks today. (Courtesy Florida State Archives.)

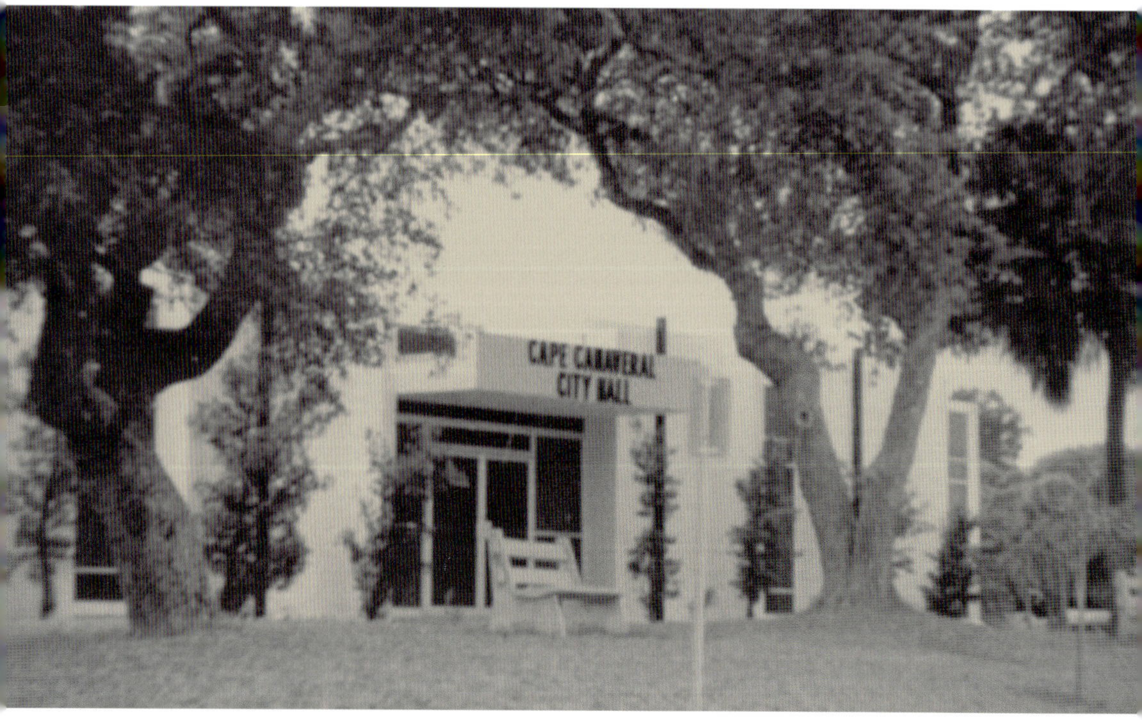

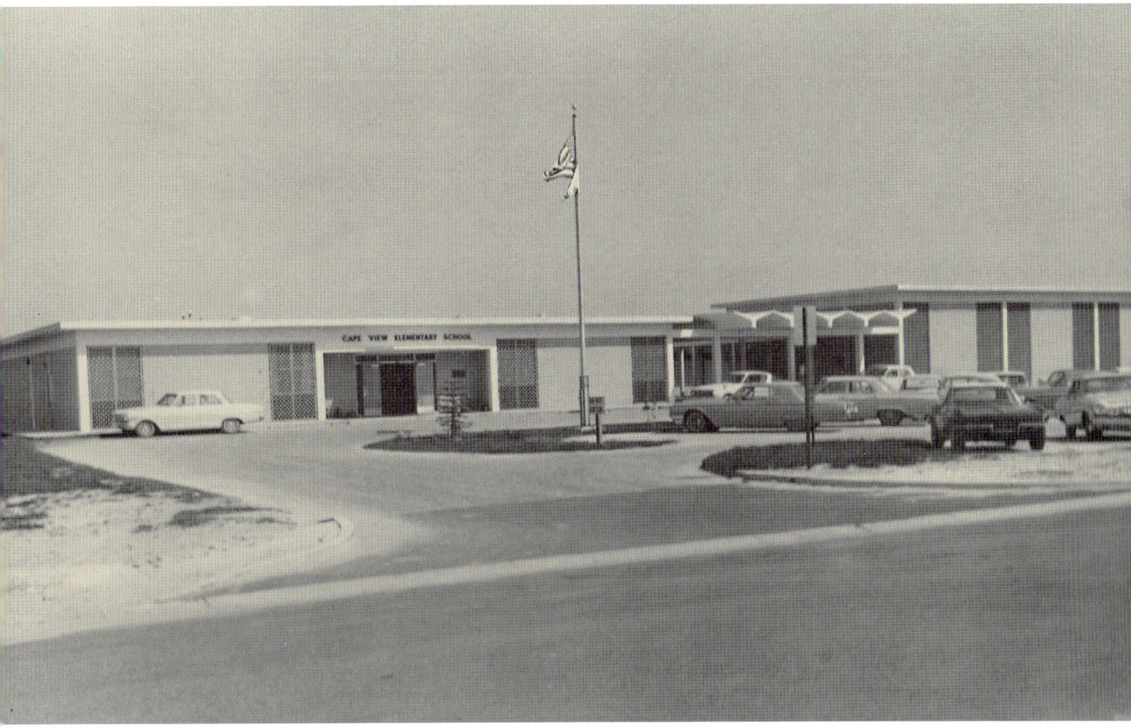


With the space race of the 1960s came a population explosion for Cape Canaveral and other Brevard County municipalities. Built in the mid-1960s at 8440 North Rosalind Avenue, Cape View Elementary taught many of the children whose parents came to the area to work for the space program. With the exception of some now-grown trees, the school looks virtually the same today. (Courtesy Cape View Elementary.)

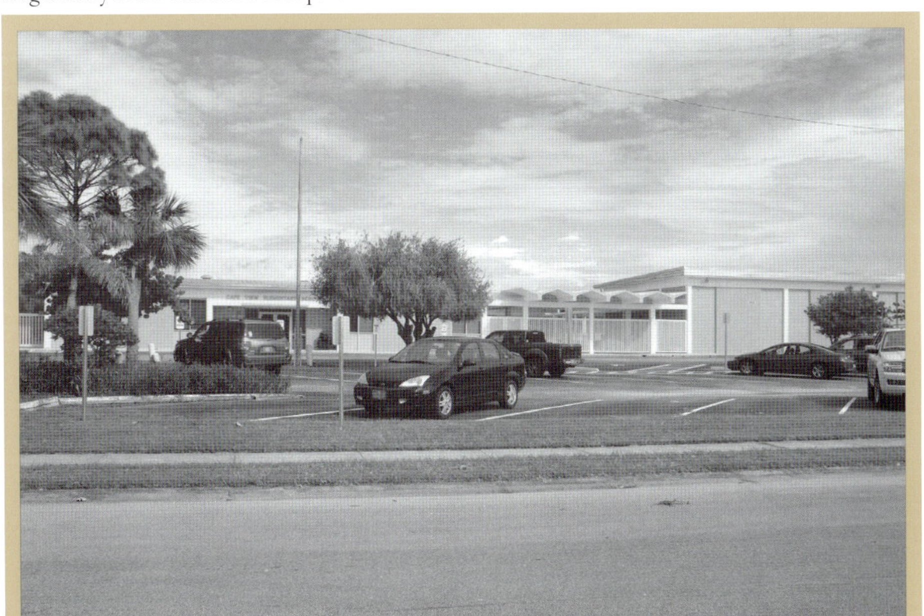

Located on Cape Canaveral Air Force Station, the Canaveral Lighthouse was built in 1847. It was originally built to help keep ships a safe distance from shore. The lighthouse went through major renovations in 2006, which cost about $750,000 and included the hoisting of an 18,000-pound roof and lamp. Today it is the only lighthouse run by the U.S. Air Force. (Courtesy NASA.)

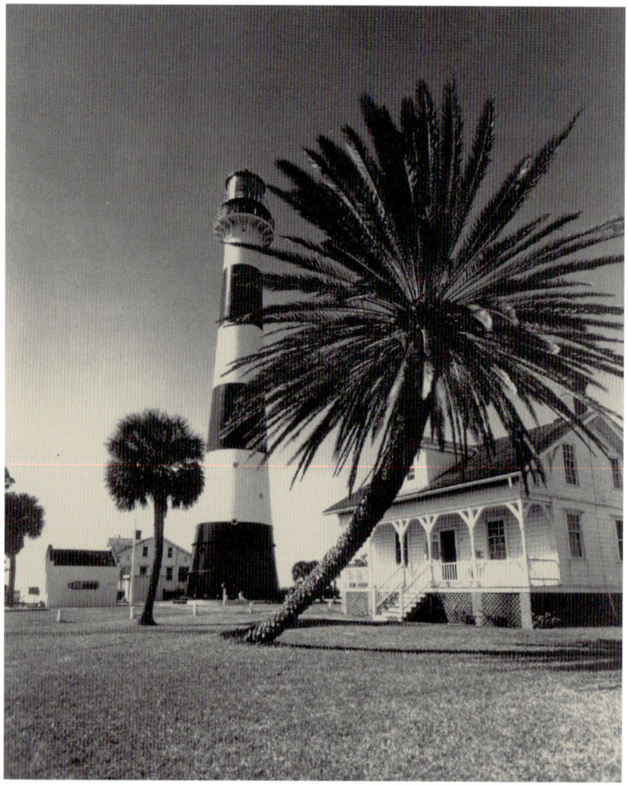

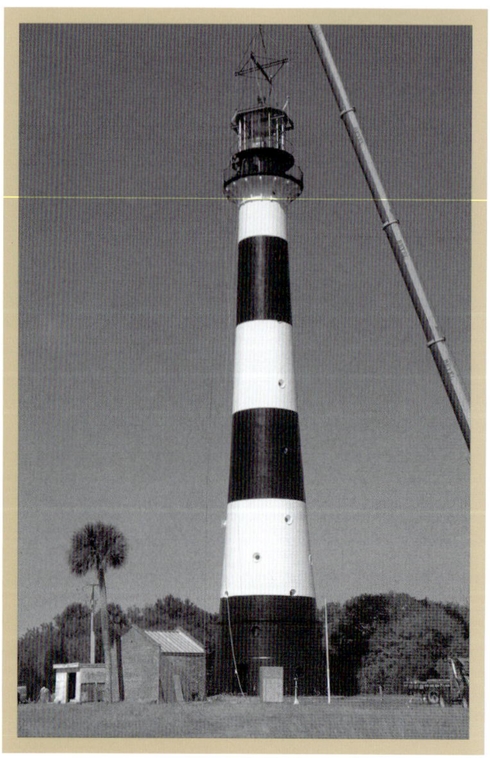

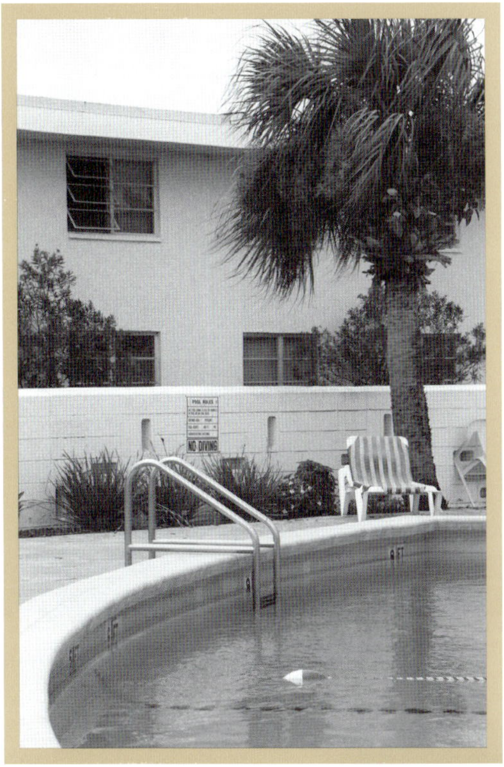


Cape View Elementary teacher Norma Cale poses for a photograph at the Palms East Apartments built in the 1960s at 211 Caroline Street in Cape Canaveral. Today the pool and buildings look almost the same, except for the color of some of the structures. Apartments, homes, and town houses take up every inch of open land that once existed around the complex. (Courtesy Cape View Elementary.)

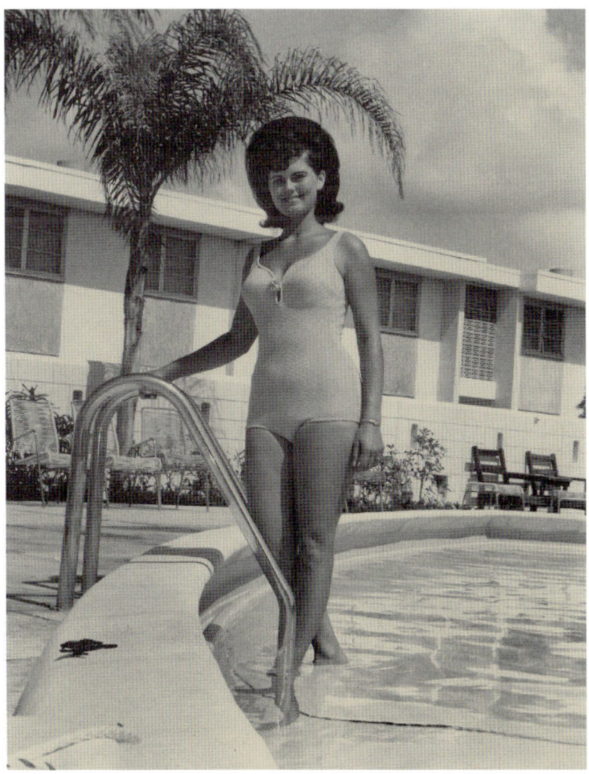

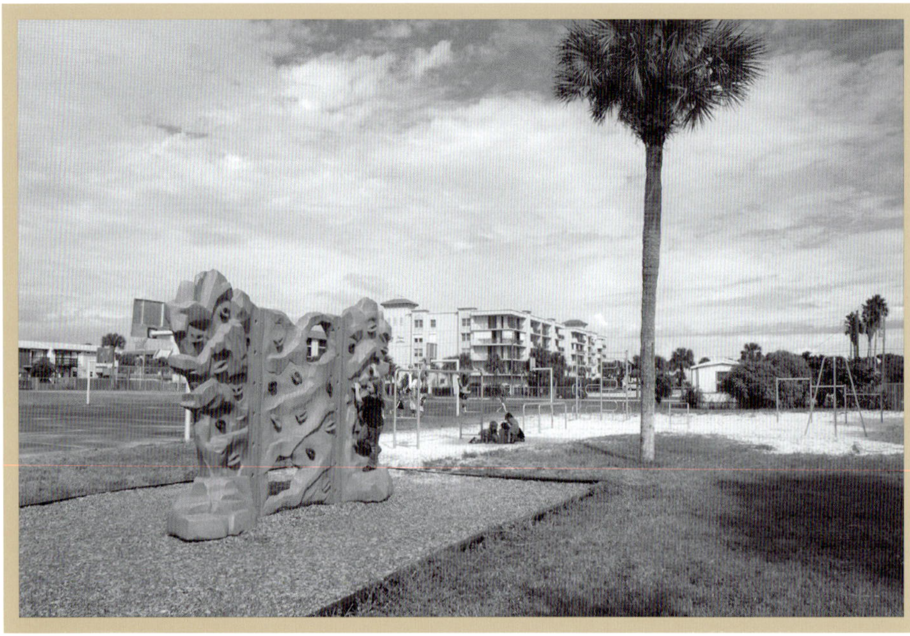

An excited first-grade class from Cape View Elementary in Cape Canaveral poses for this early-1970s photograph in back of the school, located at 8440 North Rosalind Avenue. The starkest contrast to the past that many old-timers notice is the large amount of construction on the waterfront. The empty skyline behind the students is today filled with condominiums, which take up nearly every stretch of space on the beach. (Courtesy Cape View Elementary.)

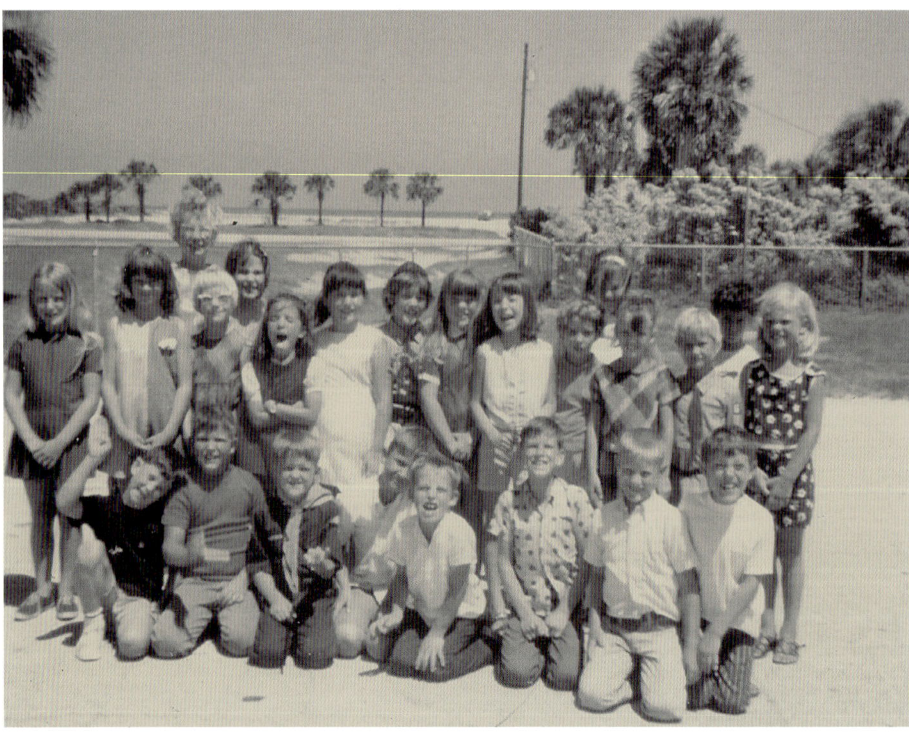

CHAPTER 4

# COCOA

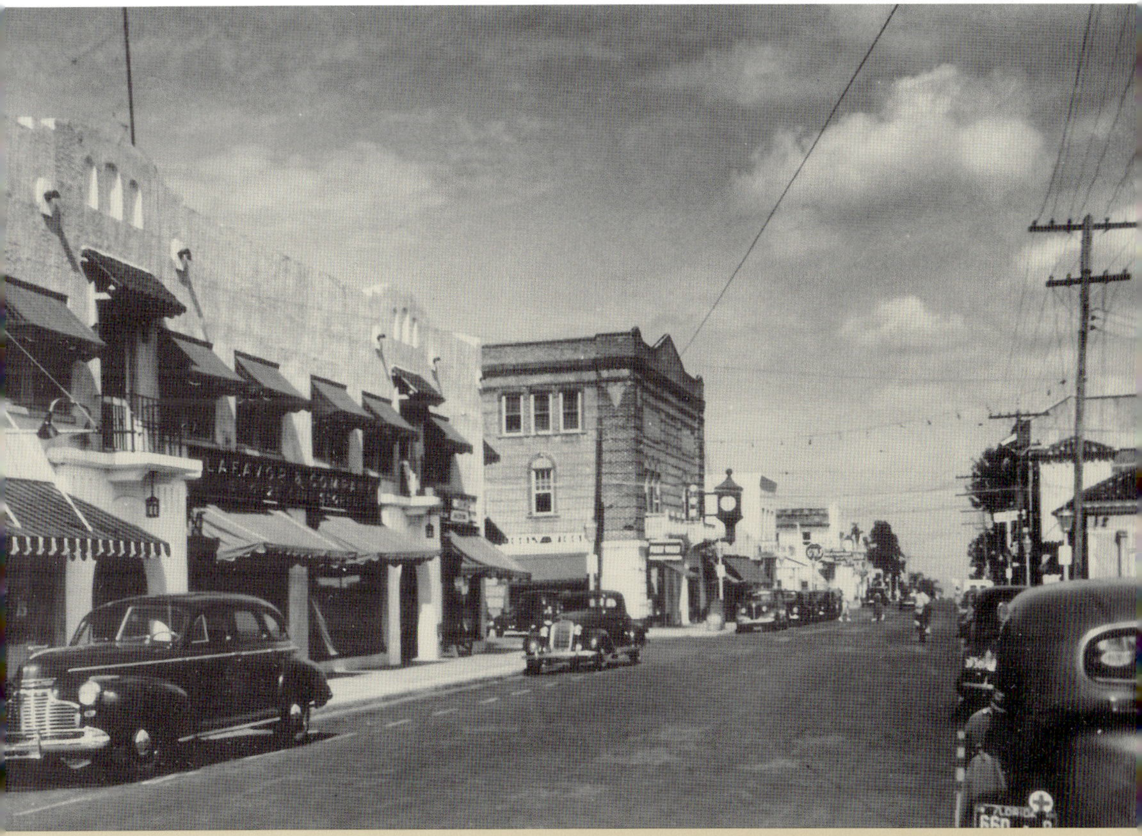

Cocoa dates back to the 1800s and is a neighbor of Cocoa Beach. Real estate pioneer Gus Edwards, who was a founder of Cocoa Beach, was originally the city attorney for Cocoa. Walking down Brevard Avenue in the 1940s would seem similar to what it is today as many of the same buildings exist. (Courtesy Florida Historical Society.)

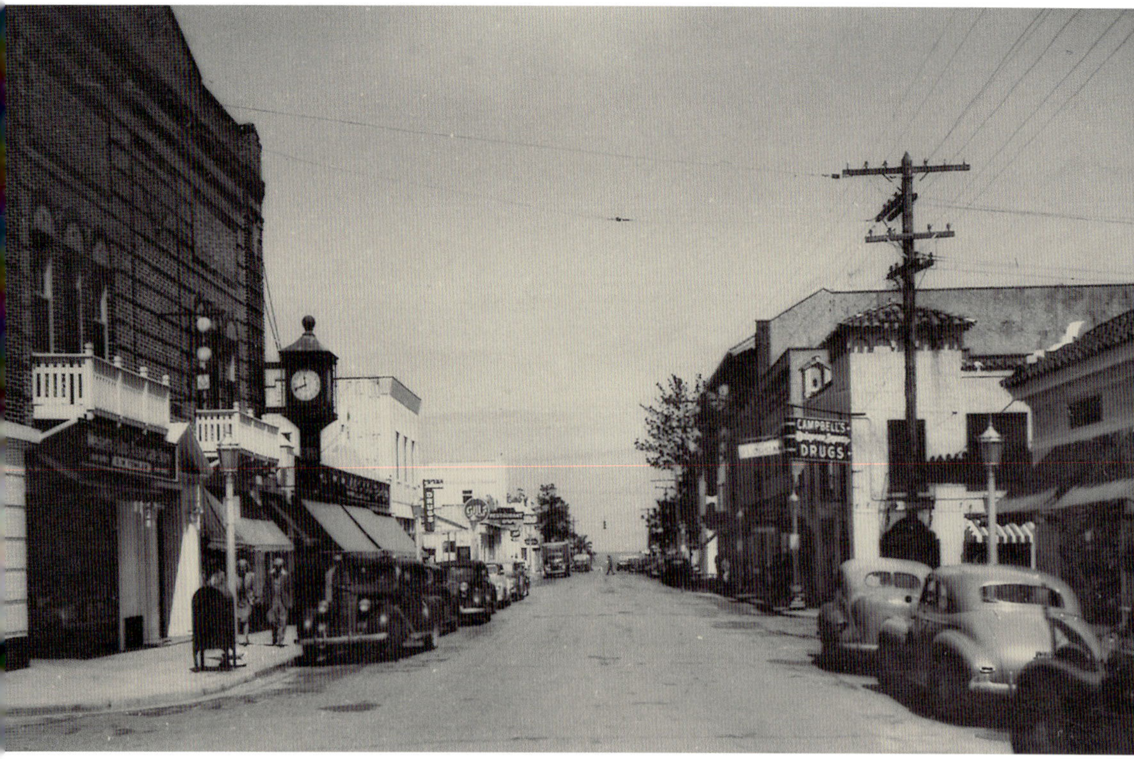


Incorporated in 1895, the town of Cocoa is one of the most historic areas near Cocoa Beach. Brevard Avenue in the 1940s showed tremendous growth from its humble beginnings as a dirt street in the late 1800s. Built in 1919, the three-story brick structure on the left is the Masonic Temple. Possibly the most recognizable building in Cocoa, it still stands today, occupied by businesses and retail stores. (Courtesy Florida Historical Society.)

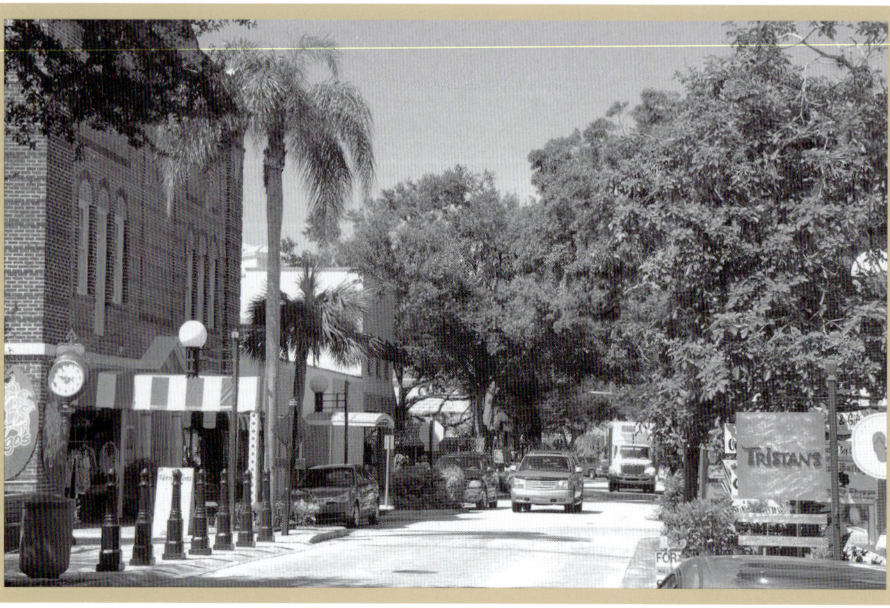

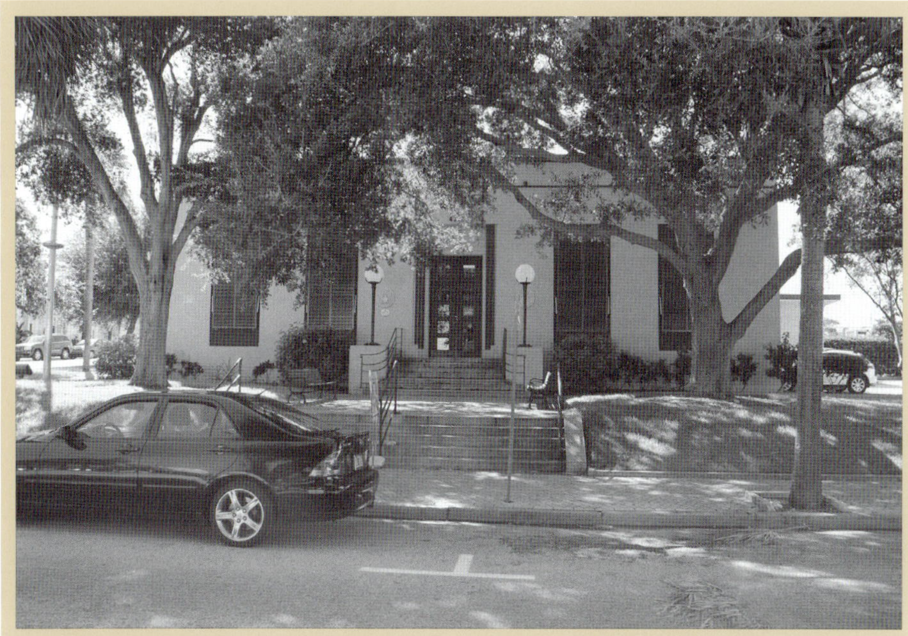

The homecoming queen of Cocoa High School passes the U.S. Post Office at 635 Brevard Avenue in 1954. The post office was built in 1940 for $70,000. The building still exists today but is now the home of the Florida Historical Society and includes a library of artifacts and books dating back hundreds of years. (Courtesy Florida Historical Society.)

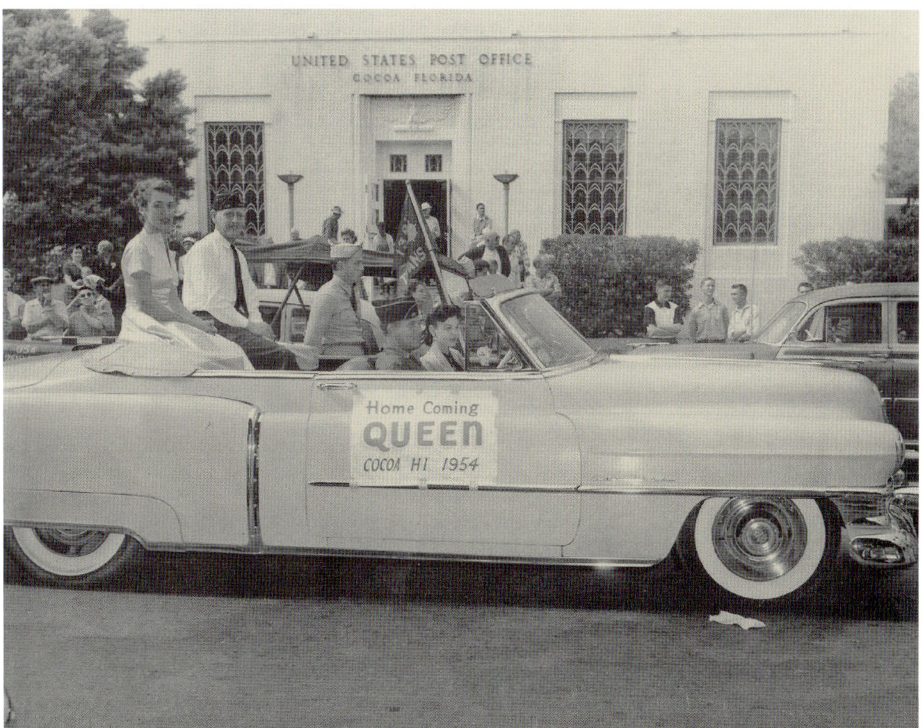

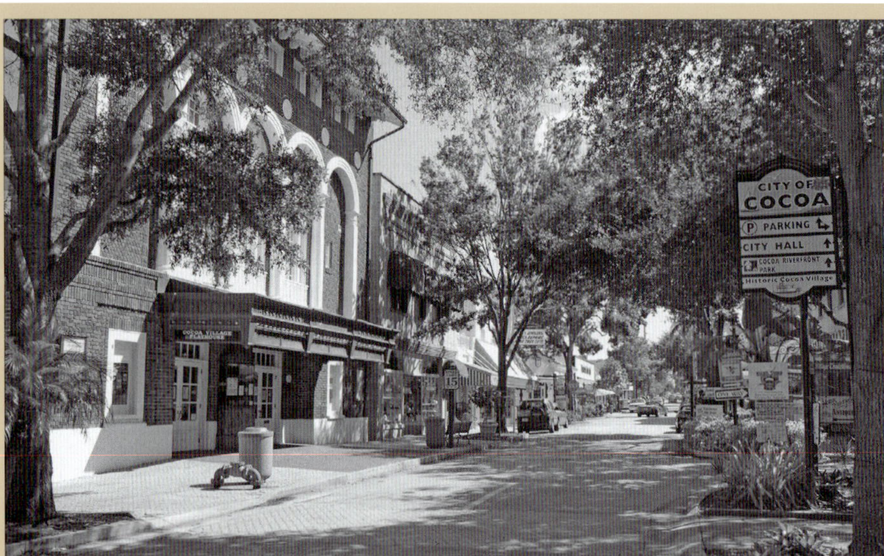


The Cocoa Village Playhouse can be seen on the left in this photograph of Brevard Avenue, probably taken in the 1940s. The playhouse was opened in 1924 as the Aladdin Theater, and in the 1940s it was a movie house called the State Theatre. In 1984, it was purchased by Brevard Community College and still exists to this day, featuring live shows with the help of hundreds of volunteers. (Courtesy Florida Historical Society.)

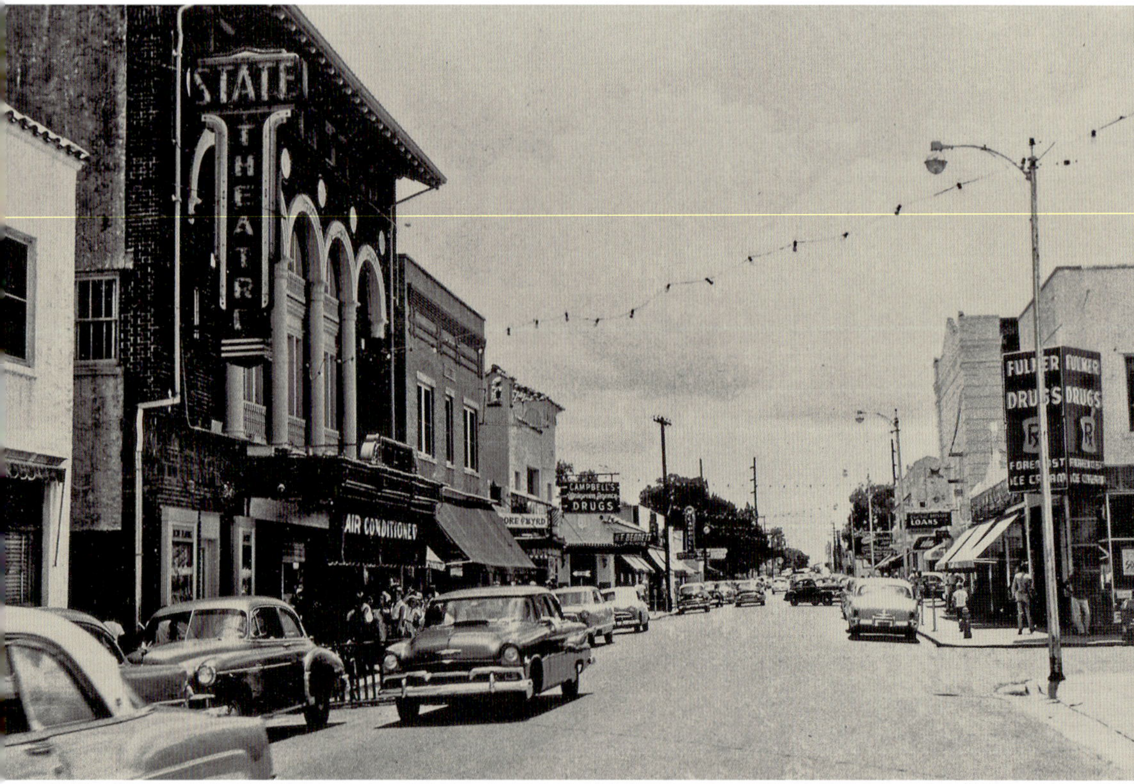

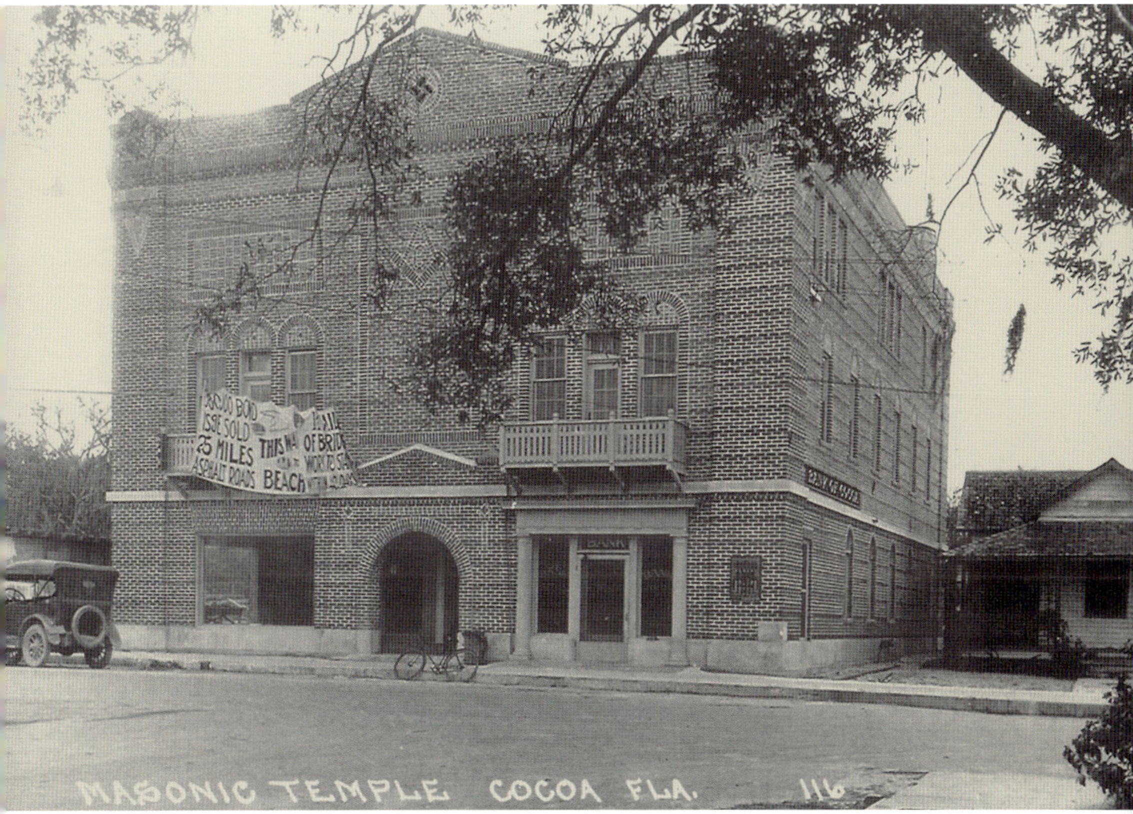


In a picture taken sometime after its 1919 construction, the Masonic Temple building still stands today and is an icon of downtown Cocoa, which is now known as Cocoa Village. The Bank of Cocoa was located downstairs, and the building was a popular watering hole during Prohibition in the 1920s. A large clock was later located on its right side but is no longer there today. Retail stores and other businesses still call the building home. (Courtesy Florida Historical Society.)

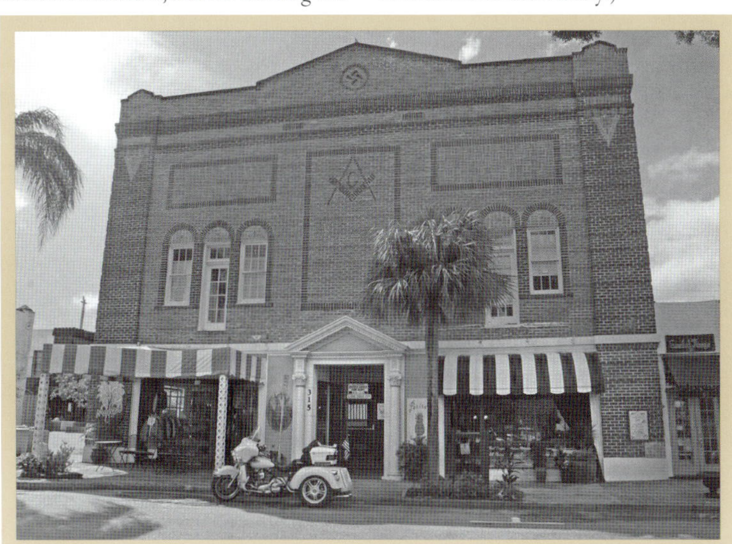

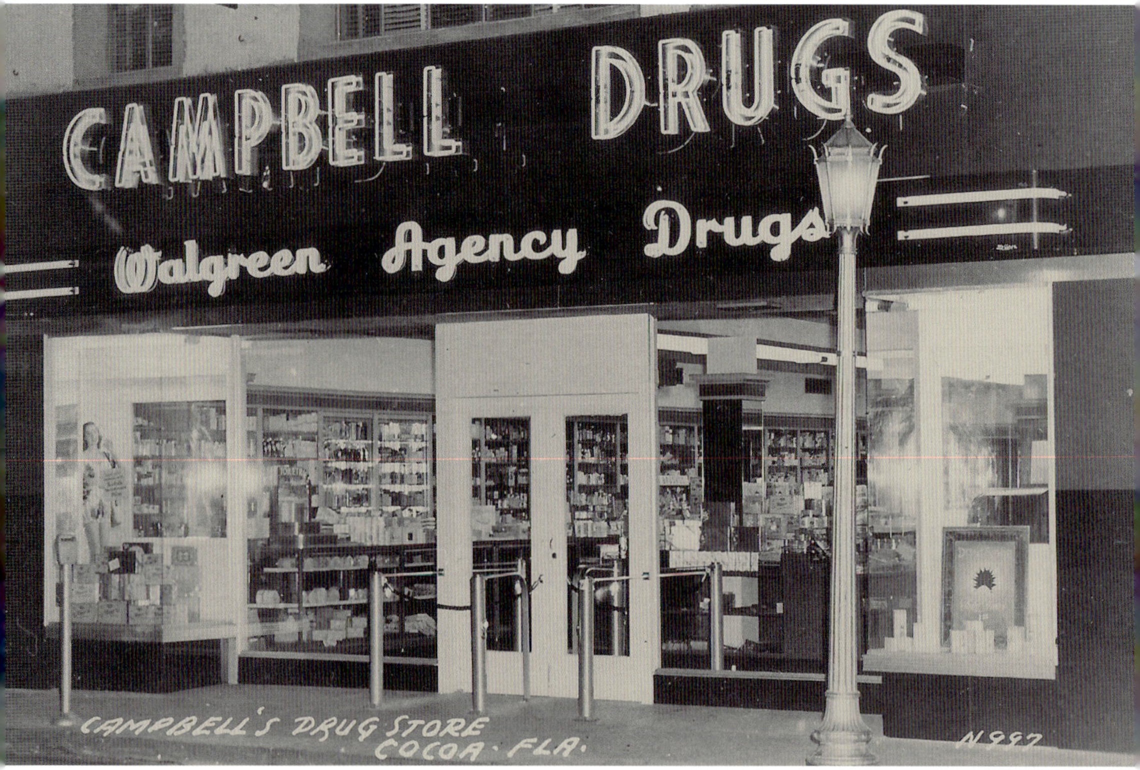


This photograph, probably taken in the late 1940s or early 1950s, shows Campbell Drugs, located on 310 Brevard Avenue in downtown Cocoa. Today it houses the Pear Tree gift shop and Bailey Jewelers. The doors at the front entrance date back to when the drugstore still existed, and were some of the first automatic doors used in Cocoa. (Courtesy Florida Historical Society.)

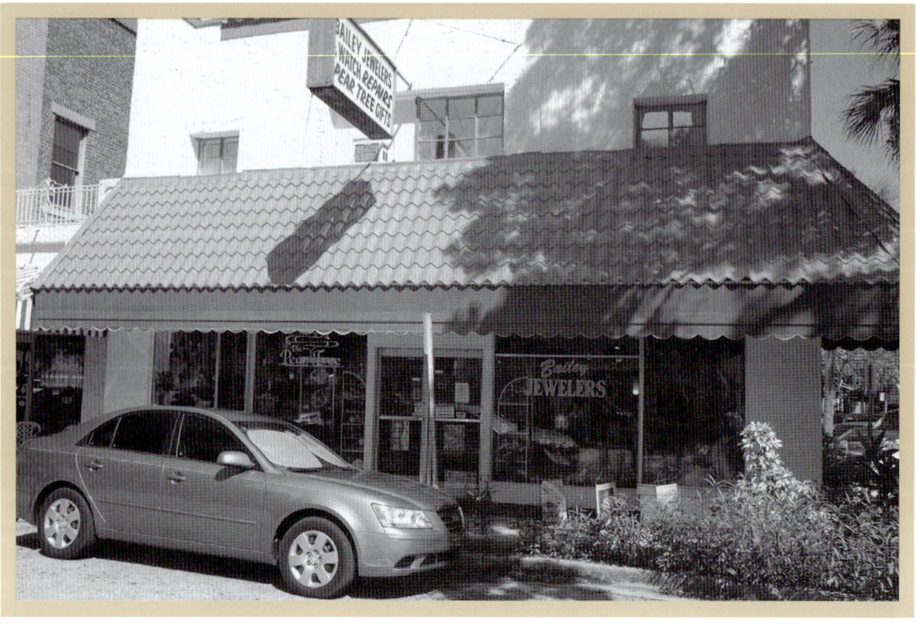

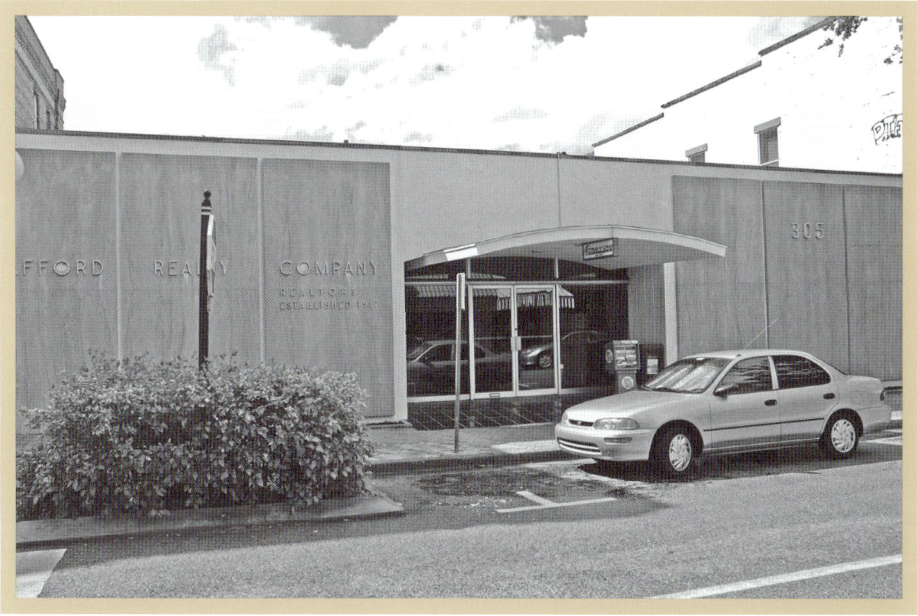


This advertisement photograph shows Trafford Realty as it existed in the 1960s. The company has been around for over 90 years, and if one hangs around Cocoa Village, he or she will probably run into Al Trafford, the son of founder A. R. Trafford. Al Trafford is a well-known elder of Brevard County, who took over running his family's company in 1954. (Courtesy Mike Ferger.)

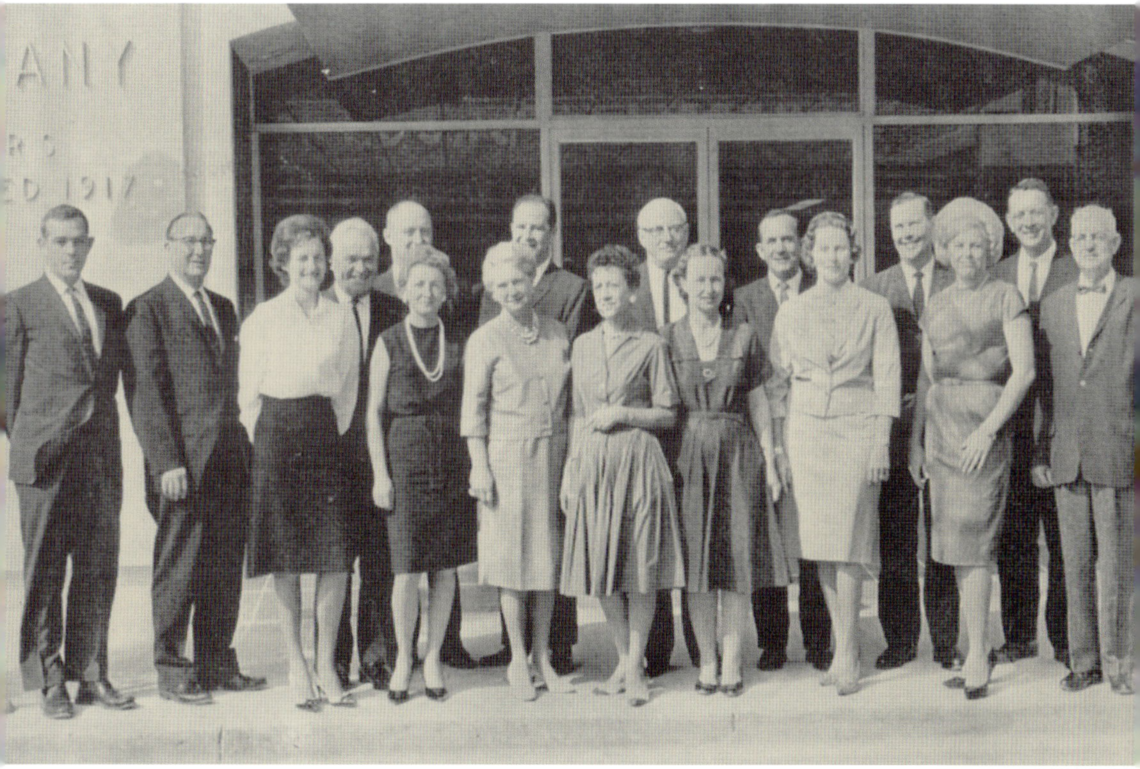

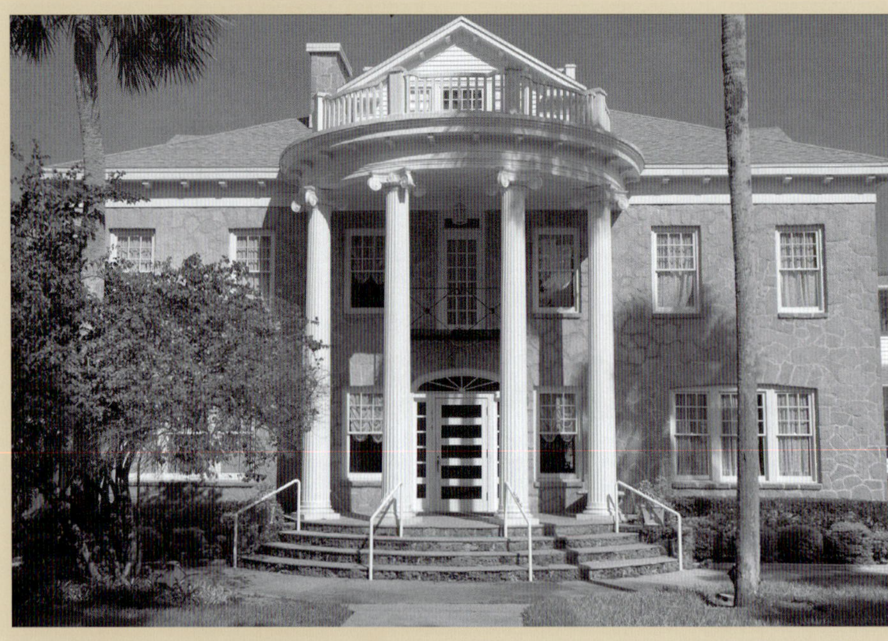

The Porcher House located at 434 Delannoy Avenue is one of the most recognizable historic homes in Cocoa. Built by citrus growers Edward and Byrnina Porcher in 1916, the house was later used as a city hall. Do not miss this wonderful structure when driving by. Today the house is open to the public and is used mainly for special events. (Courtesy Florida Historical Society.)

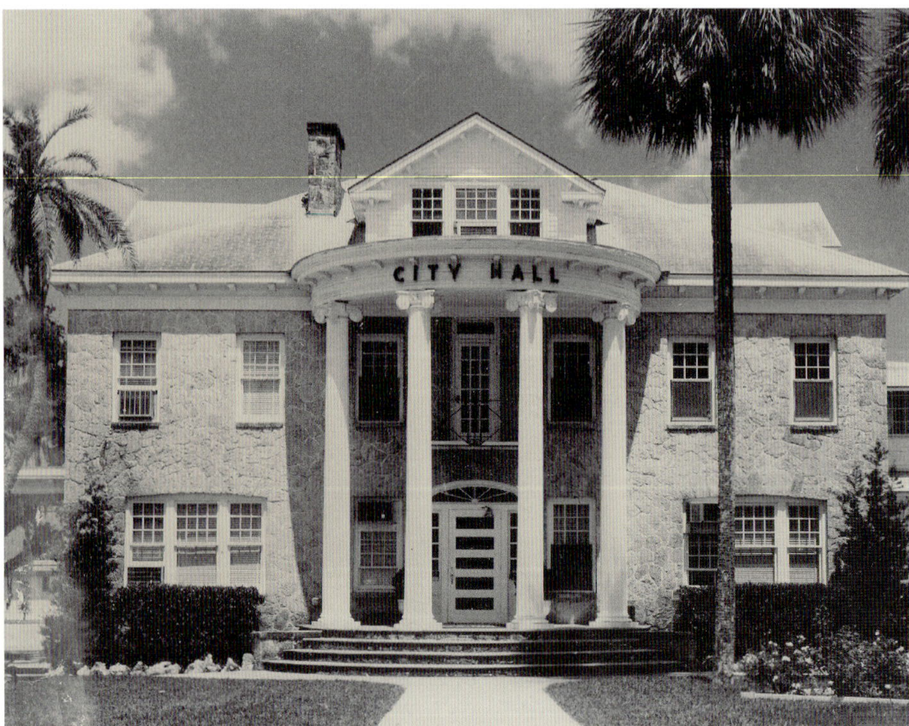

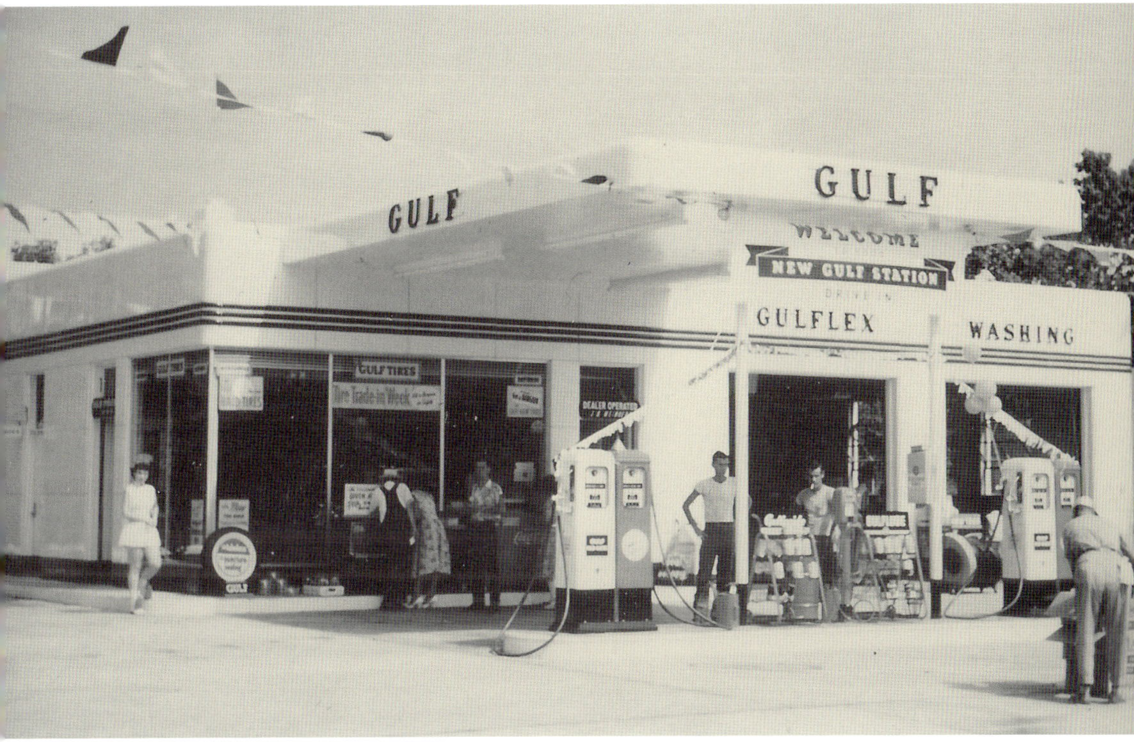


Another building that people probably drive by every day without realizing what it once was is this Gulf gas station, seen here with classic pumps of the 1950s. It once operated on the intersection of Brevard Avenue and Church Street. Later the building was turned into a dentist's office, and although it still stands, it is unoccupied today. (Courtesy Florida Historical Society.)

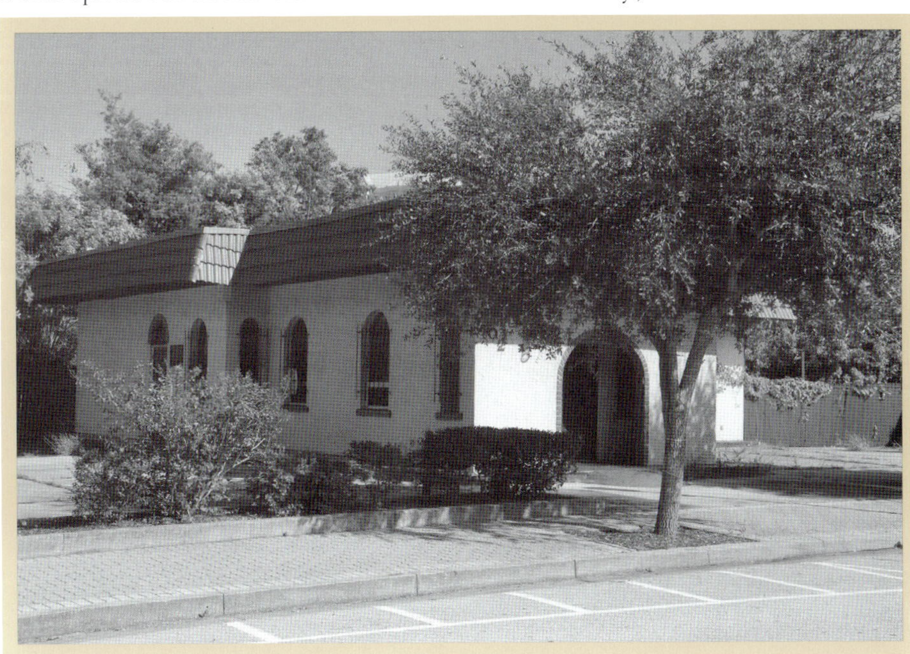

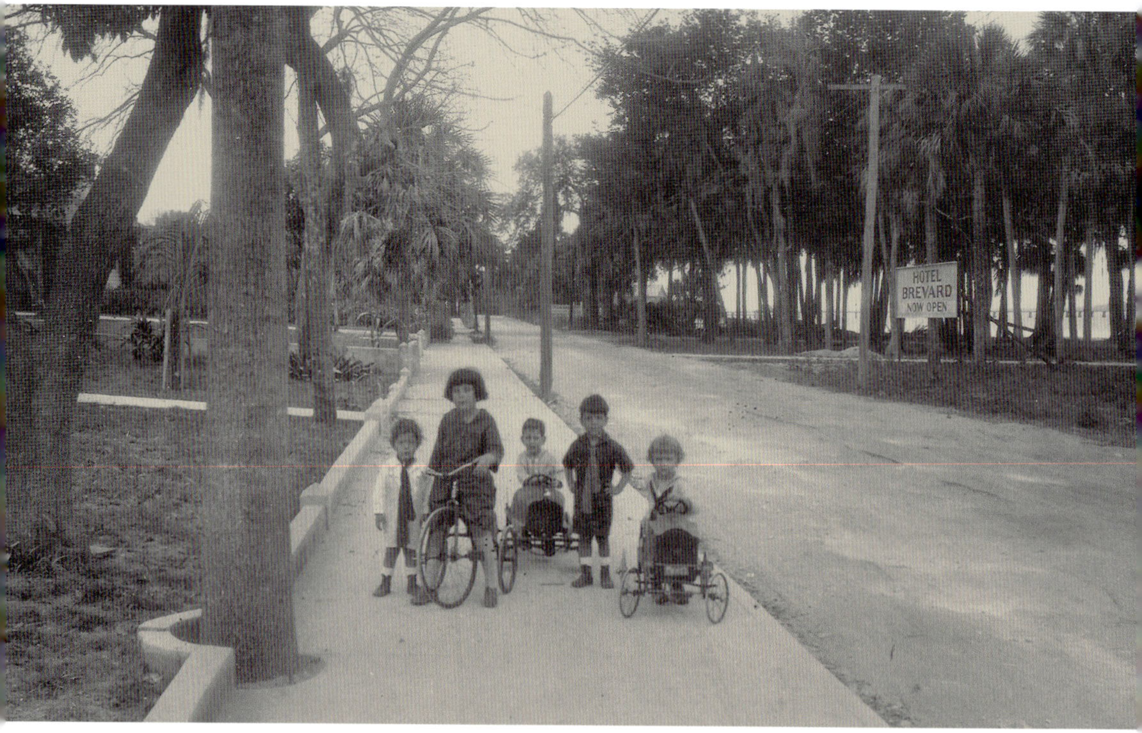


The Old Dixie Highway was once a tree-lined road used by travelers going through Cocoa. Today many condominiums line the waterfront. "We used to sit on our front lawn and count the cars from each different state that passed by on the way South," said Irv Rubin, one of the kids pictured above, in a letter to the Florida Historical Society. Also pictured are Jack Rubin, Ruth Rubin, Bernard Rubin, and Bobby Roberts. (Courtesy Florida Historical Society.)

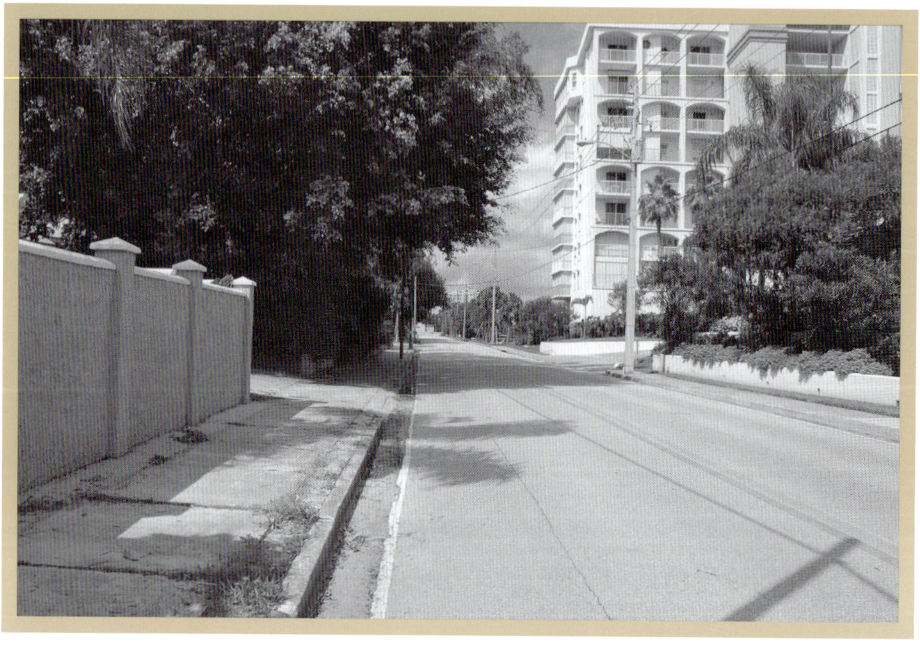

# CHAPTER 5

# MERRITT ISLAND

Merritt Island, located between Cocoa Beach and Cocoa, has seen a lot of development over the years. This photograph shows Headley's Oldsmobile dealership and gas station, located at the intersection of Highway 520 and Tropical Trail. The station no longer exists and has been replaced by a 7-Eleven store. (Courtesy Florida Historical Society.)

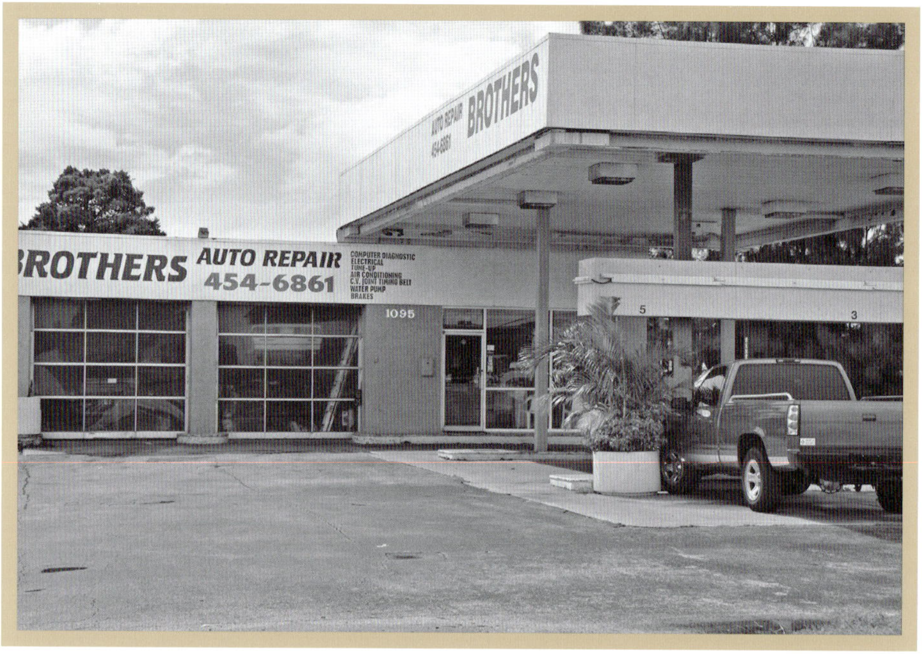


A lot has changed over the years in Merritt Island. Ed's Texaco gas station, located at 1095 North Courtenay Parkway across from Merritt Island High School, was a busy place in this 1960s advertisement photograph. Note the now classic Ford Mustang getting a fill-up. Cars are still at home there, but now the location is home to Brother's Auto Repair. (Courtesy Mike Ferger.)

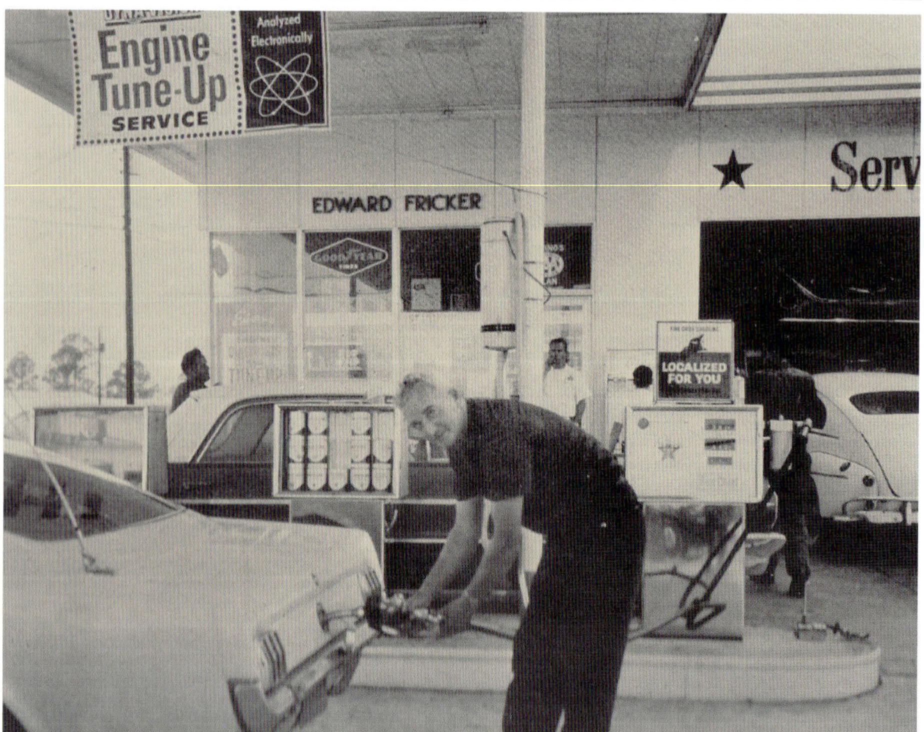

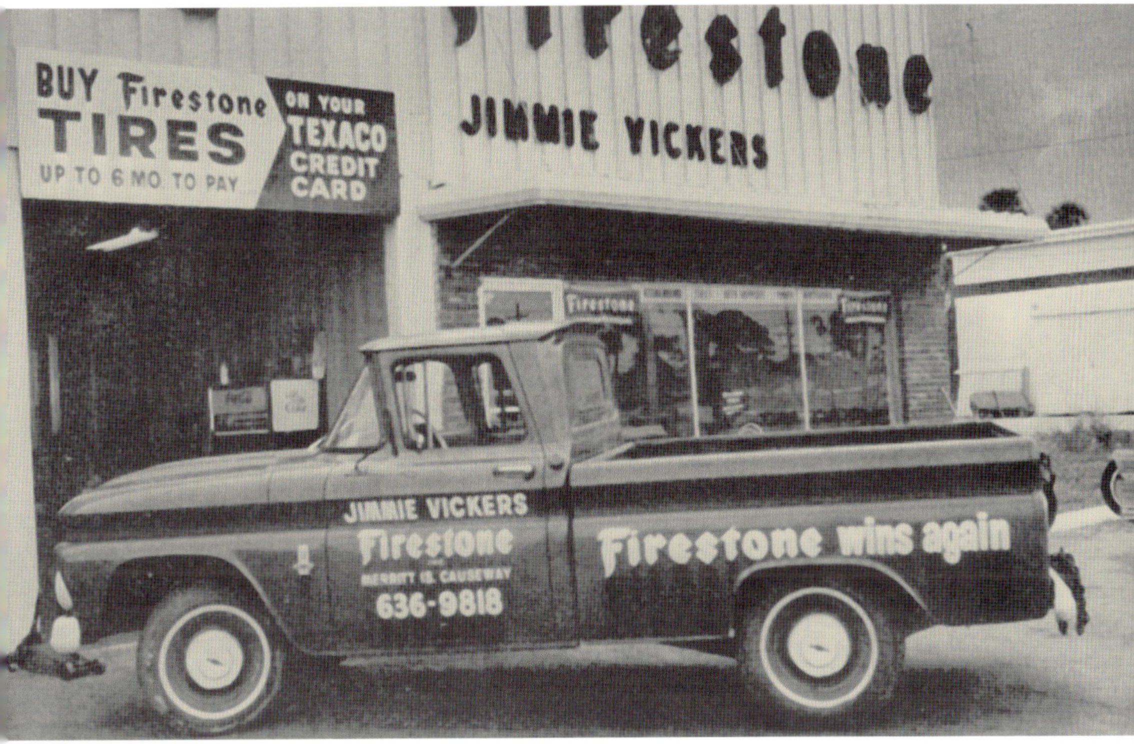


This 1960s advertisement photograph shows Jimmie Vickers Firestone, which was located on Merritt Island Causeway. Note the classic Coca-Cola vending machine that sits inside the garage. Today things have changed, but one thing is still the same. The Vickers family still operates a business that deals with automobiles, only now it is a Jeep automobile dealership located at 535 East Merritt Island Causeway. (Courtesy Mike Ferger.)

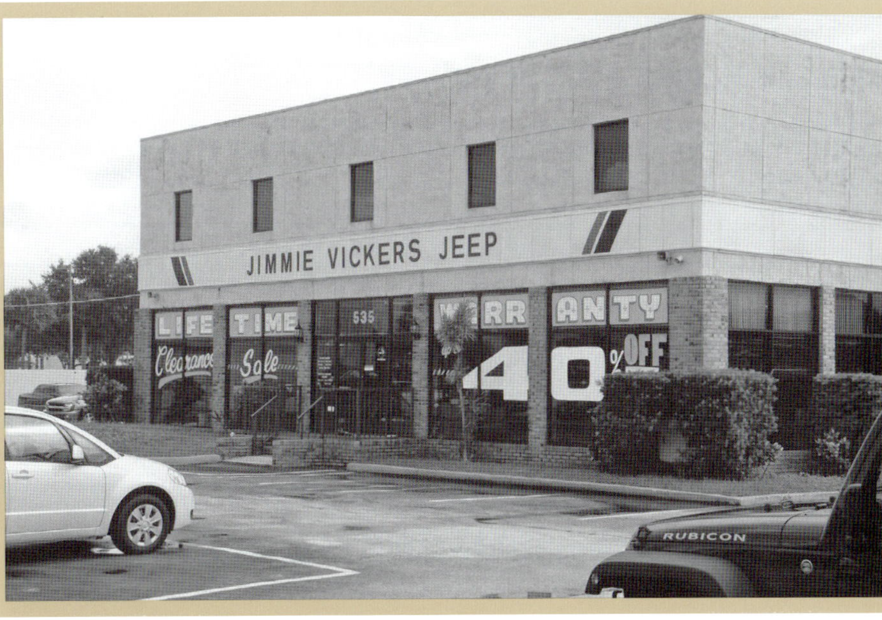

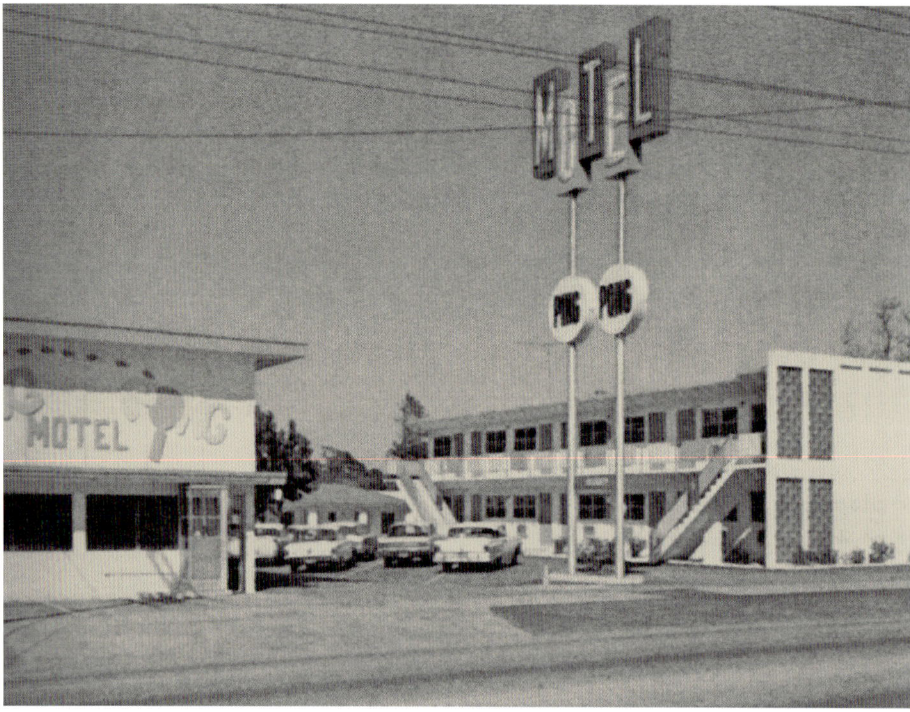


Originally Miller's Motel existed here, but the first buildings were torn down to make way for the Ping Pong Motel. It was located at 430 West Merritt Island Causeway, as seen here in an undated photograph that was probably taken in the 1960s. Today the location is the Aladdin Motel, which still exists. (Courtesy Florida Historical Society.)

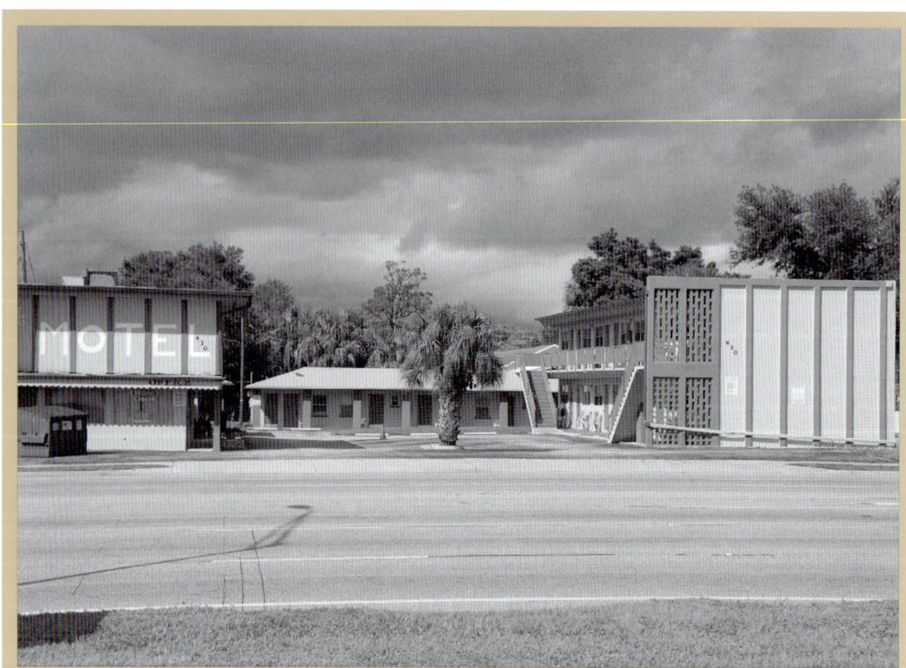

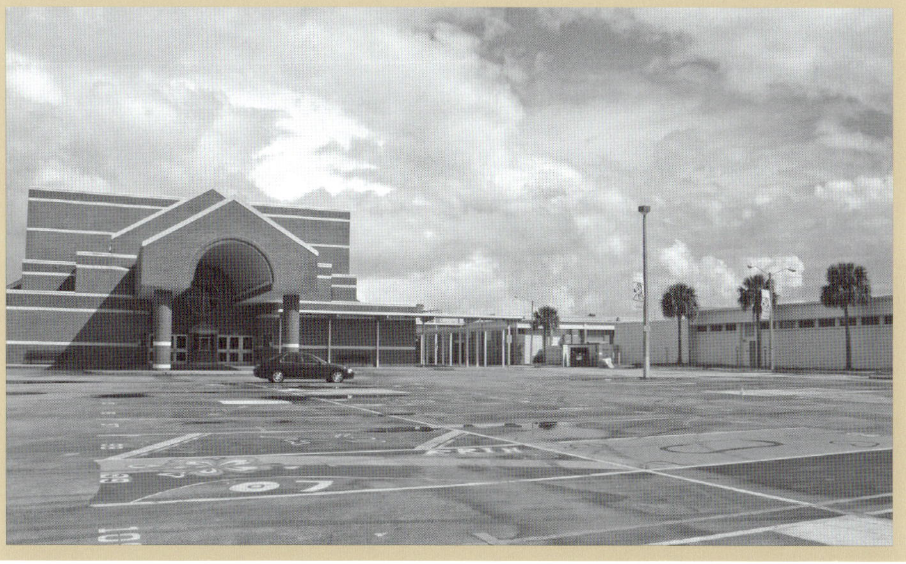

With the population growth of the 1960s came the need for more schools, churches, and infrastructure in Merritt Island. This aerial view shows the recently built Merritt Island High School, home of the Mustangs. Today the original school buildings exist, but major expansions and renovations have taken place throughout the years. The building seen on the left in this present-day photograph is the school's auditorium. (Courtesy Mike Ferger.)

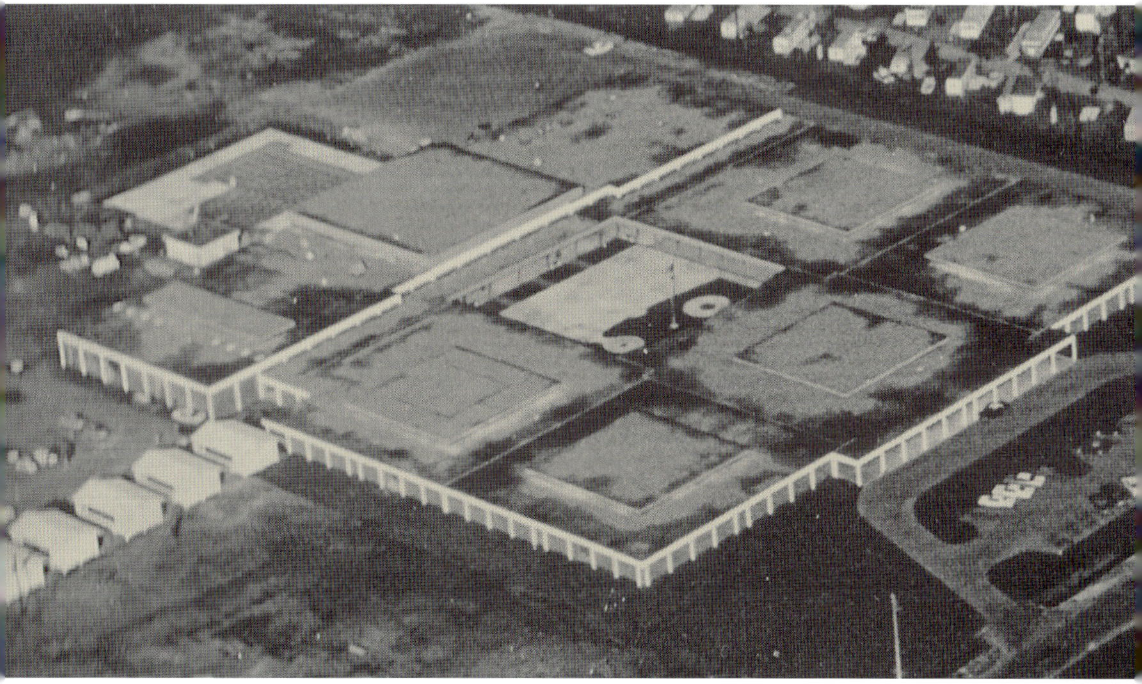

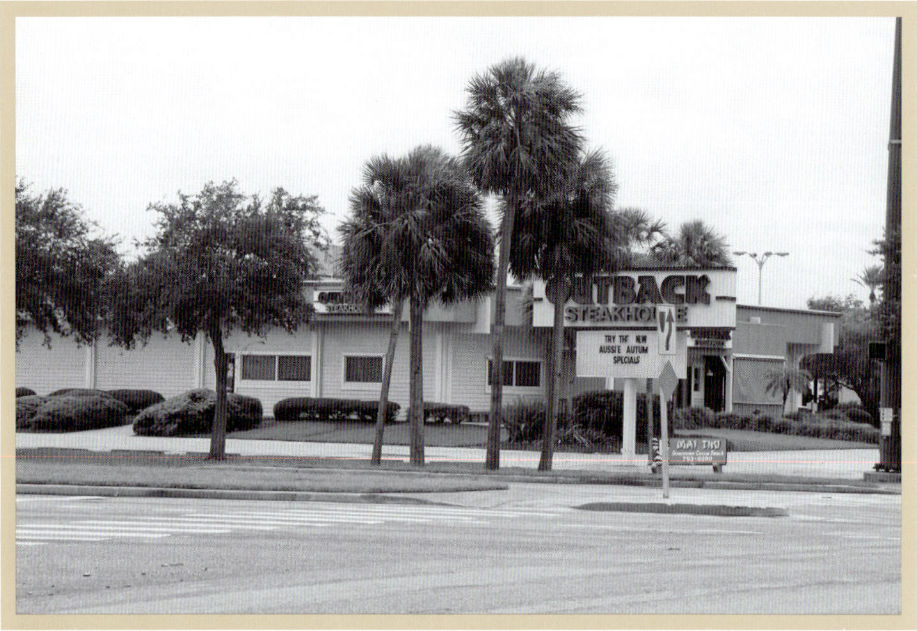


The building in this undated photograph shows a branch of Cocoa's First Federal Savings and Loan Bank, located at 777 East Merritt Island Causeway, in the parking lot of Merritt Square Mall. The mall still exists, but like many changes to Merritt Island, the area has seen a continued development of commercial businesses. An Outback Steakhouse restaurant is now at this location. (Courtesy Florida Historical Society.)

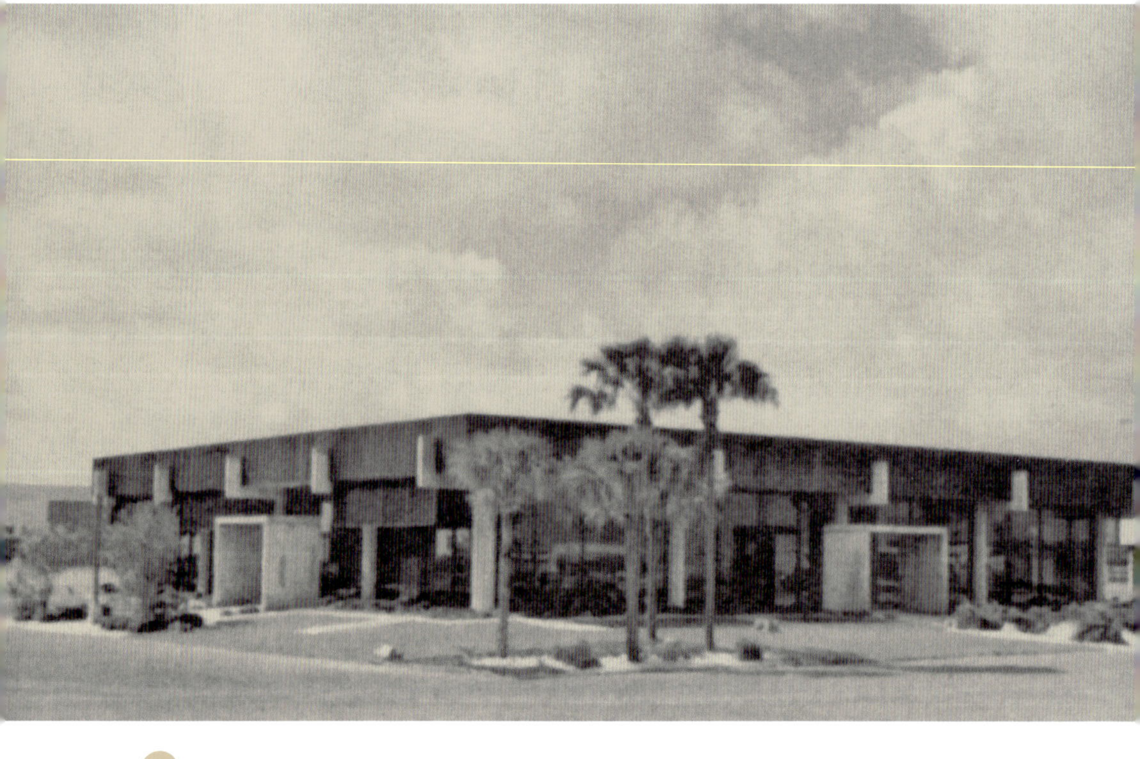

CHAPTER 6

# MELBOURNE

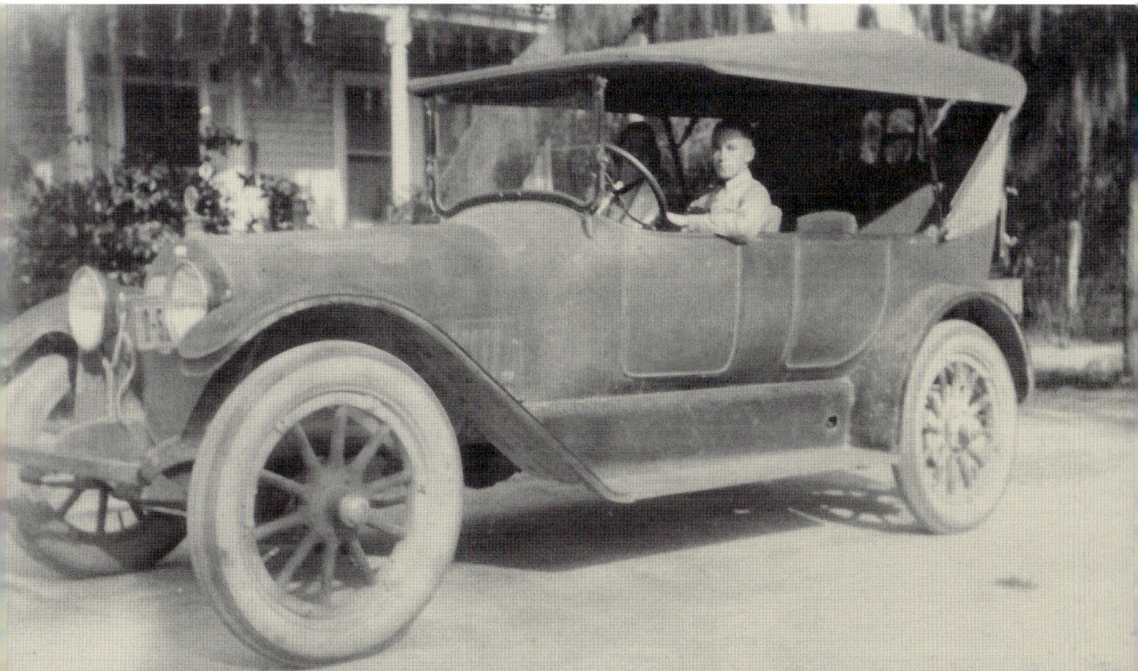

Melbourne is a neighbor of Cocoa Beach. Developed as a river town in the 19th century, it now includes the area of Eau Gallie, which was once a town itself. This 1920s photograph was taken in front of the historic James Wadsworth Rossetter House, located on Highland Avenue. The area has a lot of history. (Courtesy Historic Rossetter House Museum.)

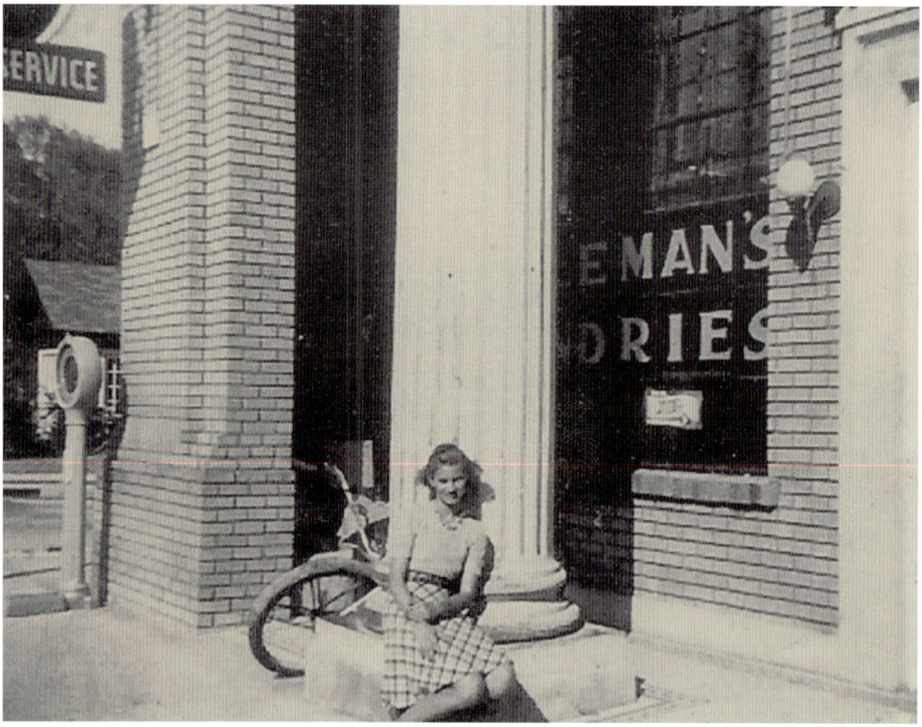


In this photograph, probably taken in the late 1940s, a girl named Christini Bell takes a rest on the front column of what was the State Bank of Eau Gallie. Constructed in 1924, the bank still looks so much like it did when it was built, one might think no time has passed at all here. The bank building is located at 1437 Highland Avenue at the intersection of Eau Gallie Boulevard and is still occupied with businesses. (Courtesy Historic Rossetter House Museum.)

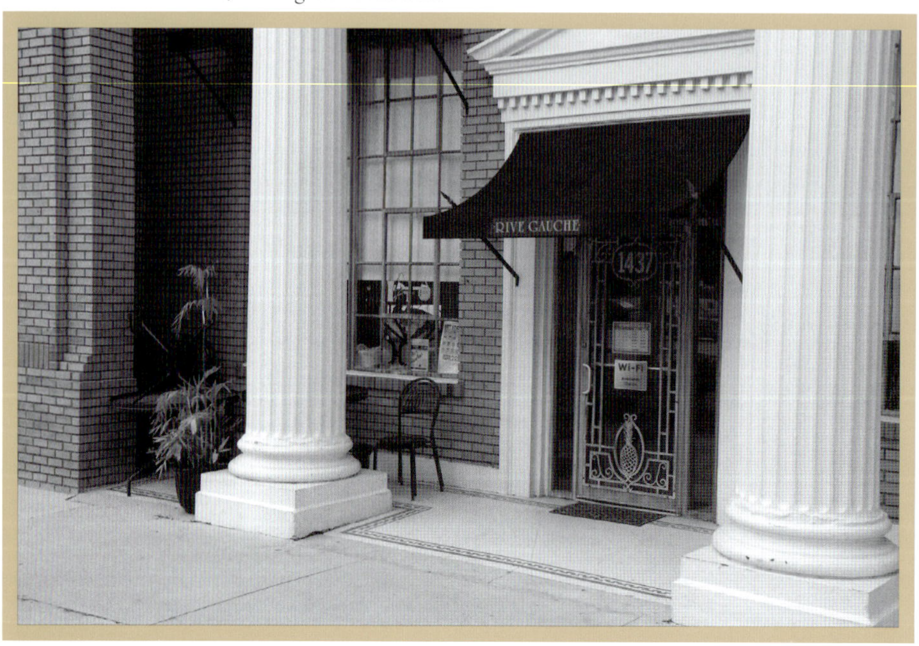

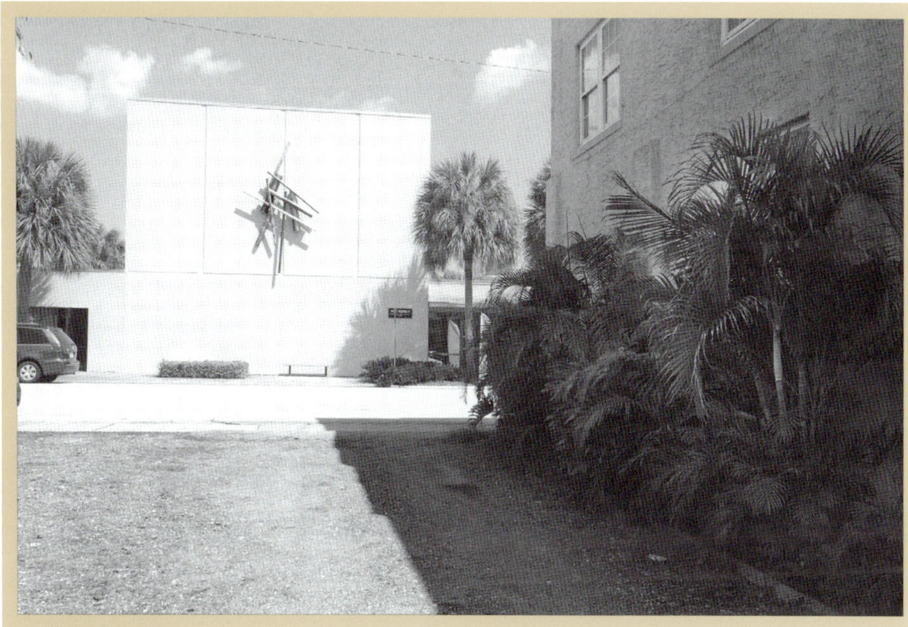

This photograph, probably taken in the 1920s, shows the alley next to 1490 Eau Gallie Boulevard, which is the location of today's Eau Gallie Florist. The city hall building, visible through the foliage, houses the Brevard Art Museum today. This area of Highland Avenue is now known as the Eau Gallie Arts District and includes art galleries and the offices of the Brevard Symphony Orchestra in addition to hosting community festivals. (Courtesy Link Johnsten.)

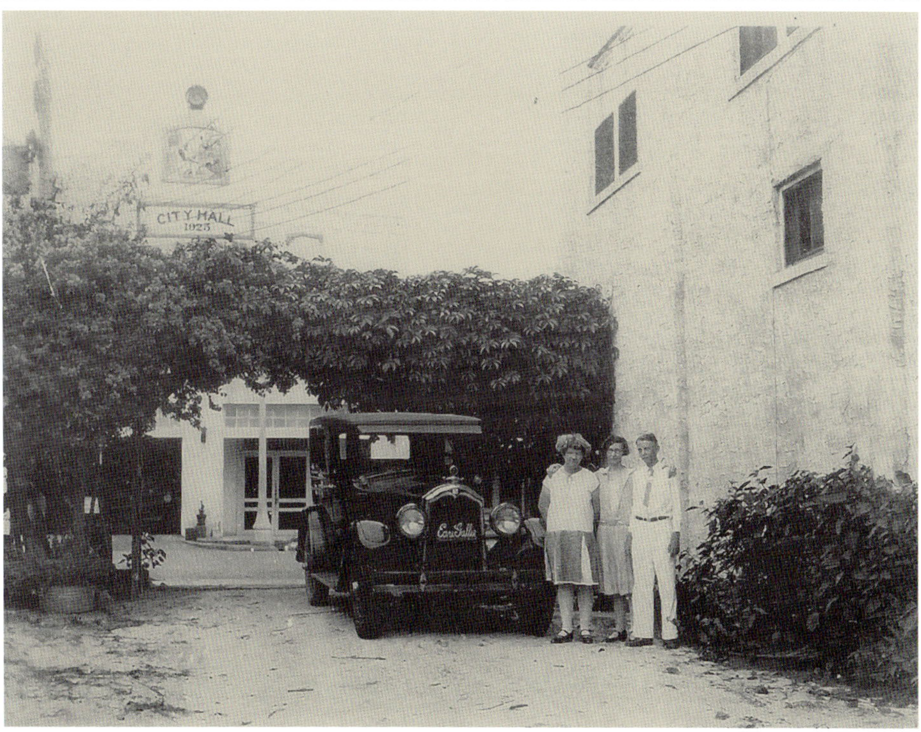

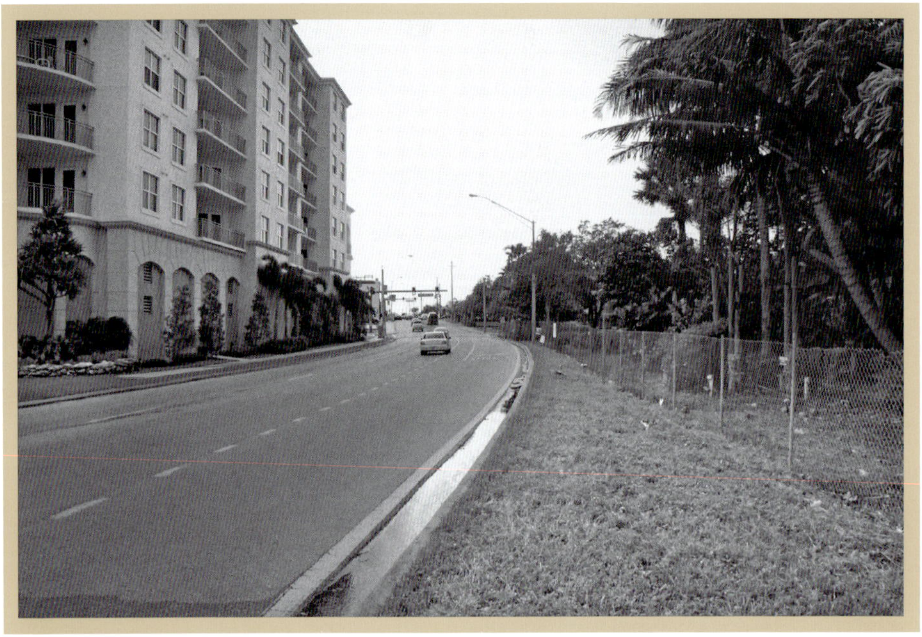

In 1925, the Oleanders (originally called the Harbor City Hotel) was located near what is now the end of Eau Gallie Boulevard, on land at Pineapple Avenue and Ninth Street. It was a beautiful hotel and had a style that made it instantly recognizable. The building was torn down in 1990, and Conchy Joe's Restaurant was built in its place. That restaurant is now closed, and the area is fenced in and unused. (Courtesy Florida Historical Society.)

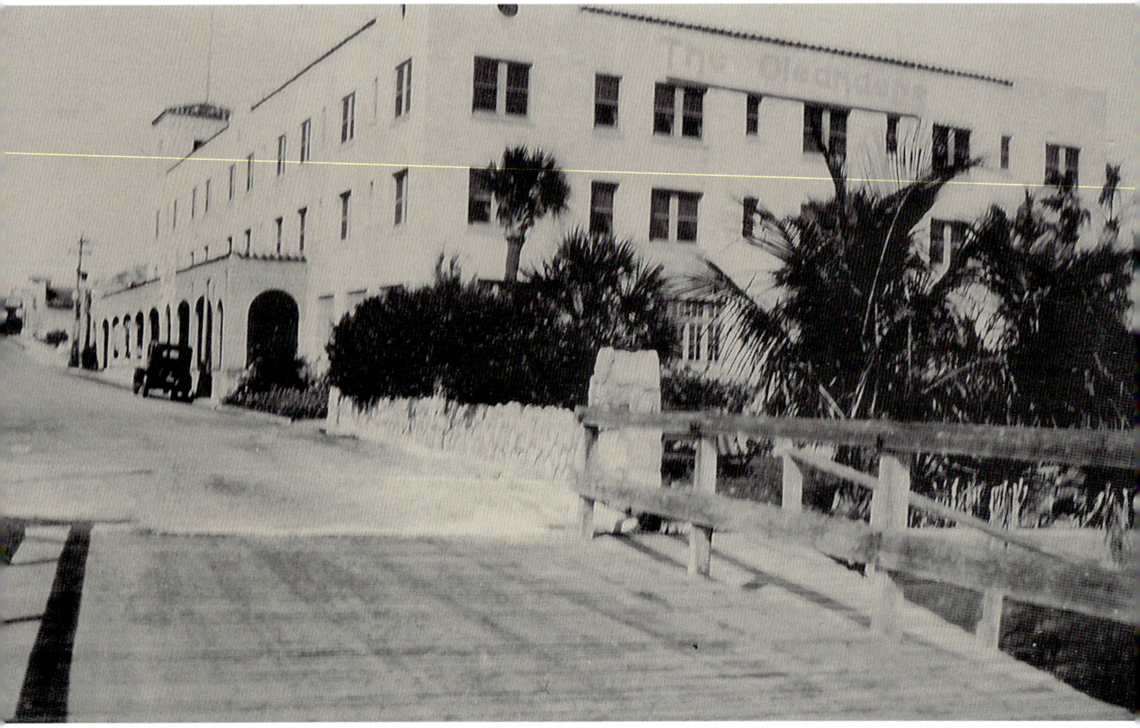

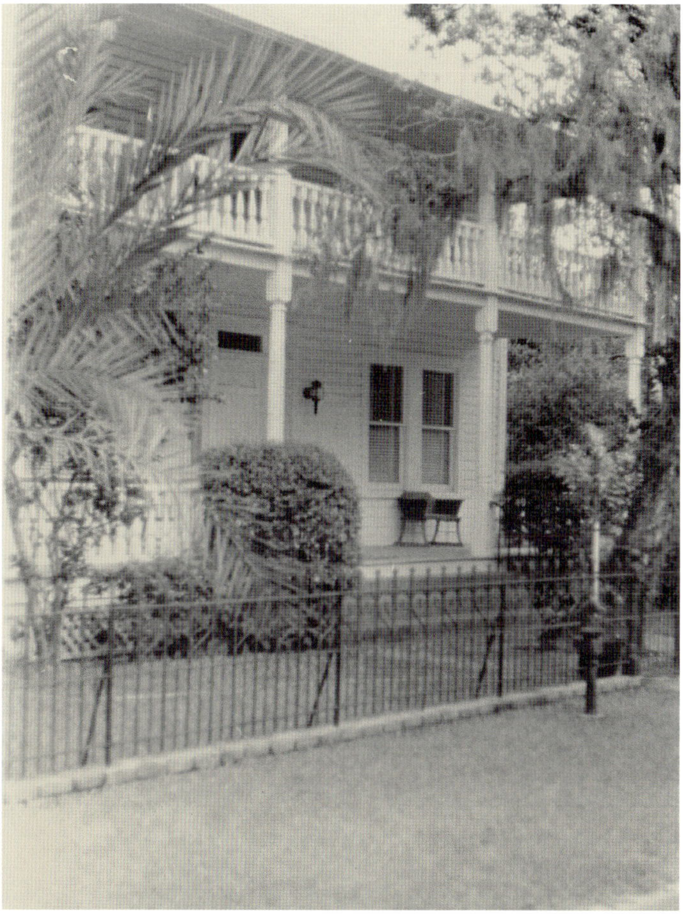

The James Wadsworth Rossetter House is a famous historical landmark located at 1320 Highland Avenue in Melbourne. James Rossetter came to Eau Gallie (now Melbourne) in 1902 and was a leader in the fishing industry. He bought the house in 1904 and expanded it for his family. He would later obtain the area's Standard Oil franchise, which his daughter Carrie would run for decades after her father's death. (Courtesy Historic Rossetter House Museum.)

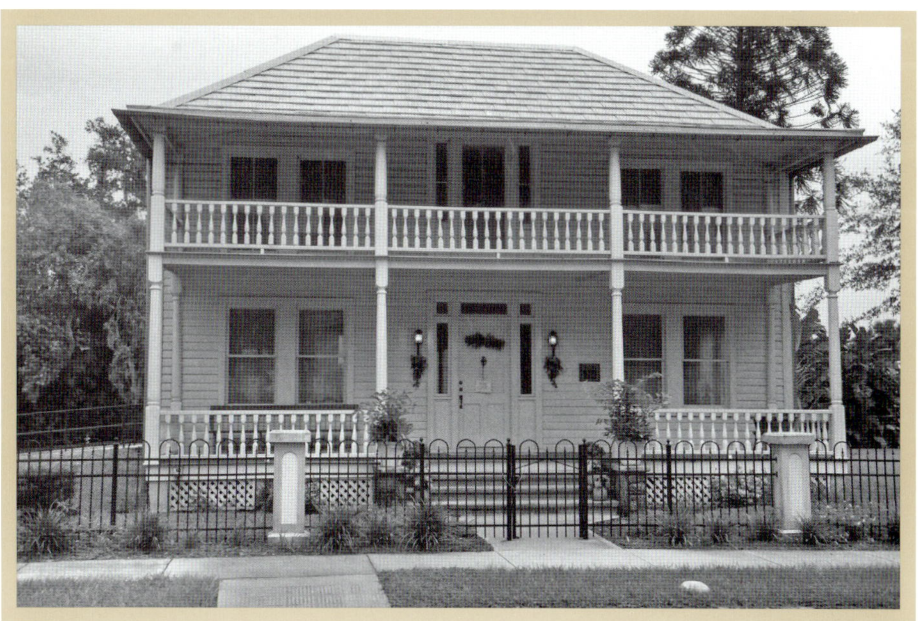

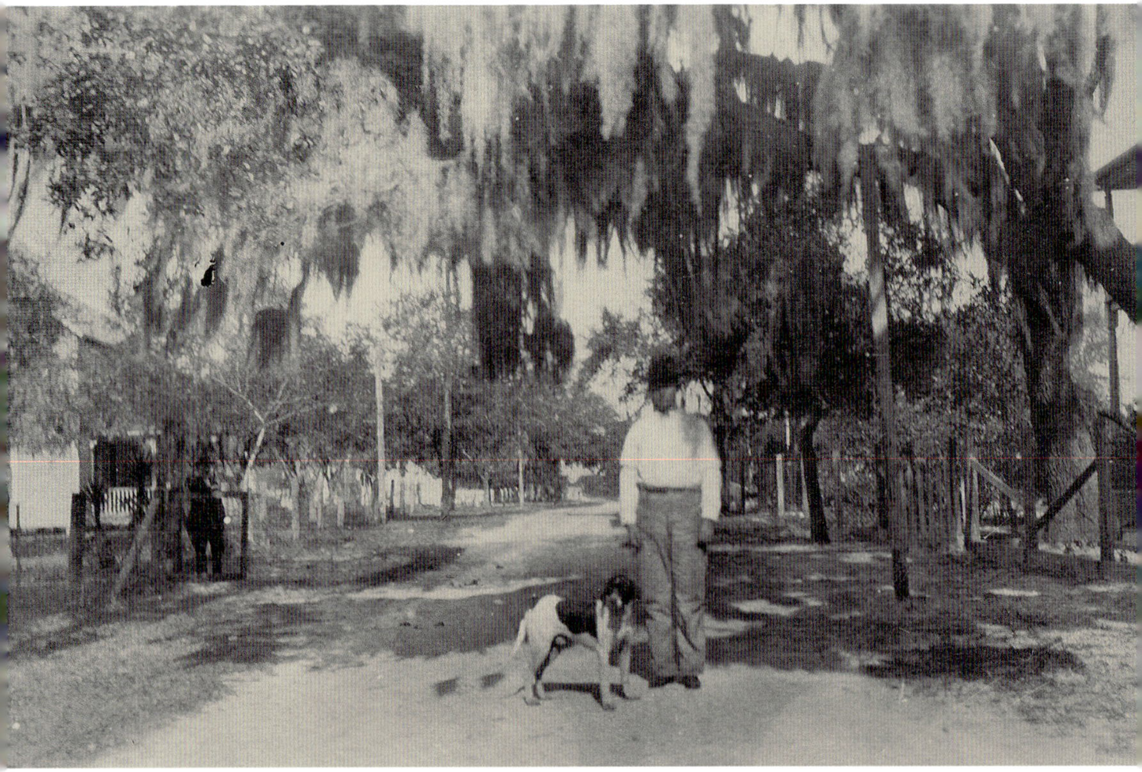

This early photograph of Highland Avenue, taken in front of the James Wadsworth Rossetter House at 1320 Highland Avenue, shows unpaved streets, lots of trees, and not much development. Today the area still has many of its historic structures, such as the William Roesch House, which is located across the street. Just a couple blocks away is the now very busy Eau Gallie Boulevard. (Courtesy Historic Rossetter House Museum.)

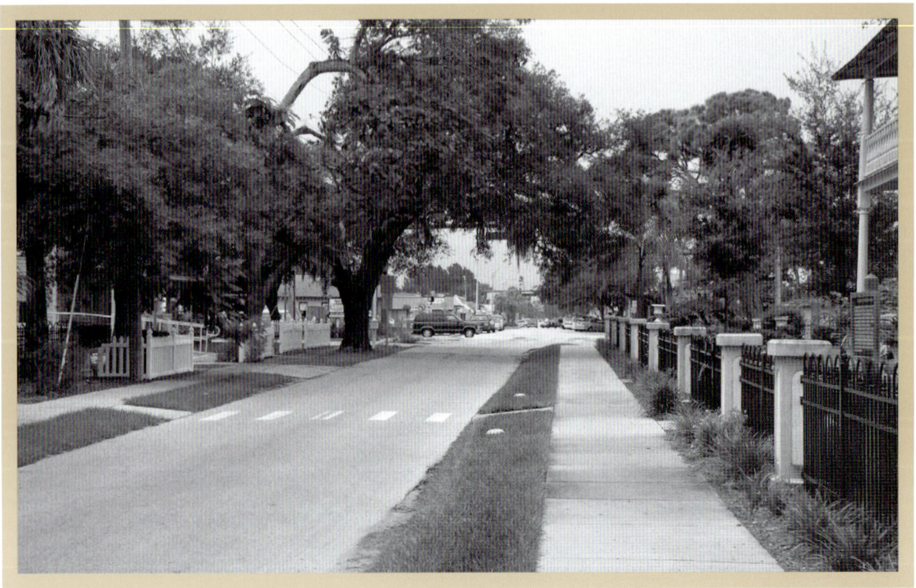

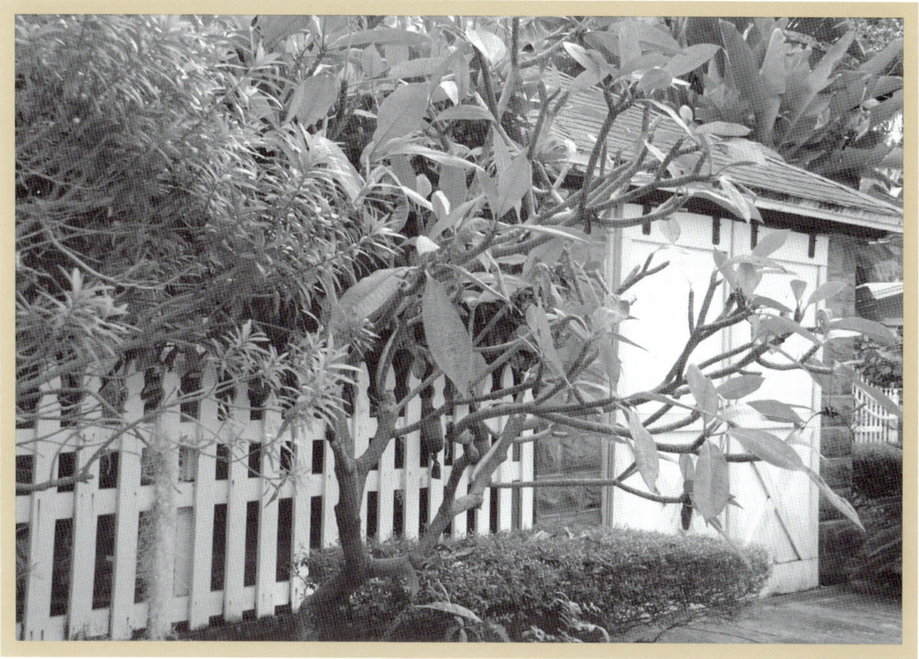

This picture was probably taken a few blocks from the James Wadsworth Rossetter House on Young Street in Eau Gallie (now Melbourne) sometime in the 1920s. Note the abundance of moss hanging from the trees and the unpaved street. It is hard to see, but the garage on the left still stands today as part of a much larger private property. (Courtesy Florida Historical Society.)

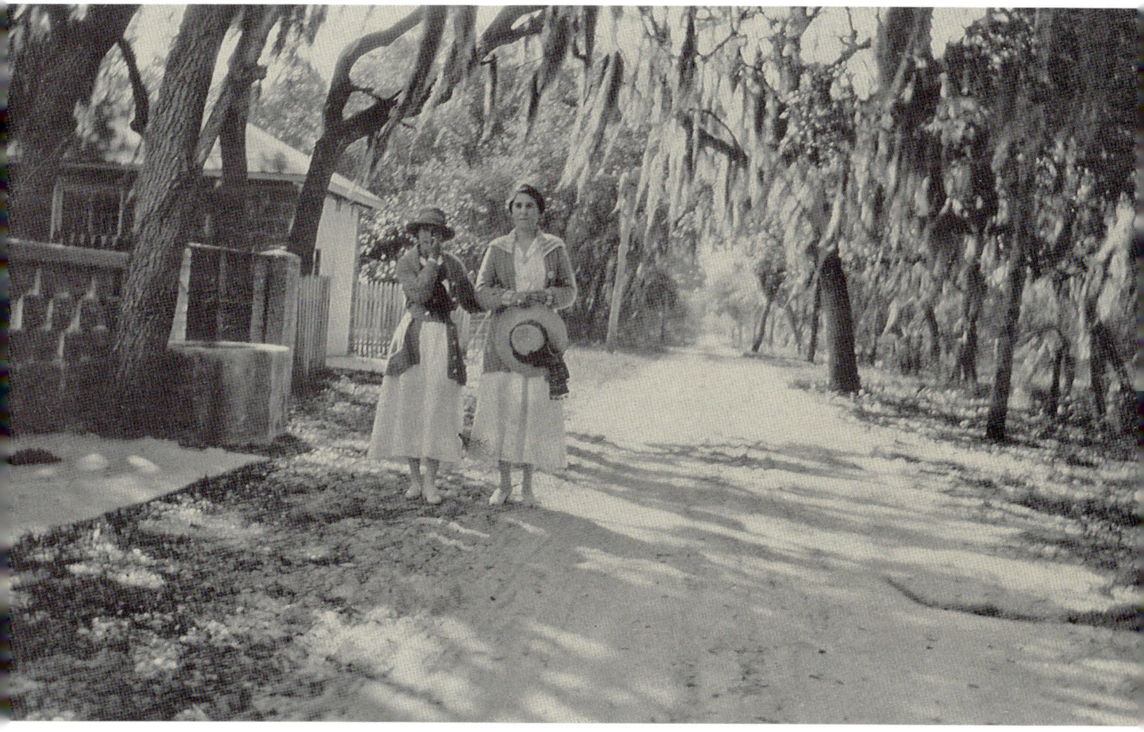

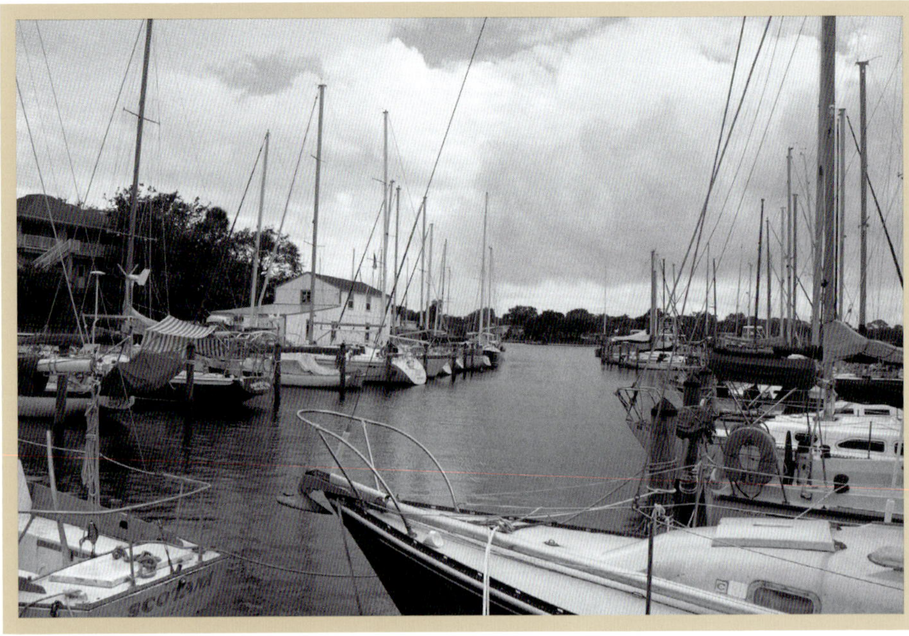

In 1896, Aaron Bennett established the Eau Gallie Yacht Basin, located at 587Young Street in Melbourne. Around 1920, the basin continued its development under the ownership of Phillip David Barbour, who was a native of Louisville, Kentucky. Barbour also established the Eau Gallie Boat Concern, and the basin was very well known in yachting circles. Today the basin still exists, and yachts from all over call the picturesque location their home. (Courtesy Florida Historical Society.)

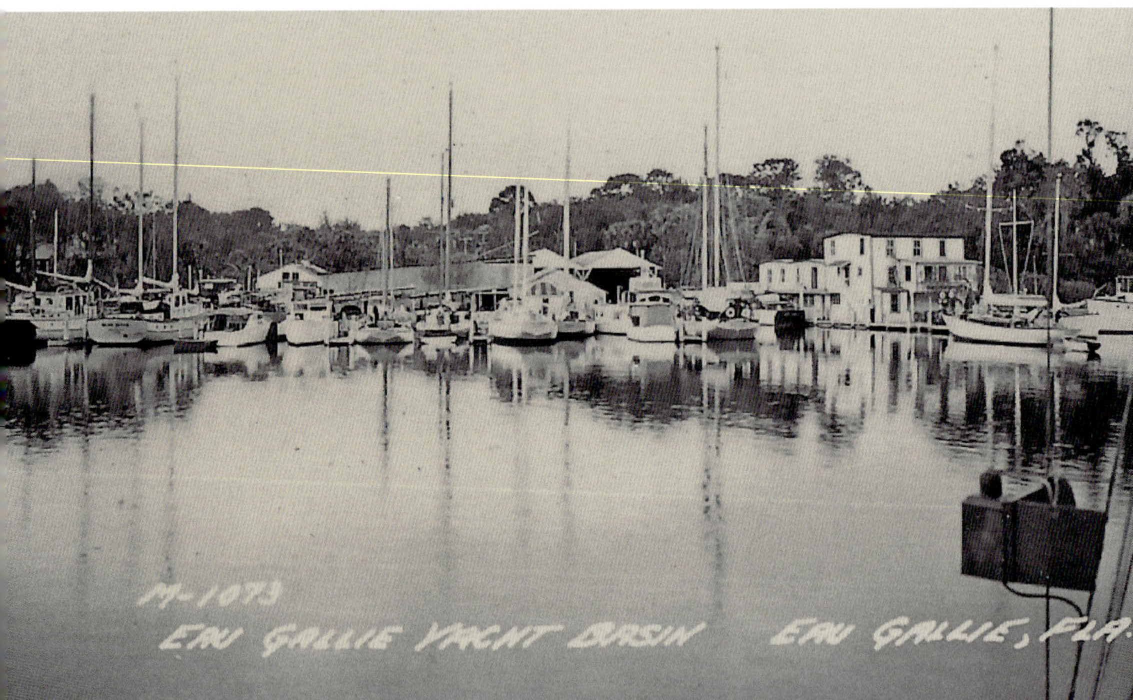

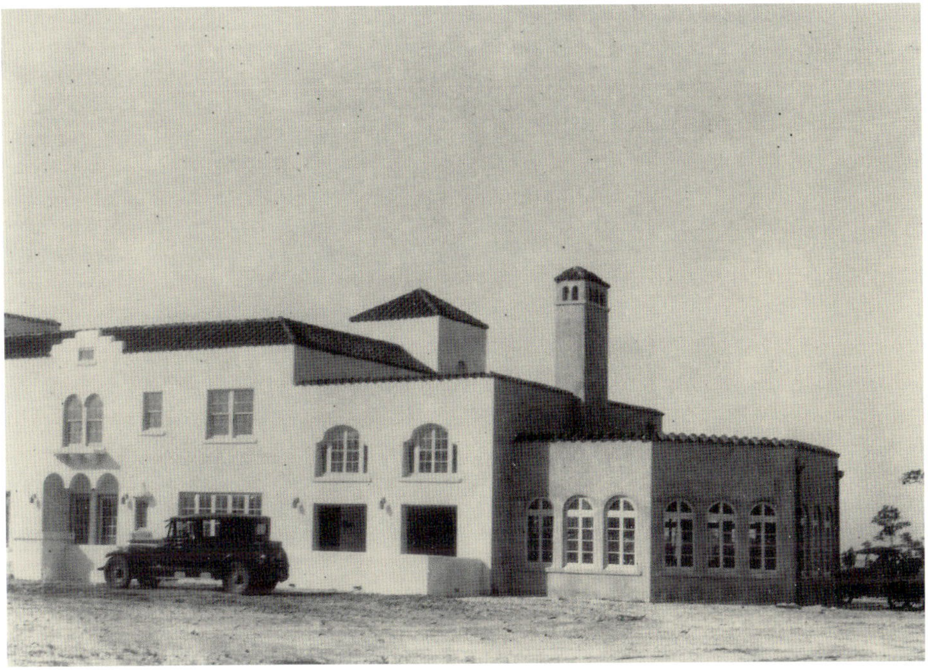

Sometime in the early 1920s, Ernest Kouwen-Hoven built his Spanish Mediterranean–style mansion, which included a fine art deco interior. Shortly thereafter, it was sold and expanded, becoming the Lincoln Hotel. Eventually, in the 1960s, it would come under the ownership of Jonathan Dwight, who used the property to found the Florida Air Academy. Today the military-style prep school is the largest military school in Florida. (Florida Historical Society.)

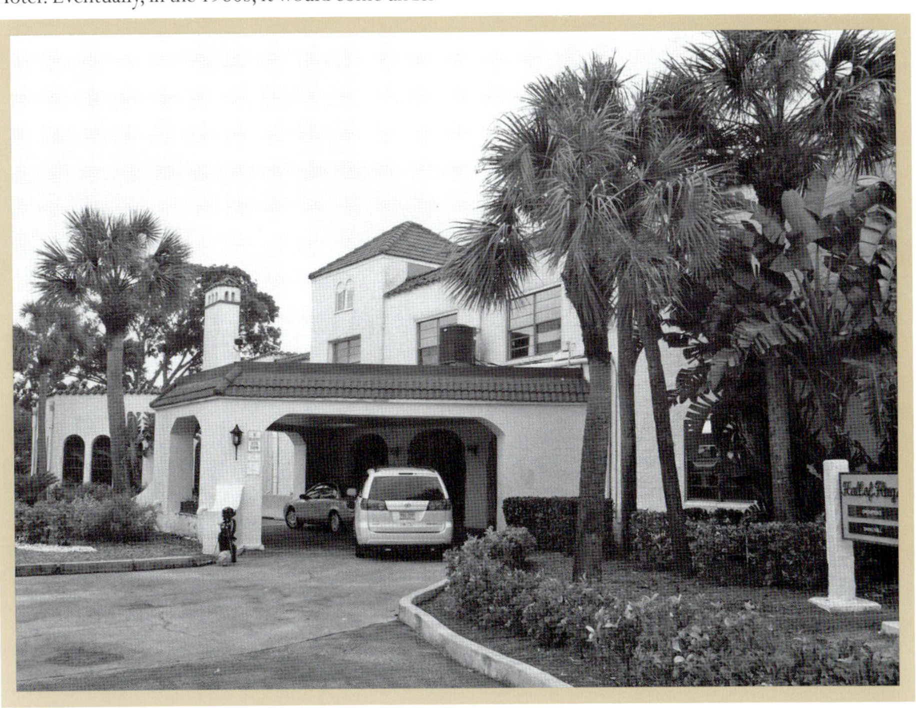

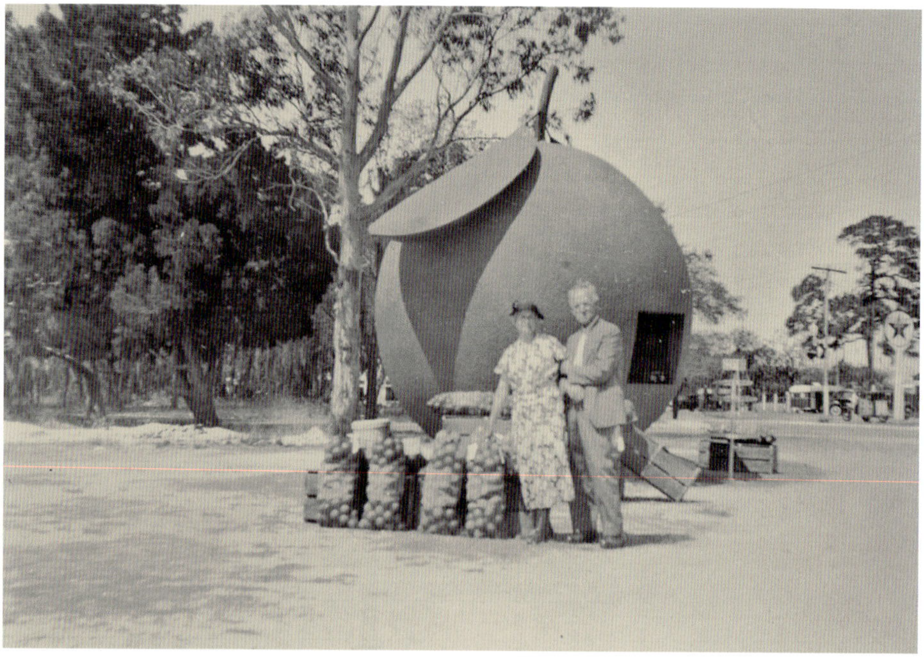

This undated photograph from the Rossetter family collection shows a unique retail stand, built in the shape of an orange, that was probably used to promote the citrus trade. Years later, the stand was in such bad shape that it lay on its side almost completely destroyed. Although some considered it an eyesore, the Melbourne Rotary Club restored the structure to its original quality, and today it is located at 2265 North Harbor City Boulevard. (Courtesy Historic Rossetter House Museum.)

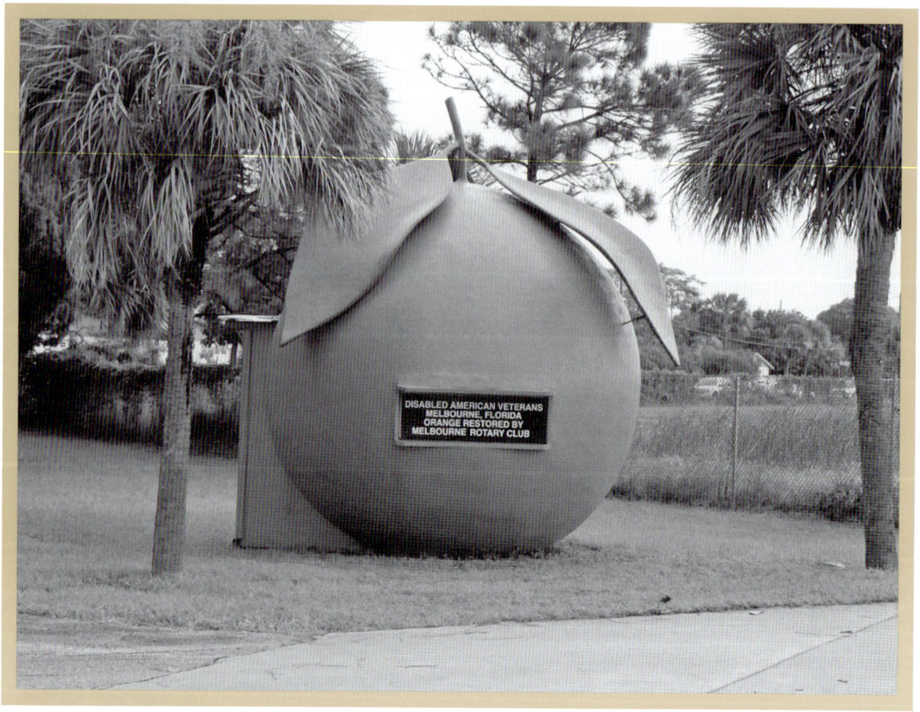

7

CHAPTER

# THE GOOD OLE DAYS

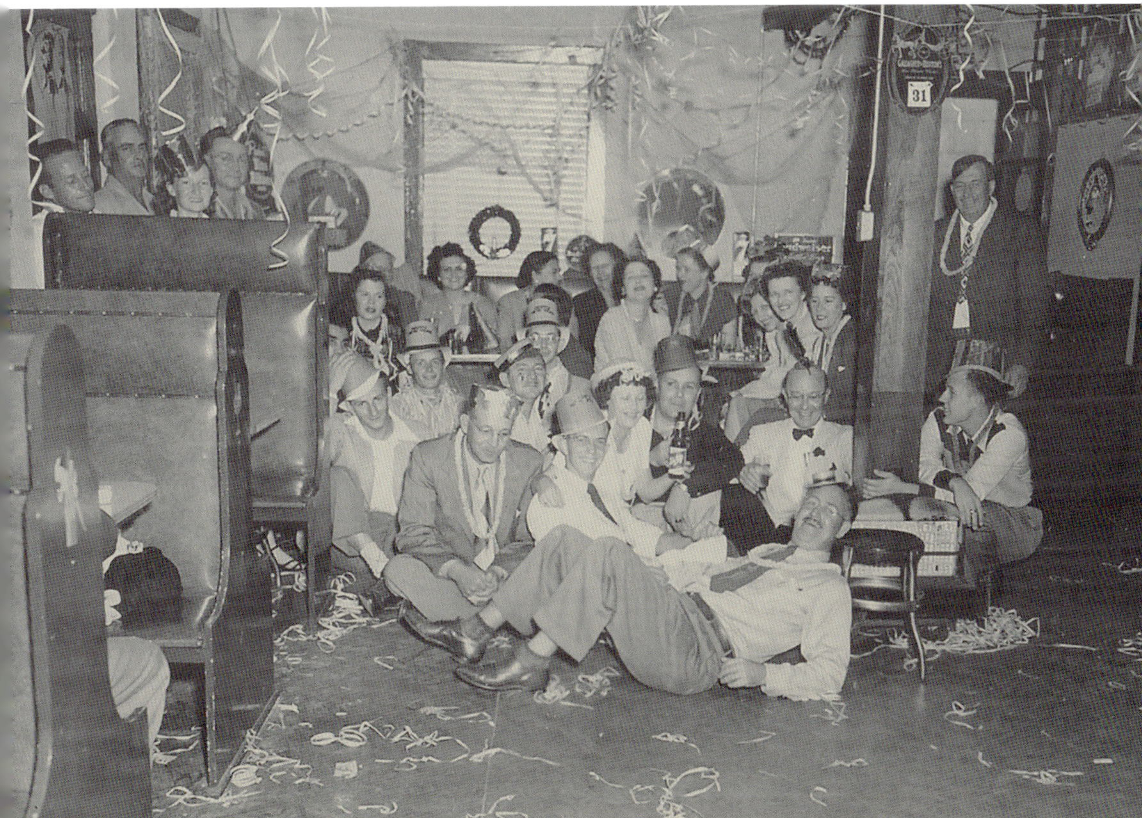

There are still old-timers who remember the good old days of Cocoa Beach and its surrounding communities. They have stories to tell, and if people would only listen, they will not be lost. This 1940s New Year's Eve celebration took place at Bernard's Surf, a famous Cocoa Beach restaurant. (Courtesy Pete Godke.)

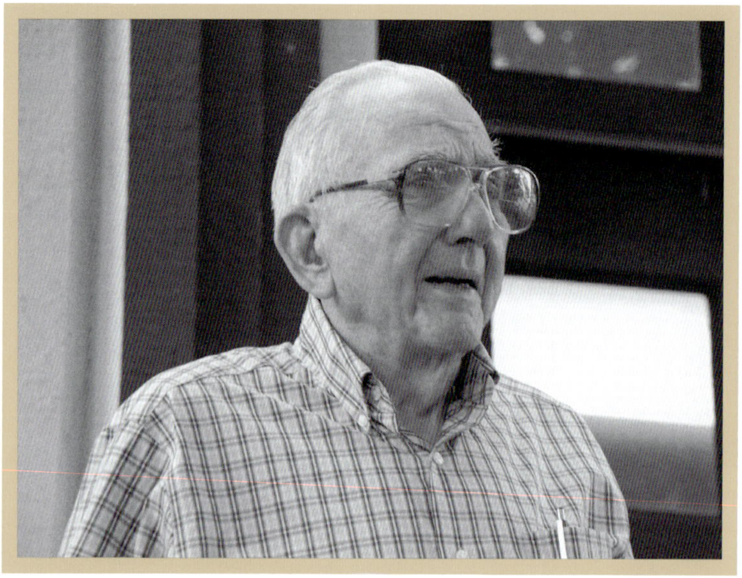

George "Speedy" Harrell is a longtime area resident who worked at the U.S. Post Office. Speedy is on the left in this 1950s beach photograph, along with friends Arthur Isaccson, W. K. Fouraker, John Gray, and George Ackroyd. Coincidentally one can still find him today at the Florida Historical Society, which is located in the old post office building on Brevard Avenue in Cocoa. This is the person to ask if one wants to know about history. (Courtesy Florida Historical Society.)

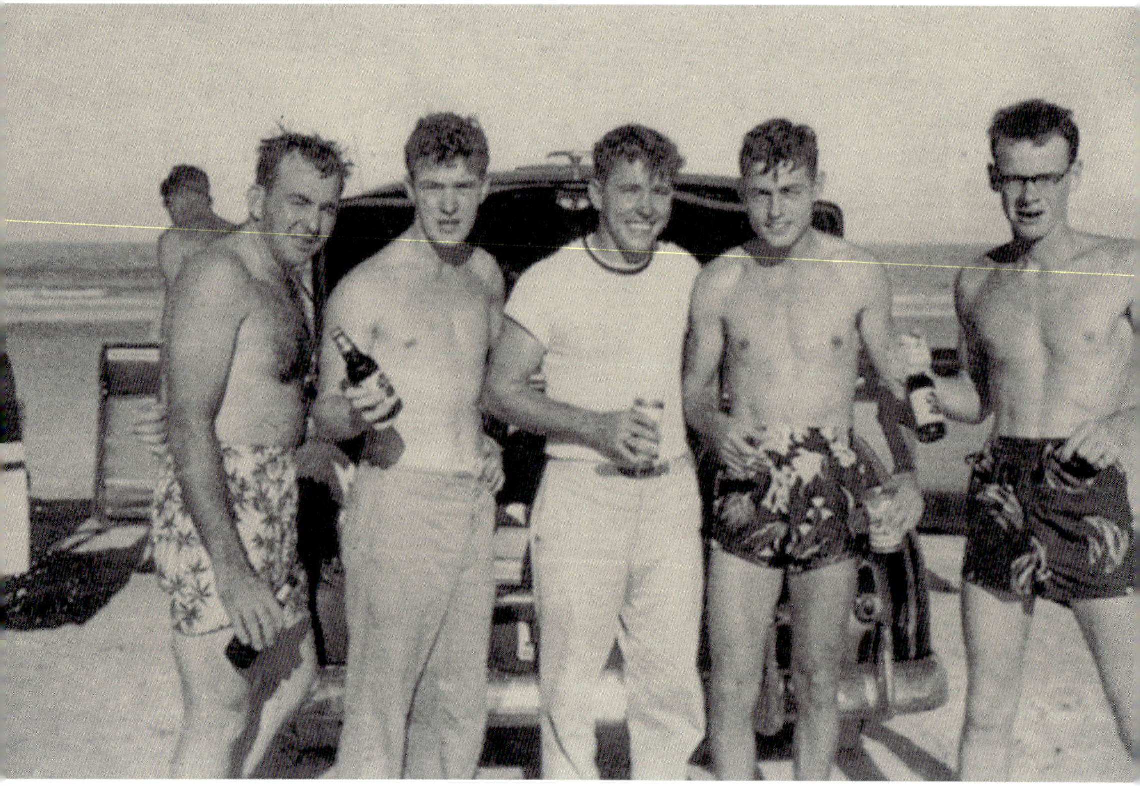

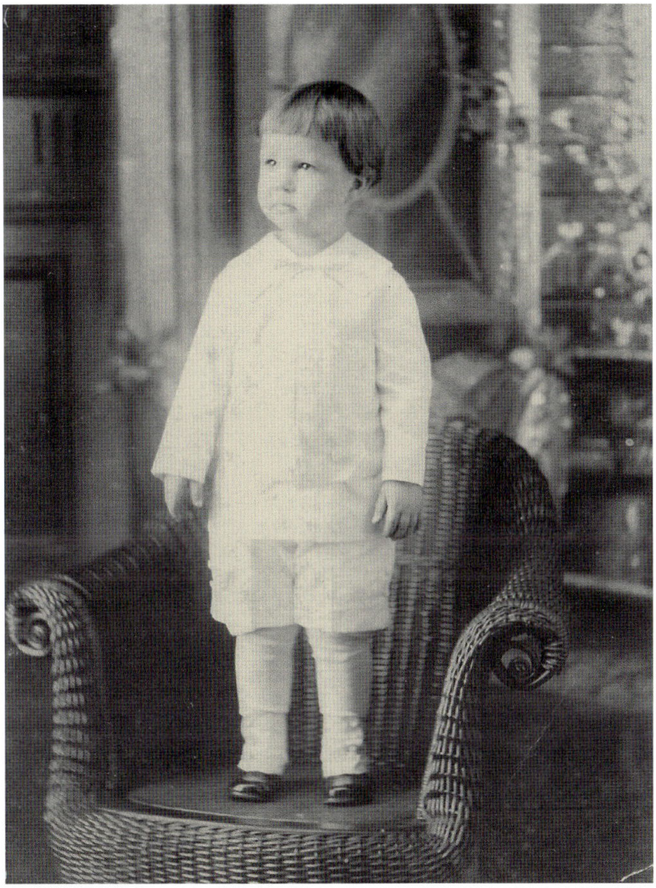

Al Trafford is a longtime elder of Brevard County and knows a lot about the area's development. He attended the University of Florida then joined his family's real estate business in 1938. After his father, A. R. Trafford, retired in 1954, Al took over running the company. He is seen here at just 28 months old, and today one can still find him at Trafford Real Estate, which to him is like spending time with family. (Courtesy Al Trafford.)

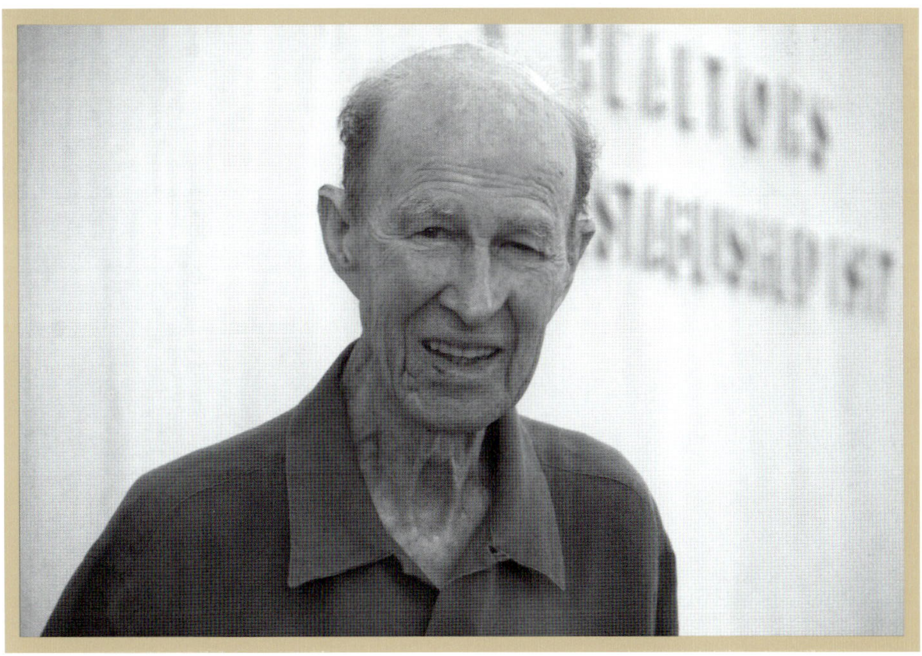

Joe Morgan was the mayor of Cocoa Beach from 1973 to 1999. He loves the city and its history and can tell anyone a lot about living there. His family started moving to the area in the 1950s. Here he is, second from the left, having some fun with his brothers Tim, Larry, and Tom back in the day. Today Joe is still involved in the community. (Courtesy Joe Morgan.)

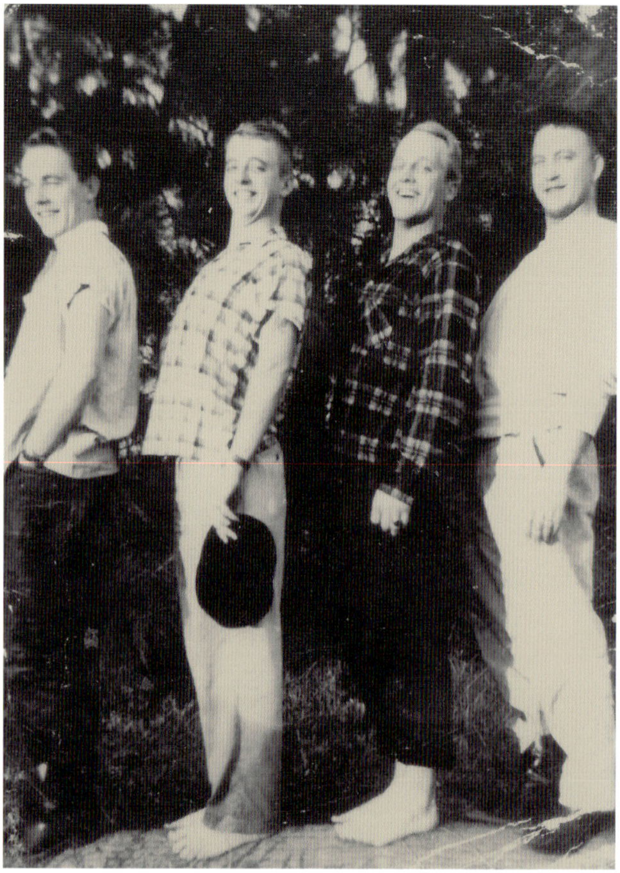

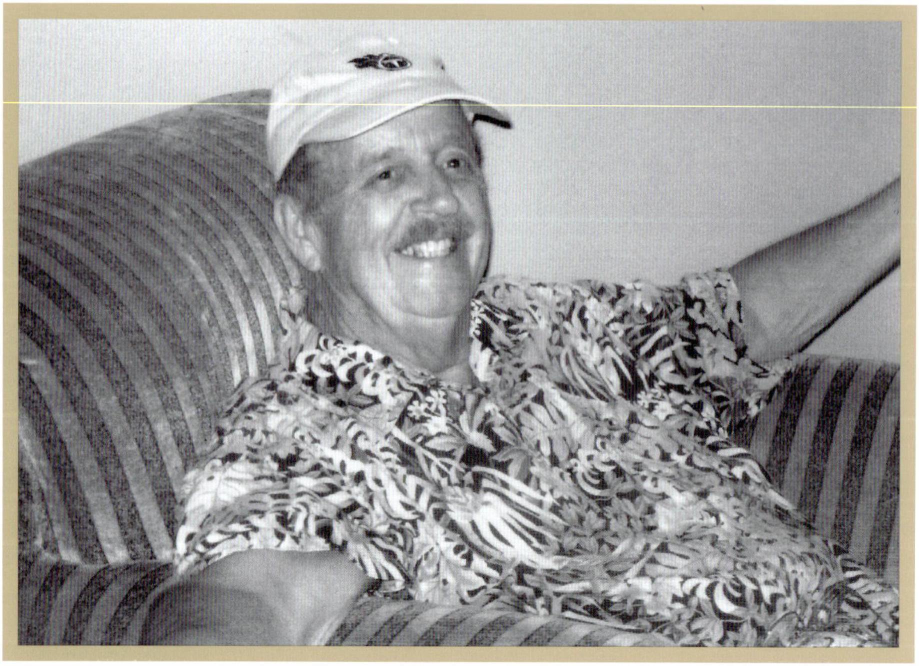

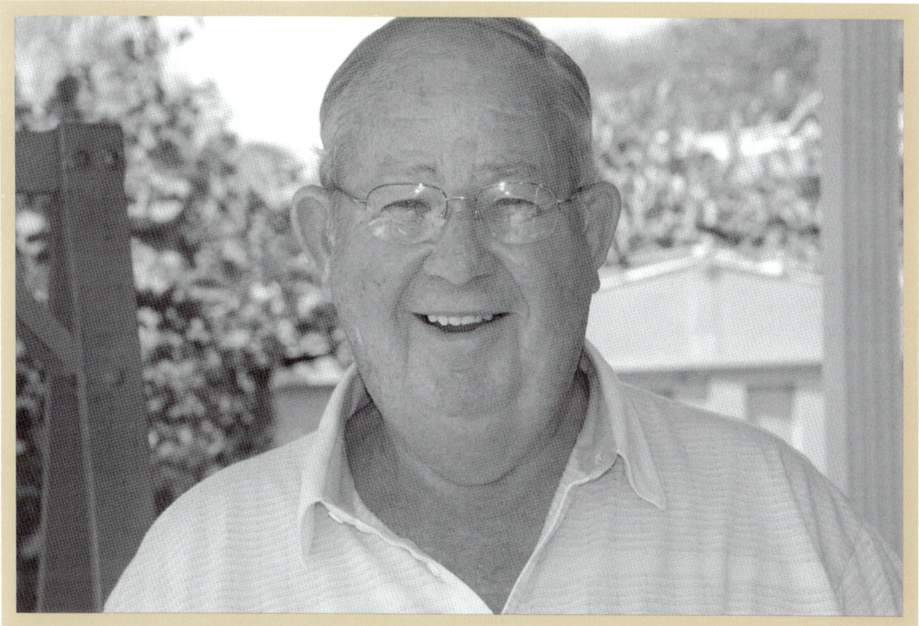

As a boy, Pete Godke would play on the beach near where his father managed the Ocean Lodge. He is pictured here with his brother Dale. He served his country in the U.S. Air Force, retired, and then returned to Cocoa Beach to run his family's store, Ann Lia's gift shop. Today he's enjoying his second retirement, but if asked, he might sit down and tell stories about Cocoa Beach. (Courtesy Pete Godke.)

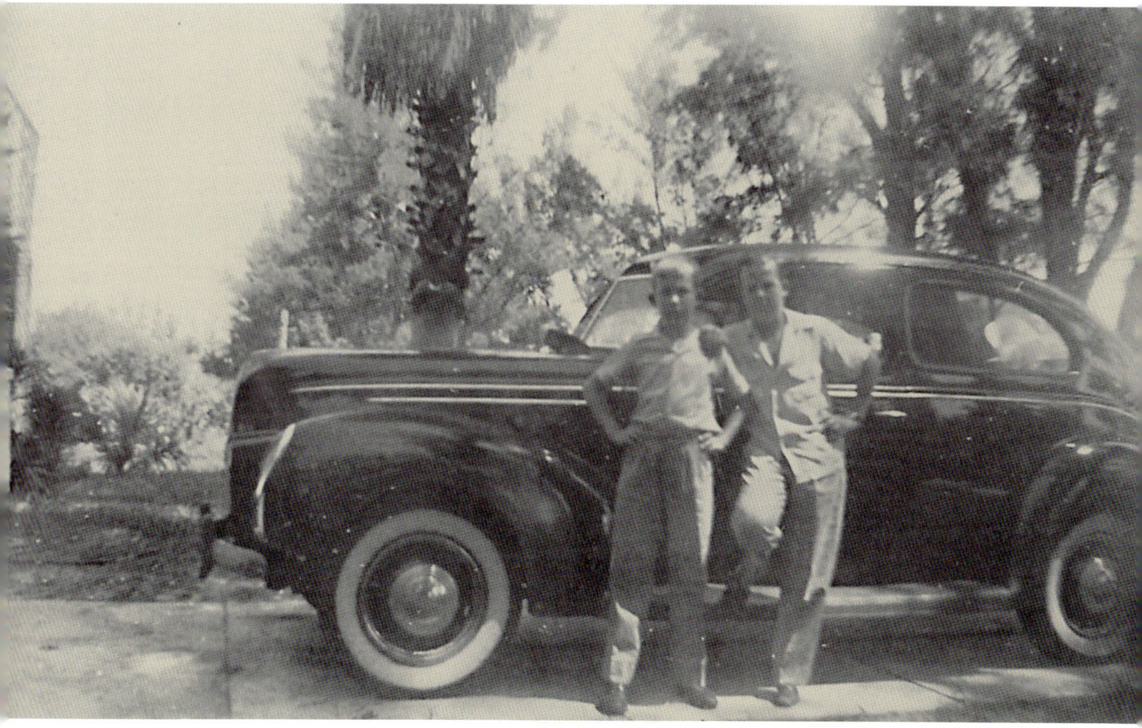

# Discover Thousands of Local History Books Featuring Millions of Vintage Images

Arcadia Publishing, the leading local history publisher in the United States, is committed to making history accessible and meaningful through publishing books that celebrate and preserve the heritage of America's people and places.

Find more books like this at
**www.arcadiapublishing.com**

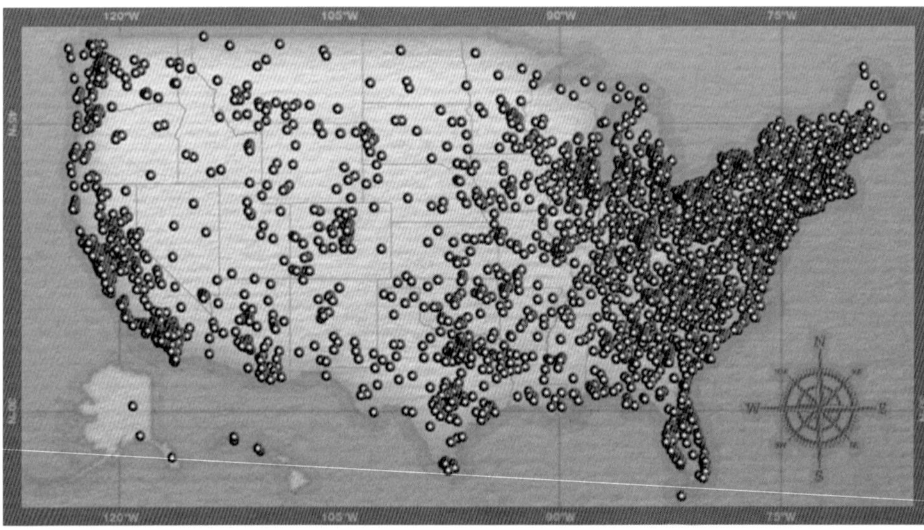

Search for your hometown history, your old stomping grounds, and even your favorite sports team.

Consistent with our mission to preserve history on a local level, this book was printed in South Carolina on American-made paper and manufactured entirely in the United States. Products carrying the accredited Forest Stewardship Council (FSC) label are printed on 100 percent FSC-certified paper.

MADE IN THE USA